Kotlin Mastery

A Comprehensive Guide for Java Developers and New Programmers

Arnika Patel
Keshav Kumar
Dr. Bishwajeet Kumar Pandey

apress®

Kotlin Mastery: A Comprehensive Guide for Java Developers and New Programmers

Arnika Patel ⓘ
Paul University, Vadodara, Gujarat, India

Keshav Kumar
Kanpur, Uttar Pradesh, India

Dr. Bishwajeet Kumar Pandey
GL Bajaj Institute of Technology and Management, Greater Noida West, Uttar Pradesh, India

ISBN-13 (pbk): 979-8-8688-1617-8   ISBN-13 (electronic): 979-8-8688-1618-5
https://doi.org/10.1007/979-8-8688-1618-5

Copyright © 2025 by Arnika Patel, Keshav Kumar, and Dr. Bishwajeet Kumar Pandey

This work is subject to copyright. All rights are reserved by the publisher, whether the whole or part of the material is concerned, specifically the rights of translation, reprinting, reuse of illustrations, recitation, broadcasting, reproduction on microfilms or in any other physical way, and transmission or information storage and retrieval, electronic adaptation, computer software, or by similar or dissimilar methodology now known or hereafter developed.

Trademarked names, logos, and images may appear in this book. Rather than use a trademark symbol with every occurrence of a trademarked name, logo, or image, we use the names, logos, and images only in an editorial fashion and to the benefit of the trademark owner, with no intention of infringement of the trademark.

The use in this publication of trade names, trademarks, service marks, and similar terms, even if they are not identified as such, is not to be taken as an expression of opinion as to whether or not they are subject to proprietary rights.

While the advice and information in this book are believed to be true and accurate at the date of publication, neither the authors nor the editors nor the publisher can accept any legal responsibility for any errors or omissions that may be made. The publisher makes no warranty, express or implied, with respect to the material contained herein.

Managing Director, Apress Media LLC: Welmoed Spahr
Acquisitions Editor: Melissa Duffy
Development Editor: James Markham
Editorial Assistant: Gryffin Winkler
Copy Editor: April Rondeau

Cover designed by eStudioCalamar

Cover image designed by Milad Fakurian on Unsplash

Distributed to the book trade worldwide by Springer Science+Business Media New York, 1 New York Plaza, New York, NY 10004. Phone 1-800-SPRINGER, fax (201) 348-4505, e-mail orders-ny@springer-sbm.com, or visit www.springeronline.com. Apress Media, LLC is a Delaware LLC and the sole member (owner) is Springer Science + Business Media Finance Inc (SSBM Finance Inc). SSBM Finance Inc is a **Delaware** corporation.

For information on translations, please e-mail booktranslations@springernature.com; for reprint, paperback, or audio rights, please e-mail bookpermissions@springernature.com.

Apress titles may be purchased in bulk for academic, corporate, or promotional use. eBook versions and licenses are also available for most titles. For more information, reference our Print and eBook Bulk Sales web page at http://www.apress.com/bulk-sales.

Any source code or other supplementary material referenced by the author in this book is available to readers on GitHub. For more detailed information, please visit https://www.apress.com/gp/services/source-code.

If disposing of this product, please recycle the paper

Table of Contents

About the Authors xiii

About the Technical Reviewer xv

Chapter 1: Introduction to Kotlin 1

1.1 Kotlin vs. Java 1

1.2 Features of Kotlin 4

1.3 Benefits and Drawbacks of Kotlin 6

    Benefits 6

    Drawbacks 7

1.4 Applications of Kotlin 7

1.5 Setting Up Your Development Environment 8

    For Command Line 8

    Running Kotlin Commands in the Command Line 9

    Development Environment for IntelliJ IDEA 13

    Creating Your First Application in Kotlin 15

1.6 Summary 18

1.7 Test Your Knowledge 18

1.8 Answers 21

Chapter 2: Fundamentals of Kotlin Programming 23

2.1 Basic Structure and Syntax 23

    Kotlin Output 24

2.2 Using Comments in Kotlin 25

    Single-Line Comments 25

    Multi-Line Comments 25

2.3 Variables 26

TABLE OF CONTENTS

- 2.4 Datatypes 26
- 2.5 Operators 27
  - Arithmetic Operators 27
  - Logical Operators 29
  - Assignment Operators 30
  - Comparison Operators 31
- 2.6 Kotlin Strings 32
  - String Length 33
  - String Functions 33
- 2.7 Kotlin Arrays 34
  - Array Length 35
  - Array Element Change 35
  - Checking If an Item Exists 36
  - Accessing Array Items Using Loop 36
- 2.8 Control Flow 37
  - if 37
  - else 38
  - else if 39
  - when 40
- 2.9 Loops 41
  - while 41
  - do..while 42
  - for 43
- 2.10 Return and Jumps 43
  - break 43
  - continue 44
  - return 45
- 2.11 Type Checks 45
- 2.12 Smart Cast 46

2.13 Real-Life Programming Practices 46

2.14 Summary 49

2.15 Test Your Knowledge 49

2.16 Answers 52

Chapter 3: Functions in Kotlin 53

3.1 A Closer Look 53

    User-Defined Functions 53

    Parameters in Functions 54

    Body of Functions 54

    Return Value of the Functions 54

    Calling Functions 55

    Standard Library Functions 56

    Advantages and Disadvantages of Using Functions in Kotlin 57

3.2 Functions with Default and Named Arguments 58

    Default Arguments 58

    Named Arguments 60

3.3 Recursive Functions 61

    Normal Function Call 61

    Recursive Function Call 63

3.4 Tail Recursive Functions 64

3.5 Programming Practices 65

3.6 Summary 68

3.7 Test Your Knowledge 69

3.8 Answers 71

Chapter 4: Object-Oriented Programming with Kotlin 73

4.1 Classes and Objects 74

    Classes 74

    Objects 75

    Nested Classes 78

    Inner Classes 79

v

TABLE OF CONTENTS

4.2 Constructors 80
    Primary Constructor 81
    Using Secondary Constructors 84
4.3 Inheritance 86
    Kotlin Override Property 87
    Kotlin Inheritance with Primary Constructor 88
    Kotlin Inheritance with Secondary Constructor 89
    Calling Base Class Secondary Constructor from Derived Class Secondary Constructor 90
4.4 Interfaces 91
    Default Values and Methods 92
    Properties in Interfaces 93
    Inheritance in Interfaces 94
    Multiple Interfaces 95
4.5 Visibility Modifiers 96
4.6 Property 99
    Class Properties 99
    Setters and Getters 100
    Access Getter and Setter 101
    Custom Setter and Getter 101
4.7 Abstract Class 102
    Overriding Non-abstract Open Member with the Abstract 103
    Multiple Derived Classes 104
4.8 Data Class 105
4.9 Sealed Class 107
4.10 Enum Class 108
    Enum Properties and Methods 109
4.11 Practical Programming Exercises 111
4.12 Summary 124
4.13 Test Your Knowledge 124
4.14 Answers 126

Chapter 5: Error Handling and Exceptions 127

5.1 Exception-Handling Basics 127

    The try-catch Block as an Expression 129

    Finally Block 130

    Throw Keyword 132

5.2 Nested try Block 133

    Multiple Catch Blocks 134

    Using When in Catch Block 136

5.3 Custom Exceptions 137

5.4 Real-Life Programming Practices 138

5.5 Summary 143

5.6 Test Your Knowledge 143

5.7 Answers 145

Chapter 6: Collections and Generics 147

6.1 Collections 147

6.2 List 148

6.3 Set 153

6.4 Maps 158

6.5 Generics 164

    Basics of Generics 164

6.6 Real-Life Programming Practices 170

6.7 Summary 172

6.8 Test Your Knowledge 172

6.9 Answers 175

Chapter 7: Kotlin Coroutines 177

7.1 Introduction 177

7.2 Creating Coroutines 177

7.3 Structured Concurrency 178

7.4 Extract Function Refactoring 179

TABLE OF CONTENTS

7.5 Scope Builder and Concurrency 179

    Scope Builder 179

    Concurrency 180

7.6 An Explicit Job 181

7.7 Coroutines Are Lightweight 182

7.8 Coroutine Exception Handling 182

7.9 Coroutine Exception Handler 183

7.10 Cancellation and Exceptions 184

7.11 Exception Aggregation 185

7.12 Real-Life Programming Practices 186

7.13 Summary 188

7.14 Test Your Knowledge 188

7.15 Answers 191

Chapter 8: Kotlin Domain-Specific Language (DSL) 193

8.1 Introduction to Kotlin DSLs 193

    Advantages of DSLs 193

8.2 Writing Our First DSL 194

8.3 DSL by Applying Builder Pattern 197

8.4 DSL with Collections 198

8.5 DSL with @DslMarker Annotation 201

8.6 Real-Life Programming Practices 202

8.7 Summary 208

8.8 Test Your Knowledge 208

8.9 Answers 212

Chapter 9: Kotlin Standard Library 213

9.1 Introduction to the Kotlin Standard Library 213

9.2 Collection Functions 213

    Sorting 213

9.3 String Functions 220

9.4 Extension Functions 224
Extended Library Classes 225
9.5 Null Safety Functions 225
9.6 File and I/O Functions 226
Create File 226
Writing to File 226
Reading from File 226
Delete File 227
9.7 Real-Life Programming Practices 227
9.8 Summary 229
9.9 Test Your Knowledge 229
9.10 Answers 233

Chapter 10: Testing in Kotlin 235
10.1 Unit Testing 235
The Significance of Unit Testing 235
Establishing the Testing Environment 236
Composing Your Initial Unit Test 236
Optimal Strategies for Unit Testing 239
Testing Frameworks 241
10.2 Kotlin Unit Testing with MockK 242
Mocking and MockK: mocking in kotlin behaves like external real dependencies and mockK is powerful and lightweight mocking library 243
MockK Annotations 243
MockK Keywords 245
10.3 Kotlin Integration Testing 245
Integration Testing in Kotlin with Ktor 248
10.4 Conclusion 248
10.5 Test Your Knowledge 250
10.6 Answers 253

Chapter 11: Kotlin Reactive Extension 255

11.1 Introduction to RxKotlin 255

11.2 Core Rx Concepts 256

    Streams: The Heart of Reactive Programming 257

    Hot and Cold Observables 257

    Flow of Hot and Cold Streams 257

11.3 Usage of Rx 258

    Basic RxKotlin Usage 258

    Using filter and distinct 259

    Observable.Interval for Periodic Emissions 260

11.4 Kotlin Coroutines 261

11.5 Reactive Programming Patterns 262

11.6 Best Practices for Testing Reactive Code 263

11.7 Conclusion 264

11.8 Real-Life Programming Practices 264

11.9 Test Your Knowledge 266

11.10 Answers 268

Chapter 12: Working with API and Networking 269

12.1 Introduction to Kotlin APIs 269

12.2 Android Development APIs 270

12.3 Networking APIs 272

12.4 Database & Storage APIs 272

12.5 UI & Graphics APIs 273

12.6 Machine Learning & IoT APIs 273

12.7 Multimedia APIs 274

12.8 Cloud & Backend APIs 275

12.9 CASE STUDY 1: Using Google Map API in Kotlin 275

    STEP 1. Enable Google Maps API 275

    STEP 2. Add Dependencies 276

    STEP 3. Add API Key to Manifest 276

STEP 4. Add a Map Fragment 276

STEP 5. Load the Map in Kotlin 277

STEP 6. Run the App 278

Extra Features 278

12.10 CASE STUDY 2: Using MQTT API in Kotlin 278

STEP 1. Create a New Kotlin Project in IntelliJ IDEA 278

STEP 2. Add MQTT Dependency 279

STEP 3. Implement MQTT Client in Kotlin 279

STEP 4. Run the MQTT Client 281

STEP 5. Explanation 281

STEP 6. Extra Features 281

12.11 Conclusion and Future Scope 281

12.12 Test Your Knowledge 282

12.13 Answers 284

Chapter 13: Advanced Kotlin Programming 285

13.1 Introduction 285

13.2 Null Safety 286

Safe Call Operator in Kotlin 287

Elvis Operator in Kotlin 288

Non-Null Assertion (!!) in Kotlin 290

Safe Cast (as?) 291

let Scope Function 292

13.3 Higher-Order Functions and Lambdas 294

Higher-Order Function with Lambda 294

Higher-Order Function Returns a Function 296

Using Lambda with List Functions 297

13.4 Lazy Initialization 299

13.5 Property Delegation 300

13.6 Conclusion 302

13.7 Future Scope 302

13.8 Real-Life Programming Practice	303
13.9 Test Your Knowledge	306
13.10 Answers	309

Chapter 14: Data Analysis with Kotlin 311

14.1 Get Started with Kotlin Notebook	311
14.2 Add Library to Kotlin Notebook	315
14.3 Working with Data Sources	316
14.4 Data Visualization in Kotlin Notebook with Kandy	320
Create Line Chart	320
Create Points Chart	322
Create Bar Chart	323
14.5 Libraries for Data Analysis in Kotlin	325
14.6 Real-Life Programming Practice	325
14.7 Summary	327
14.8 Test Your Knowledge	327
14.9 Answers	330

Chapter 15: Kotlin Multiplatform 333

15.1 Introduction to Kotlin Multiplatform	333
How It Works	334
Benefits of KMP	335
Use Cases	335
15.2 Setting Up a Multiplatform Project for iOS	336
Steps for Creating iOS Project	338
Shared Module Configuration and Implementation	339
15.3 Multiplatform Libraries	340
Dependency on a Kotlin Library	341
Dependency on Another Multiplatform Project	342
15.4 Test Your Knowledge	343
15.5 Answers	345

Index 347

About the Authors

Arnika Patel currently serves as assistant professor at Parul University, Vadodara, Gujarat, where she continues to inspire and educate future tech innovators. She was a Kotlin developer with over six months' experience in the tech industry, which was in addition to more than two and a half years as an assistant professor. Holding a master's degree in engineering, her expertise in both software development and academia is well established. In 2015, she was honored with the prestigious Devang Mehta IT Award, a testament to her contributions to the field. She is also a proud member of the Indian Society for Technical Education (ISTE), reflecting her commitment to advancing the field of engineering education. Her blend of practical experience and academic insight informs her writing, offering valuable perspectives for both technology enthusiasts and professionals. Her area of specialization includes mobile ad-hoc networks, artificial intelligence, machine learning, and so forth.

Keshav Kumar is an assistant professor at the Department of Electronics and Communication Engineering at the Pranveer Singh Institute of Technology, Kanpur, India. His areas of specialization include deep learning, hardware security, green communication, low-power VLSI design, machine learning techniques, Wireless Sensor Networks (WSN), and Internet of Things (IoT). He has experience teaching Python programming, embedded systems, IoT, computer networks, and digital electronics.

ABOUT THE AUTHORS

Dr. Bishwajeet Kumar Pandey is a professor at GL Bajaj College of Technology and Management, Greater Noida, India. He has been a senior member of IEEE since 2019. He has over 15 years of industry and teaching experience and has authored and co-authored more than 170 papers. He has experience teaching ethical hacking, application and web security, cloud migration, incident handling and response, information security, artificial intelligence, machine learning, computer networks, and digital logic.

About the Technical Reviewer

Siddharth Kumar Patel has experience in successfully building and deploying a production Android application using current technologies like Kotlin and Jetpack Compose. He also has a solid Java background and extensive experience in Agile methodologies, which positions him as a good Android developer. His proficiency in developing data-intensive, responsive applications and his skill set with relevant industry tools further underscores his suitability.

His proactive approach to continuous learning, evidenced by completing Google-designed learning pathways, indicates a dedication to staying current with evolving Android best practices.

CHAPTER 1

Introduction to Kotlin

Kotlin is an object-oriented programming language developed by Jetbrains in 2016. Sponsored by Google, and one of the official languages for Android, Kotlin has become very popular because of its compatibility with Java and different platforms, such as Windows, Mac, Linux, and Raspberry Pi. In this chapter we'll get you grounded with some basics and close by setting up your development environment.

1.1 Kotlin vs. Java

Kotlin and Java are both good programming languages, and both are object-oriented programming languages, though developed for different reasons. Kotlin is mainly used for Android application development, whereas Java is mainly used for enterprise application development.

Java, a very popular programming language, was developed in 1996. Over the years it has developed quite a large community, but Kotlin is a new programming language with some modern features, making it an attraction for developers.

One of the most important differences between Kotlin and Java is syntax. Kotlin has very concise syntax as compared to Java, so one needs to write less code than when using Java. Also, Kotlin is more readable than Java. In Kotlin there is no need to define datatypes, as the compiler will automatically define them according to the values assigned.

In Java there is the possibility of any variable facing a null value, which can result in null pointer exceptions at runtime. Kotlin differs here, as in Kotlin you can decide whether the variable can be null or not. Thus you can avoid null pointer exceptions, which are very common in Java.

Kotlin uses extension functions, which means we can use any function of a class without creating a new class and inheriting it. In Java, to use the functionality of one class you need to create other class and inherit the class whose functionality you want to use.

CHAPTER 1 INTRODUCTION TO KOTLIN

In Android, one component that belongs to one application runs in the same process and same thread, which is the main thread and is responsible for the user interface (UI). Network operations and CPU operations are very lengthy, resulting in slow performance. To avoid this type of blockage, Java uses multithreading, where all of these operations run on multiple threads, making it more complex to handle. Kotlin uses coroutines, which is more clear and concise than handling multiple threads.

In Java there is a need to create fields or variables to store the data, constructors, and getter and setter for variables or fields, in addition to other functions like `toString()`, `equals()`, and so on. These classes are mainly intended to store data rather than having any functionality. Meanwhile, Kotlin provides a very simple way to create data classes—give keyword `data` as a prefix of the class name, and the compiler will automatically generate all the getters and setters for variables, and also constructors.

Kotlin uses a smart cast feature, which means the compiler will automatically handle redundant casts using the `is-checks` keyword. But in Java, the developer must check a variable's type in compatibility operations.

In Java there is checked exception support, so there must be a `catch` statement and exception declaration as needed. This ensures robust code, because errors are handled by checked exceptions. But it can be time consuming. Kotlin doesn't have checked exception support, meaning no declaration of exceptions or catch is required.

Kotlin is a mix of object-oriented and functional programming languages. Functional programming handles computational or mathematical functions. Higher-order functions and lambdas are examples of functional programming concepts present in Kotlin. Whereas Java is purely an object-oriented programming language, Java 8 has lambda functions.

Kotlin does not have wildcards (?- question mark -unknown type of variable), ternary operators, and public fields. Java does have wildcards, ternary operators, and public fields. Table 1-1 shows the pointed differences between Java and Kotlin.

Table 1-1. *Kotlin vs. Java*

	Kotlin	**Java**
Type	Object-oriented and functional programming language	Purely object-oriented programming language
First stable version released on	15 February 2016	23 January 1996
Product of	Jetbrains	Oracle
Community Support	As it is new technology, smaller community than Java	Large Community of Developers
Use	Used for mobile application development and server-side applications	Used for enterprise applications, desktop applications, mobile applications
Extensions	.kt (kotlin source file) .kts (kotlin script file) .ktm (kotlin module)	.java (java source file) .class (class file) .jar (archived file)
Line of Code (LOC)	Less as compared to Java	More as compared to Kotlin
Datatype	No need to assign, compiler will automatically assign datatype to variable	Compulsory to assign datatype to variable
Null Safety	Available	Not Available
Extension Function	We can create extension functions	Not supported by Java
Coroutine	We can create multiple threads in Kotlin by using coroutines	In Java, coroutines are not available; we need to use multithreading for creating multiple threads, which is more complex
Data Class	We can create data class in kotlin by giving prefix "*data*"	We cannot create data classes in Java
Smart Casts	Supported	Not Supported
Checked Exception	Not Available	Available

(*continued*)

Table 1-1. (*continued*)

	Kotlin	Java
Lambdas and Higher-Order Functions	Available in Kotlin	Available after Java 8 version
Wildcards	Not Available	Available
Public Fields	Not Available	Available
Ternary Operator	Not Available	Available

1.2 Features of Kotlin

Kotlin provides many features that make it very popular among developers. The following list shows each and every feature of Kotlin:

- **Interoperability:** Kotlin is designed in such a way that it can be interoperable with Java. That means Java code can be called from Kotlin and Kotlin code can be called from Java. This allows all developers to smoothly migrate from Java to Kotlin or to use existing Java libraries in Kotlin code.

- **Concise:** In Kotlin when you declare a variable there is no need to give the datatype, as the Kotlin compiler will automatically decide it. This and other functionalities, like null safety, extension functions, and so forth, are decided by Kotlin, thus reducing the amount of code required, as compared to Java.

- **Null Safety:** In Java most developers face a common exception known as a null pointer exception, which can be very distressing. In Kotlin, the developer can mostly eliminate null pointer exceptions by using a null safety feature to decide whether the variable can be null or not.

- **Data Classes:** Data classes are generally used for storing data. In Java the developer needs to declare the variable, getter, setter, and constructors, but in Kotlin the developer just needs to create one class by giving the prefix `data` before the class name, which will automatically create constructors, getter, and setter for the given variables.

- **Smart Casts:** Kotlin uses a smart cast feature, which means there is no need to check types. All casting checks are automatically handled by compiler using the `is-checks` keyword.

- **Compilation Time:** In Kotlin compilation time depends on various factors, like usage of complex code structure, development environment, which build system the developer is using, and the use of higher order functions. These will affect the compilation speed, but as compared to other languages like Java, the compilation speed of Kotlin is still faster.

- **Extension Function:** Extension functions allow you to add new methods or functions to existing classes without extending that class or changing the code of that class; i.e., without using inheritance. By using extension functions one can use any frameworks, libraries, or classes.

- **Lambdas and Higher Order Functions:** Kotlin is a functional programming language. That means it handles all the mathematical and computational functions. Higher order functions and lambdas are one of the functional programming features.

- **Companion Objects:** In Kotlin, a companion object is used in the same way as static variables are used in Java. We can say that it is a replacement for static variables. Companion objects are defined by the `Companion` keyword. The `Companion` keyword can be accessed by using a class name. Using companion objects will improve code organization and encapsulation.

- **Kotlin Multiplatform (KMP):** Kotlin multiplatform allows you to reuse Kotlin code to create cross-platform applications usable in platforms like iOS, macOS, Linux, Windows, Android, and so on. Using KMP, you can control different functionalities on different platforms and can extend existing applications on multiplatform modules.

- **Coroutine:** Kotlin includes the way of doing asynchronous programming by using coroutines. Coroutines can be used when developing multithreaded applications, those applications in which user experience as well as scalability is required. Coroutines handle multiple threads without their blocking each other.

- **Lazy Loading:** Kotlin uses an important feature called lazy loading, mostly while developing Android applications. In Android applications having a quicker startup time will enhance the user experience, which can be achieved using the lazy loading feature. This means that the application loads only those data that are required at the time.

1.3 Benefits and Drawbacks of Kotlin

While Kotlin is a modern, concise, object-oriented, and functional programming language, like any other programming language it has its benefits and drawbacks.

Benefits

- Kotlin is easy to learn because its syntax and structure are very easy. If you have worked in Java then you will easily understand Kotlin in no time.

- Kotlin can use Java code inside Kotlin or Kotlin code inside Java. Developers can also use Java libraries or frameworks in Kotlin.

- Coroutines are beneficial for working with multithreaded applications and asynchronous programming. Kotlin handles multiple threads via coroutines without blocking another thread.

- Kotlin has some powerful features like lambdas, higher order functions, smart casts, companion objects, extension functions, and more that enhance the performance of applications.

- Kotlin is more reliable in terms of being a faulty or buggy system. There are fewer chances of bugs because before releasing the final version of Kotlin it goes through many alpha and beta versions.

- Kotlin is easy to learn for all Java developers, as the skills that a Java developer uses to develop Android applications will work for Kotlin too.

- Kotlin is also multiplatform and can be used across iOS, Android, macOS, Linux, Windows, etc.

Drawbacks

- Being a modern and new programming language, Kotlin has less community support. It will be more difficult for developers to find resources, libraries, or frameworks while developing software applications. It can also be difficult for a new developer to switch to Kotlin because resources are limited for learning purposes.

- In Android development, Kotlin applications might have a large APK size due to the usage of Kotlin's standard library.

- Despite being a very popular programming language, there are fewer skilled programmers available to recruit from all over the world.

- Though Kotlin is generally faster, in some cases where the usage of lambdas or extension functions is high one might see slow compilation speeds.

1.4 Applications of Kotlin

Following are some applications in which we can incorporate the Kotlin programming language:

- Google announced in Google I/O 17 that Kotlin is the preferred language for Android application development.

- Kotlin can also be used to develop backend web applications and services.

- Kotlin multiplatform mobile is used to develop applications for both iOS and Android platforms.

- Kotlin can be used with JavaScript; i.e., Kotlin/JS for web development.

- Kotlin has many libraries for data science and machine learning, which allows developers to use Kotlin for those purposes.

- Kotlin can also be used in game development or in cross-platform game development.

- Kotlin can be used with AWS and Google Cloud to develop serverless applications.

- Kotlin/Native can be used to develop projects for embedded systems.

1.5 Setting Up Your Development Environment For Command Line

To set up the Kotlin development environment, we need to follow four steps. First, we will install JDK, or if it's already installed we will verify the installation. Then we must download the Kotlin compiler, set up the environment variable, and then, finally, verify the installation. Here we are following the installation process for the Windows operating system. For Mac users, the steps will be same.

Kotlin runs on the Java virtual machine (JVM), so first you need to install JDK or verify if it is already installed. To install it you can download it from the official Oracle website and run that .exe file.

1. Type the commands shown in Figure 1-1. If it is installed then it will give the version name (java 18). Otherwise, it will give an error that the command `javas` is not recognized.

```
C:\Users\key>javac -version
javac 18
```

Figure 1-1. Verify Java version

CHAPTER 1 INTRODUCTION TO KOTLIN

2. Download the latest version of the Kotlin compiler, place it in the folder you want, and extract that zip file. You'll then see all the files required to run Kotlin in the "bin" folder (Figure 1-2).

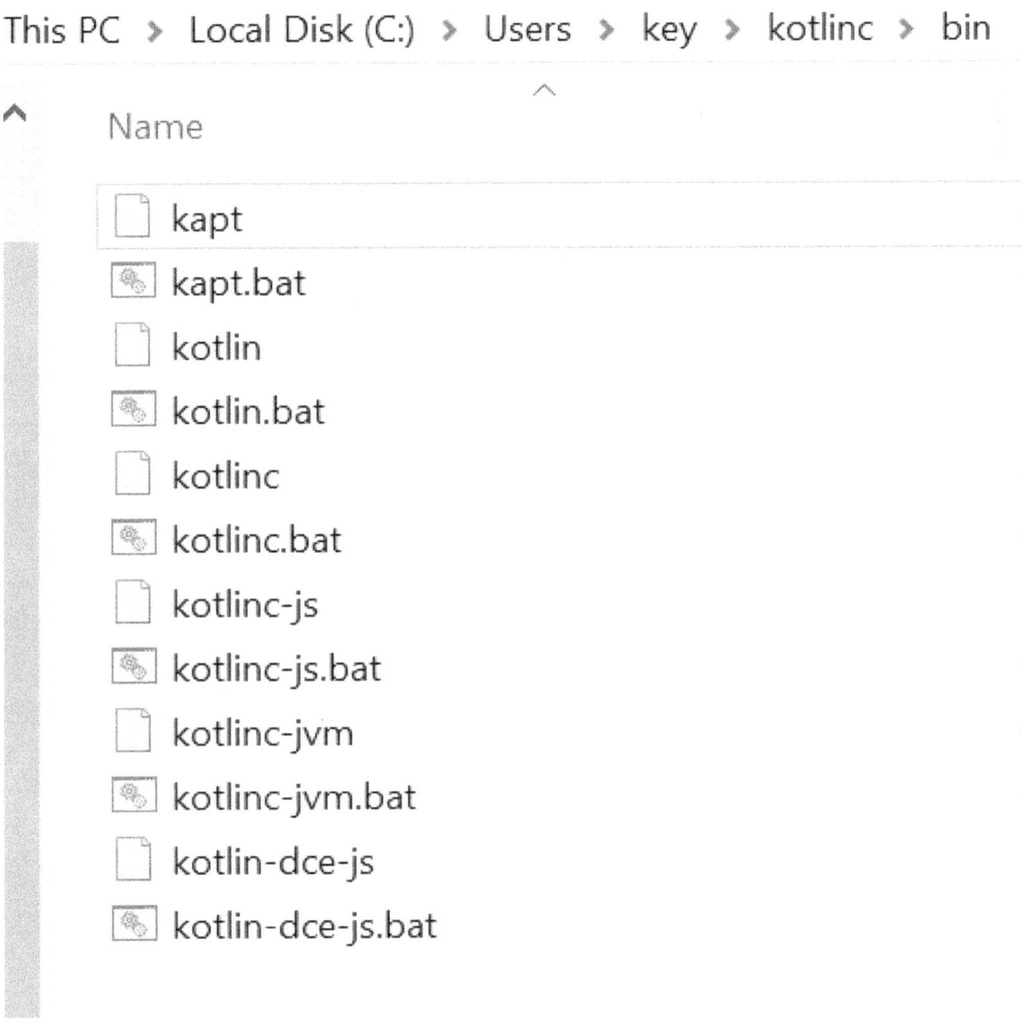

This PC › Local Disk (C:) › Users › key › kotlinc › bin

Name

- kapt
- kapt.bat
- kotlin
- kotlin.bat
- kotlinc
- kotlinc.bat
- kotlinc-js
- kotlinc-js.bat
- kotlinc-jvm
- kotlinc-jvm.bat
- kotlin-dce-js
- kotlin-dce-js.bat

Figure 1-2. *Files that run Kotlin*

Running Kotlin Commands in the Command Line

Now you need to set the PATH environment variable by location of the Kotlin compiler.

1. Right-click on "This PC" and select "Properties" (Figure 1-3).

CHAPTER 1   INTRODUCTION TO KOTLIN

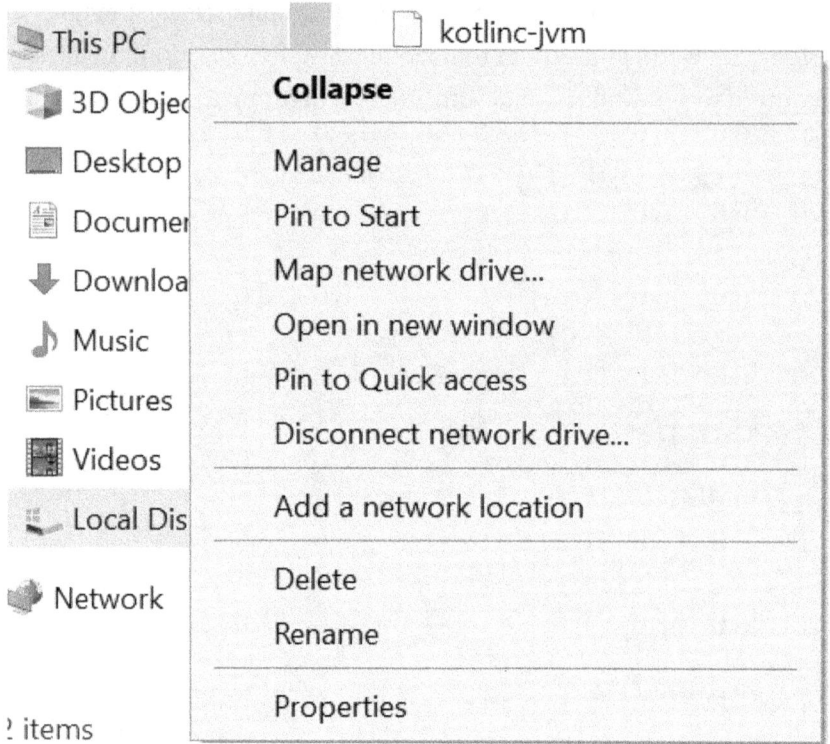

Figure 1-3. *Right-click "This PC"*

2. Select "Advanced System Settings" (Figure 1-4).

Figure 1-4. *Advanced system settings*

CHAPTER 1 INTRODUCTION TO KOTLIN

3. Select "Environment Variables" (Figure 1-5).

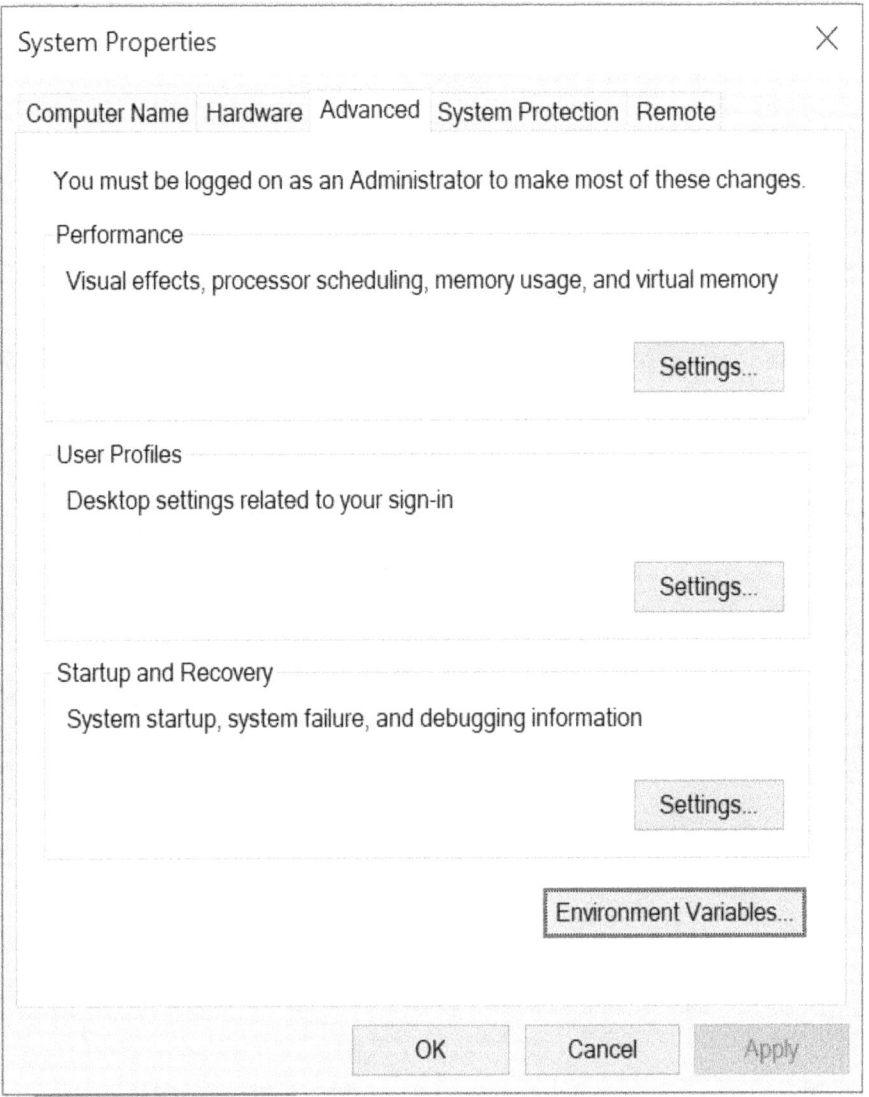

Figure 1-5. *Environment Variables*

CHAPTER 1   INTRODUCTION TO KOTLIN

4. Select "Path" under "System variables" (Figure 1-6).

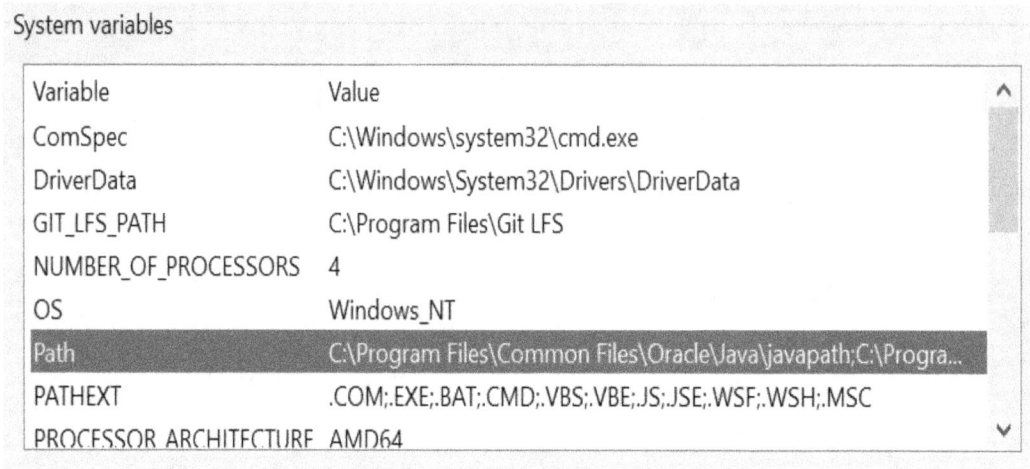

Figure 1-6. *System variables*

5. Add files that run Kotlin by clicking on the Browse button (Figure 1-7).

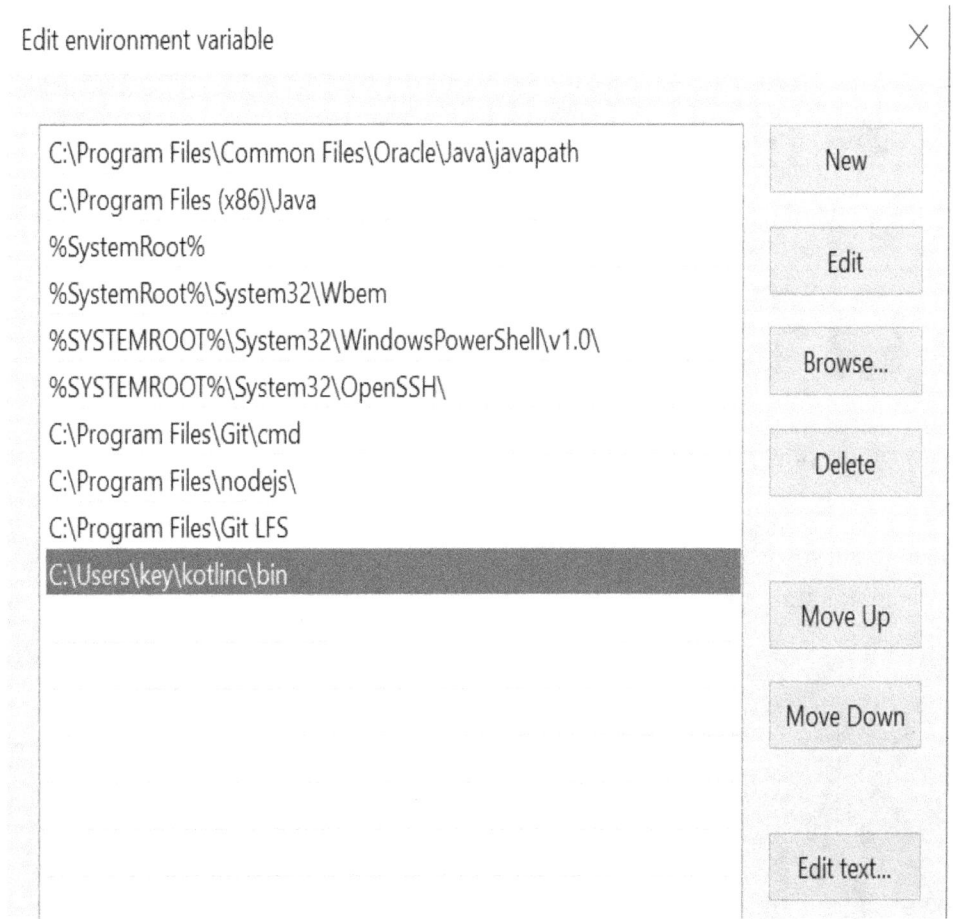

Figure 1-7. Add Kotlin-run files

Now we have successfully set up the environment variable. The next step is to download and install the development environment for kotlin.

Development Environment for IntelliJ IDEA

In this section, first we will install the IntelliJ IDEA for developing Kotlin code. We will then verify the installation by running a sample program. Note that there are two versions of IntelliJ, Ultimate and Community. The Community version is free to use. The installation steps for both of them are the same.

Kotlin is developed by JetBrains, which developed integrated development environments (IDEs) like IntelliJ IDEA. It also has a toolkit to run Kotlin.

CHAPTER 1 INTRODUCTION TO KOTLIN

1. To start installation, first download the most recent version of IntelliJ IDEA from the JetBrains website.

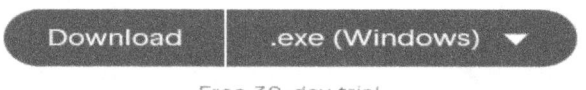

Figure 1-8. *IntelliJ IDEA*

2. Once you have downloaded the .exe file, double-click it to start the installation process. Figures 1-9 and 1-10 show the process.

Figure 1-9. *Install IntelliJ IDEA*

CHAPTER 1　INTRODUCTION TO KOTLIN

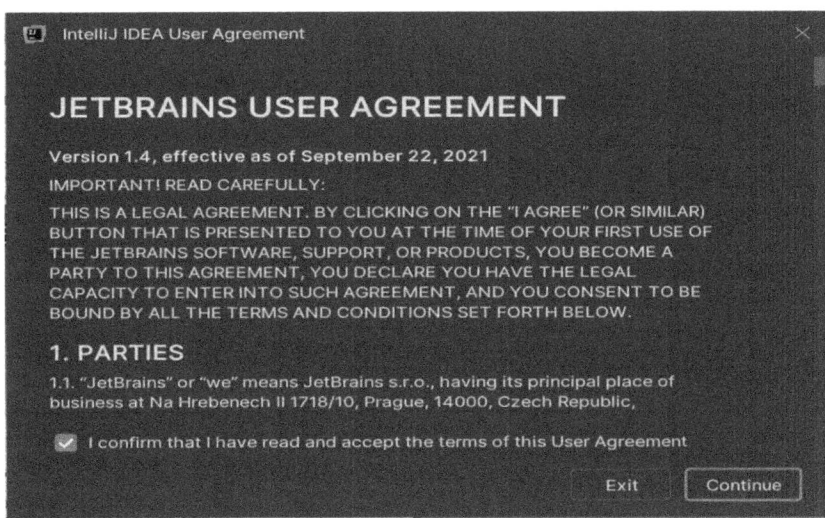

Figure 1-10. Agree to terms

Creating Your First Application in Kotlin

After installation, create a new Kotlin application by clicking on "New Project," as shown in Figure 1-11.

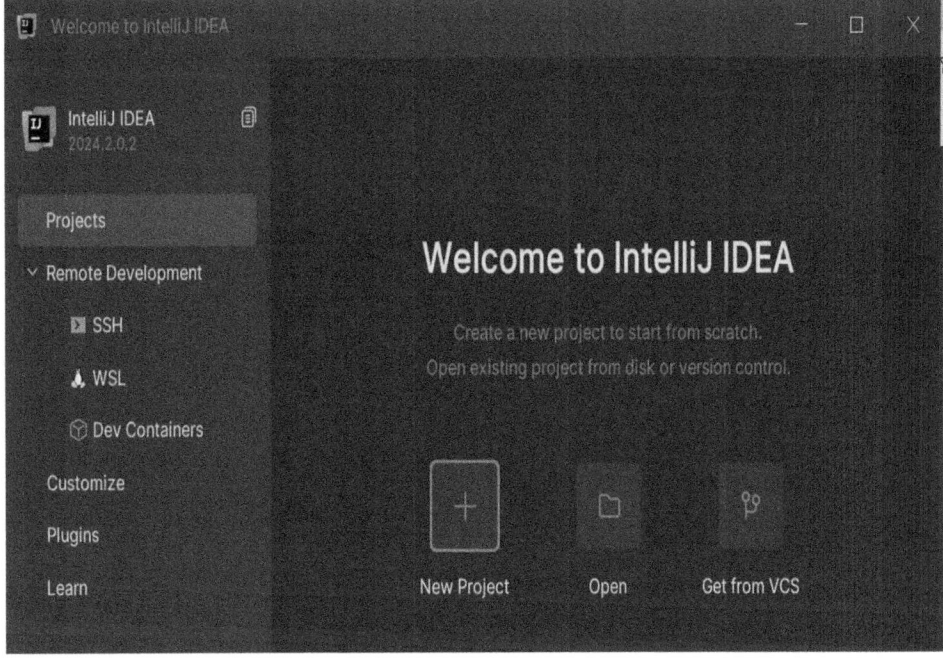

Figure 1-11. Create new project

15

CHAPTER 1   INTRODUCTION TO KOTLIN

1. Select "Kotlin" and click the Next button (Figure 1-12).

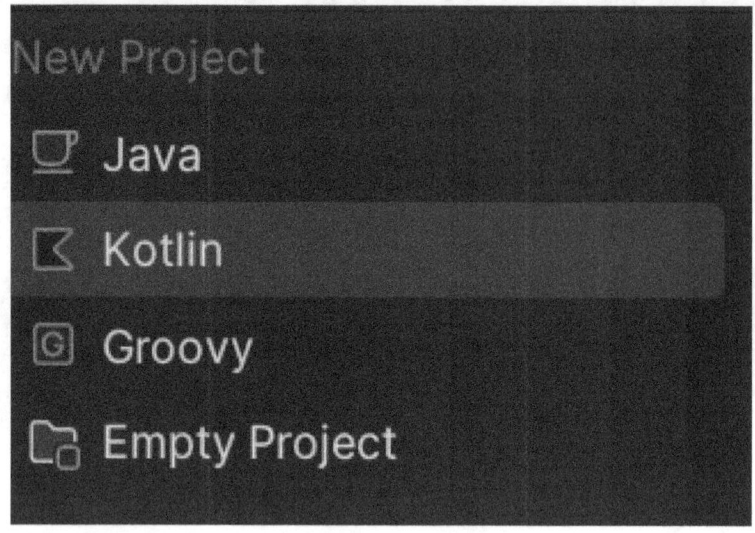

Figure 1-12. Select "Kotlin"

2. Name the project and click the Finish button (Figure 1-13).

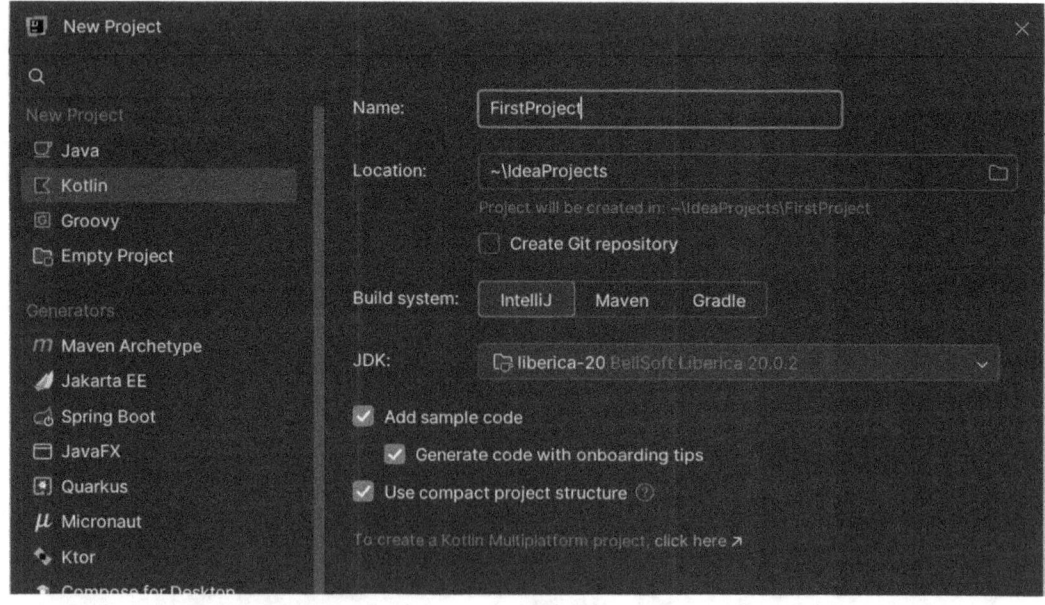

Figure 1-13. Name the project

CHAPTER 1　INTRODUCTION TO KOTLIN

3. Create a new Kotlin file under the "src" folder and name it "Mainka" (Figure 1-14).

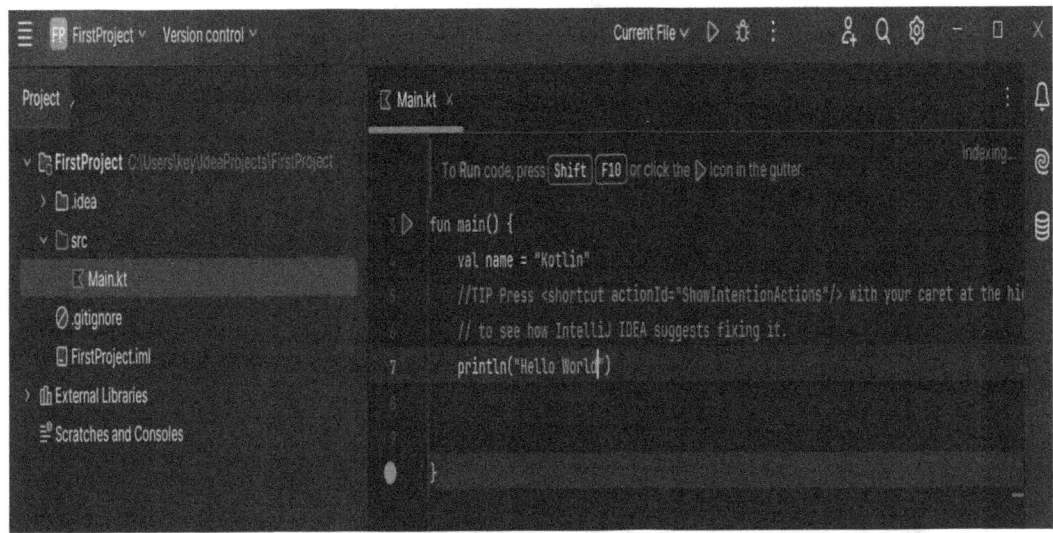

Figure 1-14. *Main.kt program*

4. Create a sample function to print "Hello world" and then test whether it runs correctly (Figure 1-15). To run the program, click on the green triangle that appears to the left of fun main(). Note that whenever you run a Kotlin program for the first time it will take some time to compile the functionalities.

CHAPTER 1   INTRODUCTION TO KOTLIN

Figure 1-15. Run program

1.6 Summary

In this chapter, we have learned about what Kotlin is, the benefits and drawbacks of Kotlin, and its features. We've seen how to set up the development environment for creating and running Kotlin programs and also have tested our installation by running a small program.

1.7 Test Your Knowledge

1. Which command is used for checking if JDK is installed or not?

    a. jdk

    b. java -i

    c. javac -v

    d. javac –version

2. Which Kotlin feature helps prevent null pointer exceptions?

    a. smart casts

    b. null safety

    c. lazy initialization

    d. lambdas

3. What is the main benefit of using the `lazy` keyword in Kotlin?

    a. It ensures that variables initialize only when they are first accessed in the program.

    b. It helps in preventing null pointer exceptions.

    c. It prevents part of the program from compiling.

    d. It optimizes the memory usage by deleting unused variables.

4. Which keyword is used to declare static-like variables in Kotlin?

    a. static

    b. final

    c. object

    d. companion

5. Which of the following is the main usage of the Kotlin programming language?

    a. web application development

    b. system programming

    c. enterprise programming

    d. Android application development

6. Which of the following is true about the Kotlin programming language?

    a. object-oriented programming language

    b. functional programming language

c. both (a) and (b)

d. none of above

7. Which of the following features is not supported by Kotlin?

   a. ternary operator

   b. smart casts

   c. extension function

   d. coroutines

8. The Kotlin programming language is fully compatible with _____?

   a. Python

   b. C

   c. Java

   d. Swift

9. Who developed the Kotlin programming language?

   a. Google

   b. Oracle

   c. Jetbrains

   d. Microsoft

10. In which year was Kotlin announced as an official programming language for Android application development by Google I/O?

    a. 2021

    b. 2017

    c. 2016

    d. 2015

1.8 Answers

1. d
2. b
3. a
4. d
5. d
6. c
7. a
8. c
9. c
10. b

CHAPTER 2

Fundamentals of Kotlin Programming

2.1 Basic Structure and Syntax

In chapter 1, we saw how to install Kotlin and run our first program to print "Hello World." For that, we use the following code:

```
fun main() {
    println("Hello world")
}
```

Where the `fun` keyword is used for declaring a function; `println()` is used for printing lines written inside brackets; and `main()` is the function that will be available in each and every Kotlin program. It indicates the starting point of code execution in a Kotlin program. Any lines of code written inside this `main()` function's curly brackets will be executed.

In previous versions of Kotlin before version 1.3 it was required to add parameters to a `main()` function. The following is an example of using a `main()` function with a parameter:

```
fun main(args : Array<String>) {
  println("Hello World")
}
```

Output:

```
Hello World
```

This is not required anymore in the upgraded versions of Kotlin, but it will not cause any harm to your program if you were previously using it and continue to use it. However, programs will run fine without it.

Kotlin Output

The println() function is used for printing output or any text or numbers in Kotlin. You can also add multiple println() functions in your program. Here, every new println() will add a new line to your output. The following shows the multiple println() functions:

```
fun main() {
   println("1. Hello Kotlin...")
   println("2. Welcome to Kotlin Learning Experience...")
   println("3. Have a great experience...")
}
```

Output:

```
1. Hello Kotlin...
2. Welcome to Kotlin Learning Experience...
3. Have a great experience...
```

However, if you want to output text without creating a new line, then you can add this with the use of the print() function instead of using println(). The following is an example of using a print() function instead of a println() function.

```
fun main() {
   print("1. Hello Kotlin...")
   print("2. Welcome to Kotlin Learning Experience...")
   print("3. Have a great experience...")
}
```

Output:

```
1. Hello Kotlin...2. Welcome to Kotlin Learning Experience...3. Have a great experience...
```

2.2 Using Comments in Kotlin

Comments are used to explain the code or to not run a particular line or block of code. There are two ways to add comments in your code.

Single-Line Comments

Single-line comments can be added by using two forward slashes (//). Any text after // in the same line will not be executed or will be ignored at runtime.

The following shows the usage of single-line comments before a line of code:

```
fun main() {
    //print hello world
    print("Hello Kotlin...")
}
```

Output:

```
Hello Kotlin...
```

The following is the usage of a single-line comment at the end of a line of code:

```
fun main() {
    print("Hello Kotlin...") //print hello kotlin
}
```

Output:

```
Hello Kotlin...
```

Multi-Line Comments

To ignore or to not run a block of code, multi-line comments are used. Multi-line comments start with /* and end with */. Any text between /*...*/ will be ignored or not run during the program run.

The following is an example of multi-line comments:

```
fun main() {
    /*
```

The following is an example that will print "Hello Kotlin":

```
    */
    print("Hello Kotlin...")
}
```

Output:

```
Hello Kotlin...
```

2.3 Variables

Variables are generally used for storing values. In Kotlin programming, we can create variables by using var or val. The following is the syntax for declaring a variable:

```
var variablename = value
val variablename = value
```

For example,

```
var bookname = "kotlin"
val bookpublisher = "apress"
```

The difference between var and val is, when we create a variable using val it cannot be changed or modified, but when we create a variable using var it can be. Using val, we can assign a value that is not going to change at any point of time in program; using var, we can assign a value that can be changed in the program. For example,

```
val pi = 3.14
var name = "kotlin"
name = "kotlin programming"
```

2.4 Datatypes

A datatype is a variable or attribute that indicates the type of data a parameter is holding. It is very important because users and programs need to know how to handle that variable or parameter.

CHAPTER 2 FUNDAMENTALS OF KOTLIN PROGRAMMING

In Kotlin programming, the type of variable is decided when we declare a variable and assign its value. For example,

```
val num = 4                // Int
val numAverage = 3.0       // Double
val word = 'k'             // Char
val isTrue = true          // Boolean
val myName = "kotlin"      // String
```

2.5 Operators

Operators in Kotlin are used to perform operations on values or variables. The operations are called operators, while the values are known as operands. Table 2-1 shows an example of the difference between operators and operands.

Table 2-1. *Difference between Operator and Operand*

Operand	Operator	Operand
30	+	40
50	-	60

There are four types of operators available in Kotlin:

1. Arithmetic operators
2. Logical operators
3. Assignment operators
4. Comparison operators

Arithmetic Operators

To perform general mathematical operations, arithmetic operators are used. Table 2-2 shows the various arithmetic operators available in Kotlin.

CHAPTER 2 FUNDAMENTALS OF KOTLIN PROGRAMMING

Table 2-2. Arithmetic Operators

Operator	Name	Example	Description
+	Addition	A + B	Use to perform addition operation
-	Subtraction	A – B	Use to perform subtraction operation
*	Multiplication	A * B	Use to perform multiplication operation
/	Division	A / B	Use to perform division operation
%	Modulus	A % B	Use to perform modulus operation
++	Increment	A++	Use to increment value by one
--	Decrement	B--	Use to decrement value by one

Let's take an example of using arithmetic operators in Kotlin code. Here I have used the string interpolation ($A, $B) to print the values of A and B, which is described in a later section (i.e., string function and Table 2-6).

```
fun main() {
    var A=40
    var B=30
    println("$A+$B="+(A+B))
    println("$A-$B="+(A-B))
    println("$A*$B="+(A*B))
    println("$A/$B="+(A/B))
    print("$A++=")
    A++
    println(A)
    print("$B--=")
    B--
    println(B)
}
```

Output:

40+30=70
40-30=10
40*30=1200

40/30=1
40++=41
30--=29

Logical Operators

Table 2-3 shows the various logical operations available in Kotlin.

Table 2-3. Logical Operators

Operator	Name	Example	Description
&&	Logical AND	A>10 && B>20	Returns true if both the operations' results are true; otherwise returns false
||	Logical OR	A>10 || B>20	Returns true if any of the operations' results are true
!	Logical NOT	A!	Returns true if the operation's result is false and returns false if the operation result is true

Let's see an example of using logical operators in Kotlin code:

```
fun main() {
    val A=40
    val B=30
    val C=20
    val D=10
    println(A>B && C>D)
    println(A>B || C<D)
    println(!true)
}
```

Output:

true
true
false

CHAPTER 2 FUNDAMENTALS OF KOTLIN PROGRAMMING

Assignment Operators

To assign values to variables, we use assignment operators. Table 2-4 shows several assignment operators.

Table 2-4. Assignment Operators

Operator	Example	Equivalent To
=	A = 2	A = 2
+=	A += 2	A = A + 2
-=	A -= 2	A = A - 2
*=	A *= 2	A = A * 2
/=	A /= 2	A = A / 2
%=	A %= 2	A = A % 2

Let's see an example of using assignment operators in Kotlin code:

```
fun main() {
    var A=50
    println("A = "+A)
    A+=2
    println("A+=2 is "+A)
    A-=2
    println("A-=2 is "+A)
    A*=2
    println("A*=2 is "+A)
    A/=2
    println("A/=2 is "+A)
    A%=2
    println("A%=2 is "+A)
}
```

Output:

```
A = 50
A+=2 is 52
A-=2 is 50
A*=2 is 100
A/=2 is 50
A%=2 is 0
```

Comparison Operators

Comparison operators are used to compare values, which will result in false or true according to the result of comparison. Table 2-5 displays the multiple comparison operators which we can use in Kotlin.

Table 2-5. *Comparison Operators*

Operator	Name	Example
==	Equal To	A == B
!=	Not Equal To	A != B
>	Greater Than	A > B
<	Less Than	A < B
>=	Greater Than or Equal To	A >= B
<=	Less Than or Equal To	A <= B

The following is an example of using a comparison operator in Kotlin:

```kotlin
fun main() {
    val A=50
    val B=20
    println("A=$A")
    println("B=$B")
    println("A == B is ${A==B}")
    println("A > B is ${A>B}")
```

```
    println("A < B is ${A<B}")
    println("A >= B is ${A>=B}")
    println("A <= B is ${A<=B}")
}
```

Output:

```
A=50
B=20
A == B is false
A > B is true
A < B is false
A >= B is true
A <= B is false
```

2.6 Kotlin Strings

Strings are generally defined as a collection of words. Kotlin strings are used to store text. We can define any variable as a string by giving its value inside double quotes, as follows:

```
var myFirstString = "Welcome Kotlin"
```

The Kotlin compiler is smart enough to understand that the type of `myFirstString` is `String` as we have assigned its value by using double quotes. However, like Java, you can assign a type to a variable as follows:

```
var myFirstString : String = "Welcome Kotlin"
```

If you want to create a string without giving its value, then the type specification is a must; otherwise, it will give an error. The following is an example:

```
var myFirstString : String
myFirstString = "Welcome Kotlin"
```

CHAPTER 2 FUNDAMENTALS OF KOTLIN PROGRAMMING

String Length

The number of characters present in a string is called its length. The following is an example of how you can find the length of a string:

```
var alphabetText = "abcdefghij"
println("The length of alphabetText is "+alphabetText.length)
```

String Functions

In Kotlin there are many functions available to perform string operations. Table 2-6 describes all the available functions.

Table 2-6. *String Functions*

Function Name	Description
compareTo()	Use for comparing two strings and returns result 0 if both strings are equal
indexOf()	Use for searching for the first occurrence of specific word
uppercase()	Use to convert string into uppercase
lowercase()	Use to convert string into lowercase
Concatenation (+)	Used for concatenation of two strings
String Templates/ Interpolation ($)	Instead of using Concatenation we can use this for merging two strings. This can also be used when you want to print the value of a variable inside println function—i.e., $varName. To print the result of some operation on a variable, it can be used with curly braces—i.e., ${varName.anyFunction}

Let's see an example of using all these functions in the Kotlin program:

```
fun main() {
    val first="Hello"
    val second="Kotlin"
    var first_second=""
    println("Length of String first: ${first.length}")
    println("String Compare: ${first.compareTo("Hello")}")
    println("Convert String to Uppercase: ${first.uppercase()}")
    println("Convert String to Lowercase:+${first.lowercase()}")
```

33

```
    first_second=first+second
    println("String Concatenation: $first_second")
    println("String Templates/Interpolation: $first$second")
   println("Finding the indexof String kotlin: ${first_second.
indexOf("Kotlin")}")
}
```

Output:

```
Length of String first: 5
String Compare: 0
Convert String to Uppercase: HELLO
Convert String to Lowercase: hello
String Concatenation: HelloKotlin
String Templates/Interpolation: HelloKotlin
Finding the indexof String kotlin: 5
```

2.7 Kotlin Arrays

Arrays are used for storing lists of items of the same type. Declaring many variables to store their values can be tedious, time-consuming, and complex, so instead we can just declare one array and store all the values in that array.

In Kotlin, the arrayOf() function is used for declaring an array, as follows:

```
val numbers = arrayOf(0,1,2,3,4,5,6,7,8,9)      //array of integers
val colors = arrayOf("red","green","blue","orange","yellow")  //array of strings
```

Example:

```
fun main() {
    val colors = arrayOf("red","green","blue")
    println(colors[0]) //print value from array at position 0
    println(colors[1]) //print value from array at position 1
    println(colors[2]) //print value from array at position 2
}
```

Output:

```
red
green
blue
```

The preceding example declares the array of colors and prints it using its index. To access the values of an array we need to use the name of the array followed by indices of the element we need to access.

Array Length

To find how many elements are stored in an array, we can use the size property of an array, as follows:

```
fun main() {
    val colors = arrayOf("red","green","blue")
    println(colors.size)
}
```

Output:

```
3
```

Array Element Change

Following is an example of how we can change an existing element of an array:

```
fun main() {
    val colors = arrayOf("red","green","blue")
    println("colors[0] is: ${colors[0]}")
    colors[0]="black"
    println("colors[0] is: ${colors[0]}")
}
```

Output:

```
colors[0] is: red
colors[0] is: black
```

CHAPTER 2 FUNDAMENTALS OF KOTLIN PROGRAMMING

In the preceding example, it will first print the existing value of index 0 in the colors array. After that, we change the value of that by assigning new value to index 0. Last, it will print the newly assigned value.

Checking If an Item Exists

The in operator is used to check if a particular item exists in an array, as follows:

```
fun main() {
    val colors = arrayOf("red","green","blue")
    if("red" in colors){
        println("It exists")
    }else{
        println("It does not exists")
    }
}
```

Output:

```
It exists
```

This example uses the in operator so see if red is exists in the colors array, and it prints the value accordingly.

Accessing Array Items Using Loop

We can access array elements by using loops instead of using indices all the time. The following shows this:

```
fun main() {
    val colors = arrayOf("red","green","blue","purple","white")
    for(color in colors){
        println(color)
    }
}
```

Output:

```
red
green
blue
purple
white
```

This example shows that by using a `for` loop we can access all the elements of an array. It will loop through the colors array and print all the elements present in the array.

2.8 Control Flow

In Kotlin, programmers can use conditions to complete different actions. Following are the conditional statements available in Kotlin.

if

The `if` statement will check the condition inside the `if` statement, and if it is true then the block of code written inside the `if` will run; otherwise it will not.

Syntax:

```
If( condition ){
    // block of code to execute if condition is true
}
```

Example:

```
fun main() {
    val Age=80
    if(Age > 60){
        println("Senior Citizen")
    }
}
```

Output:

```
Senior Citizen
```

In the preceding example, first we define the variable Age. After that, we use the `if` statement to check whether the age is greater than 60 or not. If the age is greater than 60, than it will print "Senior Citizen"; otherwise it will not.

else

The block of code written inside `else` will run when the condition inside the `if` statement is false.

Syntax:

```
If( condition ){
    // block of code to execute if condition is true
}else{
    // block of code to execute if condition is false
}
```

Example:

```
fun main() {
    val Age=40
    if(Age > 60){
        println("Senior Citizen")
    }else{
        println("Not Senior Citizen")
    }
}
```

Output:

```
Not Senior Citizen
```

In the preceding example, if the age is greater than 60 than it will print "Senior Citizen," and if the age is not greater than 60 then the `else` block will run and it will print "Not Senior Citizen."

else if

An `else if` statement will give a new condition to test if the previous or first condition is false.

Syntax:

```
If( conditionA ){
    // block of code to execute if conditionA is true
}else if(conditionB){
    // block of code to execute if conditionA is false and
conditionB is true
}else{
    // block of code to execute if conditionA is false and conditionB
is false
}
```

Example:

```
fun main() {
   val Age=19
    if(Age > 60){
        println("Senior Citizen")
    }else if(Age >30 && Age < 60){
        println("Middle Age")
    }else if(Age <30 && Age > 17){
        println("Young")
    }else{
        println("Kid")
    }
}
```

Output:

Young

In the preceding example, first it will check if the age is greater than 60; if it's true then it will print "Senior Citizen," otherwise a second condition will be checked. If the age is greater than 30 and less than 60 then it will print "Middle Age"; otherwise, the next condition will be checked. If the age is greater than 17 and less than 30 then it will print "Young"; and lastly, if all conditions are false then it will print "Kid" inside the else block.

when

A when statement provides multiple blocks of code to run with different conditions.

Syntax:

```
when( condition that needs to check){
    condition1 -> { // run if condition1 is true }
    condition2 -> { // run if condition2 is true }
    condition3 -> { // run if condition3 is true }
    else -> { // run if above all conditions are false }
}
```

Example:

```
fun main() {
    val Month=8
    when(Month){
        1 -> {println("January")}
        2 -> {println("February")}
        3 -> {println("March")}
        4 -> {println("April")}
        5 -> {println("May")}
        6 -> {println("June")}
        7 -> {println("July")}
        8 -> {println("August")}
        9 -> {println("September")}
        10 -> {println("October")}
        11 -> {println("November")}
        else -> {println("December")}
    }
}
```

Output:

August

In the preceding example, first we assign the value of the month, which is 8. After assigning the value the when statement will check for all the cases from 1 to 7, all of which are false, and then check 8, which is true, so it will print "August." Similarly, when there are multiple choices available in a program then instead of using multiple else..if statements we can use when.

2.9 Loops

In programming languages, loops are used for performing a specified block of code until the condition matches. In Kotlin, multiple types of loops are available, like while, do.. while, and for.

while

A while loop runs the block of code until the given condition inside the while block is true.

Syntax:

```
while(condition){
    // block of code will be executed until above condition is true
}
```

Example:

```
fun main() {
    var number = 1
    while(number <= 10){
        print(" "+number)
        number++
    }
}
```

Output:

1 2 3 4 5 6 7 8 9 10

This example will print values of numbers from 1 until the given condition number <=10 is true.

do..while

In a do..while loop, the block of code will be executed once; after that, it will check the condition. Until the condition is true, the code written inside the do block will be executed.

Syntax:

```
do {
     // block of code will be executed until below condition is true
}while(condition)
```

Example:

```
fun main() {
    var number = 1
    do{
        print(" "+number)
        number++
    }while(number <= 10)
}
```

Output:

1 2 3 4 5 6 7 8 9 10

In the preceding example, first the block of code written inside the do will be executed, which will print a number and increment the value by one. After that, it will print numbers until the condition written in the while is true, so the output of the program will be numbers from 1 to 10.

for

In programming languages when we use arrays and want to perform operations on them, we can use a for loop to iterate and perform the required operations.

Syntax:

```
for(range){
    // operation needs to perform for given range
}
```

Example:

```
fun main() {
    val days = arrayOf("Sun","Mon","Tue","Wed","Thu","Fri","Sat")
    for(day in days){
        print(" $day")
    }
}
```

Output:

```
Sun Mon Tue Wed Thu Fri Sat
```

The preceding example will print each day one by one from the array "days." The output will be all the elements from that array.

2.10 Return and Jumps

To perform a jump out of the loops or a return from functions, Kotlin has three structural types of jump and return statements available.

break

The break statement is used for jumping out of the enclosing loop.

Example:

```
fun main() {
    var i=1
    while(i<8){
```

```
        print("$i ")
        i++
        if(i==6){
        break
        }
    }
}
```

Output:

1 2 3 4 5

This will print numbers from 1 to 5, and when the value of *i* will be equal to 6 it will be jumped out from the loop.

continue

Use `continue` to move to the next step after jumping out of the loop.

Example:

```
fun main() {
    var i=1
    while(i<8){
        print("$i ")
            i++
            if(i==6){
            i++
            continue
        }
    }
}
```

Output:

1 2 3 4 5 7

This will print numbers from 1 to 7 and skip the number 6 because of the `continue` statement written inside the `if` code block.

return

This will return from the enclosing function.

Example:

```
fun main() {
   for(i in 1..5){
      print("$i ")
      if(i==4){
          return
      }
   }
}
```

Output:

1 2 3 4

In this example, when the value of *i* is equal to 4, then it will return from the enclosing loop and print the values from 1 to 4 and skip the 5.

2.11 Type Checks

In Kotlin we use type checks to enable users or programmers to check the type of the variable. To do so at runtime use is or !is operators.

```
fun main() {
    val first="Hello"
   if(first is String){
      println("Length of String first: "+first.length)
   }
   if(first !is String){
      println("These will not print as the type of first is String")
   }
}
```

Output:

Length of String first: 5

2.12 Smart Cast

In Kotlin, most of the time you don't need to use casting of the type, because Kotlin will automatically cast the datatype of the variable according to the assigned value. This is known as a smart class feature.

```
fun main() {
   var A:Any
    A="variable now cast to string"
    println(A)
}
```

Output:

```
variable now cast to string
```

In the preceding example, at the time of declaration we did not specify the value of the variable. That's why the type of the variable is not decided. In the next line we gave the value to the variable *A* which is of type string, so it will automatically cast to the string type.

2.13 Real-Life Programming Practices

The following are some examples that can be developed after learning the fundamental concepts of Kotlin.

1. Calculate the ticket price for an amusement park according to the age of visitor. Table 2-7 shows the prices according to the age of visitor.

   Table 2-7. Price List

Age	Price
0 to 5 years	Free entry
5 to 14 years	$5
15 to 25 years	$7
Above 25 years	$10

Solution:

```
fun main() {
    val age=30
    if(age<5 && age>0){
        println("There is no Ticket for Age:$age")
    }else if(age>5 && age<14){
        println("Ticket Price for the Age:$age is $5")
    }else if(age>14 && age<25){
        println("Ticket Price for the Age:$age is $7")
    }else{
        println("Ticket Price for the Age:$age is $10")
    }
}
```

Output:

Ticket Price for the Age: 30 is $10

2. Write a program that evaluates a student's grade according to the percentage. Table 2-8 shows the criteria for evaluating.

Table 2-8. Grade with Score

Total Score	Grade
>=90	A
>=75	B
>=60	C
>=50	D
<50	FAIL

Solution:

fun main() {
    val score=65
    when{

```
            score >= 90 -> {println("Grade for $score is A")}
            score >= 75 -> {println("Grade for $score is B")}
            score >= 60 -> {println("Grade for $score is C")}
            score >= 50 -> {println("Grade for $score is D")}
            score < 50 -> {println("FAIL")}
        }
    }
```

Output:

Grade for 65 is C

3. Write a program that evaluates a student's eligibility for the exam based on their attendance in the classroom; i.e., if attendance is greater than 75% then student is allowed to sit in exam; otherwise they are not.

Solution:

```
fun main() {
    val attendance = 60
    if(attendance>75){
        println("You are allowed to sit in exam because your attendance is $attendance%")
    }else{
        println("You are not allowed to sit in exam because your attendance is $attendance%")
    }
}
```

Output:

You are not allowed to sit in exam because your attendance is 60%.

4. Write a program that calculates the total price of products available in cart.

   Solution:

   ```
   fun main() {
       val cart = arrayOf(19.34,56.33,32.45,23.33,6.90,
       200.90,347.90,235.00)
       var totalPrice=0.0
       for(item in cart){
           totalPrice+=item
       }
       println("Total Cart Price is: $totalPrice")
   }
   ```

   Output:

   Total Cart Price is: 922.15

2.14 Summary

In this chapter, we have learned all the core topics of Kotlin, like the structure of the program, using comments, data types, variables, arrays, strings, loops, return-jumps, conditional statements, and more, with some real-life programming examples.

2.15 Test Your Knowledge

1. Which of the following operators is used for comparing two values?

   a. ==

   b. >

   c. <

   d. =

CHAPTER 2 FUNDAMENTALS OF KOTLIN PROGRAMMING

2. Which property is used for finding the length of the string?

   a. sizeOf

   b. len

   c. size

   d. length

3. Which symbol is used for string interpolation?

   a. .

   b. #

   c. $

   d. ++

4. What is a correct syntax to output "Hi there!!" in Kotlin?

   a. println("Hi there!!")

   b. cout << "Hi there!!"

   c. system.out.println("Hi there!!")

   d. console.writeline("Hi there!!")

5. How can you insert a single-line comment in Kotlin?

   a. //

   b. /*

   c. #

   d. <!--

6. Which keyword is used to declare a variable in Kotlin?

   a. fun

   b. val

   c. class

   d. define

CHAPTER 2　FUNDAMENTALS OF KOTLIN PROGRAMMING

7. How do you declare a floating point number 3.4 in Kotlin?

    a. num = 3.4

    b. double num = 3.4

    c. val num = 3.4

    d. float num = 3.4

8. What will be the output of the following code: (4>3 && 3<5)?

    a. True

    b. False

9. In Kotlin programming code, a semicolon is necessary at the end of the statement.

    a. True

    b. False

10. What will be the output of the following code?

    val x = 8
    val y = 16
    println(y%x)

    a. 2

    b. 0

    c. 8

    d. 1

CHAPTER 2   FUNDAMENTALS OF KOTLIN PROGRAMMING

2.16 Answers

1. a
2. d
3. c
4. a
5. a
6. b
7. c
8. a
9. b
10. b

CHAPTER 3

Functions in Kotlin

Having learned the fundamentals of Kotlin, in this chapter you will learn how to create functions. This will help you minimize the code inside the main method. You can also use functions that are already available.

3.1 A Closer Look

Functions are generally used to perform repetitive tasks, also known as methods. In many programming languages, functions are used to perform special tasks and break the main program into smaller chunks, making it more manageable.

For example, we can call `average(A,B,C)` multiple times, and it will print the average of three numbers.

There are two types of functions available in Kotlin: user defined and standard library. Let's take a closer look at them now.

User-Defined Functions

A function that is made or defined by a user is known as a user-defined function. Following is the syntax of a user-defined function:

```
fun function_name(argument: datatype): return_type if any{
    // block of code that needs to run
    return if any
}
```

- **fun:** `fun` is the keyword that is used for creating functions.
- **function_name:** `function_name` is the name of the function, which is given by the user.

- **argument:** This is also known as a parameter, which is given to the function for performing desired operations.
- **return_type:** This is used for specifying or telling the datatype of the return value of the function, if available.
- **{.....}:** Curly braces are used to show the function boundary or the block of code that defines the function, as follows:

```
fun addition(number1:Int,number2:Int): Int{
    var addition=0
    addition = number1+number2
    return addition
}
```

Parameters in Functions

Function parameters are also known as arguments and are given to the function to perform the desired operation.

In preceding example, two parameters are given to the function `addition`. The first parameter is `number1` and is of the integer type. The second parameter is `number2`, which is also of the integer type.

Body of Functions

The body of the function is what we write inside the function block. In the preceding example, statements declare the variable addition; assign the value of addition of two numbers to the declared variable; and represent the returned value of addition as the body of the function.

Return Value of the Functions

The return value for the function is the value that is returned from the function after performing the desired operations. In the preceding example, after assigning the value for the function, the variable `addition` is returned from the function as the output of the function.

The preceding example is a Kotlin function that has the same type of parameters. Next, let's see a Kotlin function that has different types of multiple arguments:

```
fun student(name:String,roll_no:Int){
    println(name)
    println(roll_no)
}
```

In this case, we have different types of arguments for the function named student; i.e., `name` as string and `roll_no` as integer.

Calling Functions

To execute a function, you need to call that function from the `main()` function. When the line with the function call comes in the main program, the control of the main program transfers to the function to execute that function and returns the value of that function to the main program. The execution of the main program then resumes from where it left off. Following is an example of calling an addition function with two integer arguments that return the sum of two integers:

```
fun main() {
    var result=0
    result=addition(5,2)
    println("Addition is: "+result)
}
fun addition(number1:Int,number2:Int):Int{
    var result=0
    result=number1+number2
    return result
}
```

Output:

```
Addition is: 7
```

CHAPTER 3 FUNCTIONS IN KOTLIN

Standard Library Functions

In Kotlin there are multiple library functions available. These functions are built-in functions, so users just need to follow the structure and use it, without defining it. One of the common examples of this kind of function is `println()`, which is a built-in function of Kotlin and is used for printing on the console screen whatever is written inside the brackets. Table 3-1 shows some other built-in functions that are available for use in Kotlin's standard library.

Table 3-1. Additional Built-in Functions

Function	Description	Example
println()	Prints anything written inside the bracket and returns with new line	*println("Hello from Kotlin")*
print()	Prints anything written inside the bracket and returns without new line	*print("hello from Kotlin")*
arrayOf()	Declares the array of values written inside the bracket	*arrayOf(1,2,3,4,5,6,7,8,9)*
toInt()	Converts the string value to an integer	*"2024".toInt()*
toLong()	Converts the integer value to Long	*val a:Int=6* *a.toLong()*
toString()	Converts the value to String	*2024.toString()*
toLowerCase()	Converts the value of given string to lowercase	*"HELLO FROM KOTLIN". toLowerCase()*
toUpperCase()	Converts the value of given string to uppercase	*"hello from Kotlin". toUpperCase()*
sum()	Used for adding all the values of an array	*arrayOf(1,2,3,4).sum()*
rem()	To get remainder of numbers when divided by each other	*var num1 = 26* *var num2 = 3* *var result = num1.rem(num2)*

Advantages and Disadvantages of Using Functions in Kotlin

Following are some advantages and disadvantages when we use functions in Kotlin. This also gives you an idea of when to use functions in your program.

Advantages:

- Reusability: Once the function is written, it can be used multiple times in the code without worrying about the internal working of that function.

- Readability: Using functions will enhance the readability of the code, as the code will be divided into multiple functions. Hence, it will be easier for the programmer to comprehend it.

- Modularity: Functions will divide the code into smaller chunks, making it modular. Modular programs will be more manageable and easy to change.

- Abstraction: Functions will hide the complex logic, and users just need to write the name of the function and use it, without worrying about internal implementation.

- Avoid Code Repetition: Functions can be used in programs multiple times, which will save users lines of code and effort as well as repetitive code.

- Reduce Program Size: Functions will be helpful for programmers by reducing lines of code, because once the function is written there is no need to write that function again in that program.

Disadvantages:

- Complex Debugging: Functions can make your program debugging complex, if you have used multiple functions that call one another for execution.

- Poor Memory Management: Memory management is an important aspect of programming. While working with complex programs, if programmers fail to manage it properly it will result in memory leaks.

3.2 Functions with Default and Named Arguments

In traditional programming languages, programmers need to specify all the parameters at the time of that function's being called. In Kotlin, one of the most important features is that a programmer does not need to do this. We can make the function's parameters optional. There are two types of arguments that are passed to a function in Kotlin:

1. Default Arguments
2. Named Arguments

Default Arguments

In Kotlin, the programmer can add a default value that needs to be used for that parameter, using a default argument. This means that if the parameter's value is not passed at the time that function is called, then the default value will be used, and if the parameter value is passed then the given value will be used. The following example shows how the function call is executed without any argument:

```
fun main() {
  person()
}
fun person(name: String ="James",age: Int = 23, designation: String = "Developer") {
   println("Name is $name")
   println("Age is $age")
   println("Designation is $designation")
}
```

Output:

```
Name is James
Age is 23
Designation is Developer
```

In the preceding example, the default argument for the name is "James," for age is "23," and for designation is "Developer." It will print all the default arguments, as shown in the output, when called without any arguments. Now let's see an example of calling a function with partial arguments:

```kotlin
fun main() {
    val name="Jacob"
    val age=28
    person(name,age)
}
fun person(name: String ="James",age: Int = 23, designation: String = "Developer") {
    println("Name is $name")
    println("Age is $age")
    println("Designation is $designation")
}
```

Output:

```
Name is Jacob
Age is 28
Designation is Developer
```

In this example, the function is called with the arguments of name and age, so it will be used as given, and for designation, the default argument will be used, as shown in the output. Let's see an example of a function called with all the arguments:

```kotlin
fun main() {
    val name="William"
    val age=35
    val designation="Manager"
    person(name, age, designation)
}
fun person(name: String ="James",age: Int = 23, designation: String = "Developer") {
    println("Name is $name")
    println("Age is $age")
    println("Designation is $designation")
}
```

CHAPTER 3 FUNCTIONS IN KOTLIN

Output:

```
Name is William
Age is 35
Designation is Manager
```

In this example, the function is called with all the arguments so it will be used as given in arguments, as shown in the output.

Named Arguments

In Kotlin, while working with named arguments, if we do not follow the proper order of arguments then it will give an error due to type mismatch, or it will take it in the order of the parameters as it is defined. The following example shows the mismatch of arguments:

```
fun main() {
  val name="William"
  val designation="Manager"
  person(name, designation)
}
fun person(name: String ="James",age: Int = 23, designation: String = "Developer") {
    println("Name is $name")
    println("Age is $age")
    println("Designation is $designation")
}
```

Output:

```
Error: Argument type mismatch: actual type is 'kotlin.String', but 'kotlin.Int' was expected.
```

To overcome the preceding error, we need to use named arguments so that the compiler knows which value is related to which argument. The following shows the usage of named arguments in the preceding example:

```
fun main() {
  val name="William"
```

```
    val designation="Manager"
  person(name=name, designation=designation)
}
fun person(name: String ="James",age: Int = 23, designation: String =
"Developer") {
   println("Name is $name")
   println("Age is $age")
   println("Designation is $designation")
}
```

Output:

```
Name is William
Age is 23
Designation is Manager
```

Now the compilation error is solved as the compiler has the information about the name of the arguments that need to be used for the given value.

3.3 Recursive Functions

In Kotlin programming, recursive functions are available as in all the other programming languages. A function that calls itself is known as a recursive function. The process of calling functions repeatedly is known as **recursion**.

In Kotlin, there are two types of function calls possible:

1. Normal Function Call
2. Recursive Function Call

Normal Function Call

A normal function call is when a function is called only from the `main()` method. If we want to execute the function multiple times, then we need to call it from `main()` method again and again. Let's see an example of a normal function call:

```
fun main() {
    println("Function call 1")
```

```kotlin
    student("Alice",11,18)
        println("Function call 2")
    student("Jeh",24,19)
        println("Function call 3")
    student("Jacob",34,20)
        println("Function call 4")
    student("Jaya",2,18)
}
fun student(name:String, rollno:Int, age:Int){
    println("Name is $name")
    println("Roll No is $rollno")
    println("Age is $age")
    println("")
}
```

Output:

```
Function call 1
Name is Alice
Roll No is 11
Age is 18

Function call 2
Name is Jeh
Roll No is 24
Age is 19

Function call 3
Name is Jacob
Roll No is 34
Age is 20

Function call 4
Name is Jaya
Roll No is 2
Age is 18
```

Recursive Function Call

When a function calls itself from the same function, then it is known as a recursive function. Note that every recursive function must have one condition to terminate the function call or else that function call will run infinitely, which will give an error of stack overflow. Let's see an example of a recursive function without a terminating condition:

```kotlin
fun main() {
    val n=1
    countNumber(n)
}
fun countNumber(number:Int){
    println(number)
    countNumber(number+1)
}
```

Output:

Error: Exception in thread "main" java.lang.StackOverflowError

In the preceding example, we did not use a condition to exit from the recursive call. That's why the function runs infinitely and the output of the function is an error, as exception f stack overflow occurs.

Now let's add a condition to exit from the preceding example:

```kotlin
fun main() {
    val n=1
    countNumber(n)
}
fun countNumber(number:Int){
    println(number)
    if(number<10){
        countNumber(number+1)
    }
}
```

Output:

1
2
3
4
5
6
7
8
9
10

To overcome the example's exception, we have added one condition. In this example, when the value of a number exceeds the value 10, then it will not execute recursive calls. Hence, we get the output that prints the value from 1 to 10.

3.4 Tail Recursive Functions

In recursive functions, we execute the function call first and then calculate the value of the result. Instead of this, in tail recursion, we calculate the result first and then execute the function calls. This will result in no more stack overflow exceptions or errors in the program. The rule of tail recursion is: The recursive function call must occur at the last line of the function. Let's see an example of a tail recursive function:

```
fun main() {
    val n = 1
    val result = Factorial(5,n)
    println("Factorial of 5 is: $result")
}
fun Factorial(number: Int, r:Int):Long{
    return if(number==1){
     r.toLong()
    }else{
     Factorial(number-1,r*number)
    }
}
```

Output:

```
factorial of 5 is: 120
```

In the preceding example, first it executes the exit condition value, and after that the recursive function call occurs. This will eliminate the stack overflow exception because the function call occurs at the last line of the function, so there is no need to save the current function call in the memory.

3.5 Programming Practices

In this section we will see some real-life examples where you can use your knowledge of functions and build real-life applications.

1. **Write a program that converts the temperature from Celsius to Fahrenheit and Fahrenheit to Celsius.**

    Solution:

    ```
    fun celsiusToFahrenheitConverter(celsiusTemp: Double): Double {
        return (celsiusTemp * 9 / 5) + 32
    }
    fun fahrenheitToCelsiusConverter(fahrenheitTemp: Double): Double {
        return (fahrenheitTemp - 32) * 5 / 9
    }
    fun main() {
        val celsiusTemp = 34.0
        val fahrenheitTemp = 45.0
        val convertedFahrenheitTemp = celsiusToFahrenheitConverter
        (celsiusTemp)
        println("$celsiusTemp °C is $convertedFahrenheitTemp °F")
        val convertedCelsiusTemp = fahrenheitToCelsiusConverter
        (fahrenheitTemp)
        println("$fahrenheitTemp °F is $convertedCelsiusTemp °C")
    }
    ```

Output:

```
34.0 °C is 93.2 °F
45.0 °F is 7.222222222222222 °C
```

2. **Write a program that finds the area of a circle.**

   Solution:

   ```
   fun areaOfCircle(radius: Double): Double {
       return (3.14 * radius * radius)
   }
   fun main() {
       val radius = 4.0
       val area = areaOfCircle(radius)
       println("Area of Circle is $area")
   }
   ```

   Output:

   ```
   Area of Circle is 50.24
   ```

3. **Write a program to find the maximum from two numbers.**

   Solution:

   ```
   fun max(number1:Int,number2:Int) {
      if(number1>number2){
          println("Maximum number from $number1 and $number2 is
          $number1")
      }else{
          println("Maximum number from $number1 and $number2 is
          $number2")
       }
   }
   fun main() {
       max(10,12)
   }
   ```

Output:

```
Maximum number from 10 and 12 is 12
```

4. **Write a program to check if a given number is even or odd.**
   Solution:

```
fun evenOrOdd(number:Int) {
   if(number%2==0){
       println("$number is EVEN number")
   }else{
       println("$number is ODD number")
   }
}
fun main() {
    evenOrOdd(17)
}
```

Output:

```
17 is ODD number
```

5. **Write a program that creates a simple calculator that calculates arithmetic operations like addition, subtraction, division, multiplication, and modulus.**
   Solution:

```
fun addition(number1: Int, number2: Int): Int{
    return number1+number2
}
fun subtraction(number1: Int, number2: Int): Int{
    return number1-number2
}
fun multiplication(number1: Int, number2: Int): Int{
    return number1*number2
}
```

```
fun division(number1: Int, number2: Int): Double{
    if(number2!=0){
        return (number1/number2).toDouble()
    }else{
        return 0.0
    }
}
fun modulus(number1: Int, number2: Int): Int{
    return number1%number2
}
fun main() {
    println("Addition of 12 and 13 is: ${addition(12, 13)}")
    println("Subtraction 15 and 10 is: ${subtraction(15, 10)}")
    println("Multiplication 2 and 6 is: ${multiplication(2, 6)}")
    println("Division of 22 and 2 is: ${division(22, 2)}")
    println("Modulus of 22 and 2 is: ${modulus(22, 2)}")
}
```

Output:

```
Addition of 12 and 13 is: 25
Subtraction 15 and 10 is: 5
Multiplication 2 and 6 is: 12
Division of 22 and 2 is: 11.0
Modulus of 22 and 2 is: 0
```

3.6 Summary

In this chapter we have learned all about functions in Kotlin, which enables you to write your own functions and use already available functions. We have also seen some real-life examples where you can apply knowledge of functions to create different applications.

3.7 Test Your Knowledge

1. Which keyword is used to define a function in Kotlin?

    a. function

    b. fun

    c. define

    d. def

2. Which of the following is the correct syntax for declaring a function in Kotlin?

    a. fun fun_name(): return_type{}

    b. function fun_name(): return_type{}

    c. fun fun_name(argument1:type, argument2:type): return_type{}

    d. fun fun_name(): {return_type}

3. Which of the following statements is applicable for Kotlin standard library functions?

    a. They are built-in functions, available to use without defining them.

    b. They need to be defined by user.

    c. They do not return values.

    d. They only work with string inputs.

4. Which of the following is a Kotlin standard library function that converts values to strings?

    a. toVal()

    b. toChar()

    c. toInt()

    d. toString()

5. What is the advantage of using functions in Kotlin programming?

    a. Reduce memory usage

    b. Make debugging easier

    c. Reduce code duplication

    d. Increase complexity

6. Which of the following is a disadvantage of functions in Kotlin programming?

    a. Poor memory management in complex programs

    b. Faster execution

    c. Increased readability

    d. Modularity

7. Which of the following functions is used to convert a string into uppercase?

    a. toUpper()

    b. toUpperCase()

    c. toStringUpper()

    d. toStringUpperCase()

8. What will happen if we do not provide the correct order of arguments in a function call with named arguments?

    a. The program will execute successfully.

    b. The program will run but will give wrong values.

    c. There will be a type mismatch error.

    d. It will give runtime error.

9. What will be the output of the following code?

```
fun countNumber(number: Int) {
    println(number)
    countNumber(number + 1)
}
```

```kotlin
fun main() {
    countNumber(8)
}
```

    a. Infinite loop without error

    b. 1

    c. StackOverFlowError

    d. 1,2,3,4,5,6,7,8,9,10

10. Which of the following function prints the text to the console without adding a new line?

    a. println()

    b. output()

    c. printWithoutLine()

    d. print()

3.8 Answers

1. b
2. c
3. a
4. d
5. c
6. a
7. b
8. a
9. c
10. d

CHAPTER 4

Object-Oriented Programming with Kotlin

Object-oriented programming (OOP) supports programming based on objects. Instead of using functions or logic, programming is dependent upon objects, which contain data or code. Figure 4-1 shows the key concepts included in an object-oriented programming language.

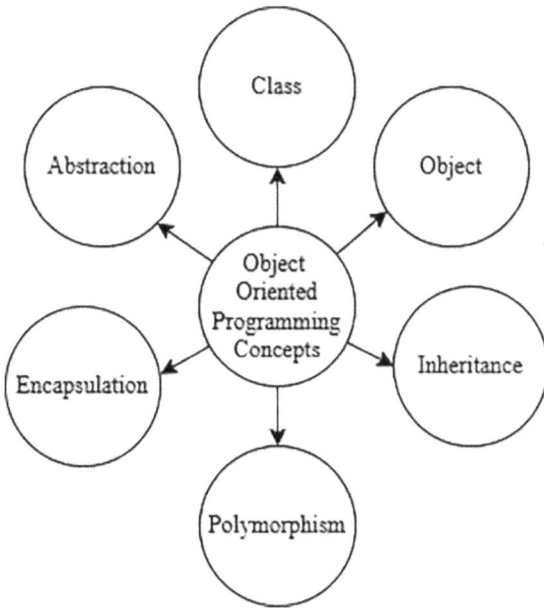

Figure 4-1. *Object-oriented programming concepts*

- **Classes and Objects** are the basic elements of OOP. They are generally used for representing real-world objects. A class is a collection of methods or properties with which multiple objects can be created. Objects are real-life entities and are visible to users.
- **Abstraction** is a property that can give access to only required information to a user. Information that is confidential or private will not be visible to the user.
- **Encapsulation** refers to "data hiding." Using this property, we can protect data from the outside world.
- **Inheritance** is a property that allows the inheriting of methods of one class by another class.
- **Polymorphism** is the ability to appear in many forms. This can be achieved using methods with the same name and different parameters.

In this chapter, we will learn how these OOP concepts are applied to the Kotlin programming language.

4.1 Classes and Objects

Classes

Classes are a collection of methods and properties, which in turn are used for creating multiple objects. To create multiple objects, first we need to define the class, using the `class` keyword. Class definition includes the name of the class, header of the class, and members and properties included inside the class (which is also known as the body of the class) enclosed within the curly braces. The following is the syntax of a class declaration:

Syntax:

```
class class_name{        //class header
    //class property
    //class methods
}
```

- **Class Name:** We can give any name to the class. Each and every class has a unique name.

- **Class Header:** Header of the class includes parameter or constructor of the class.

- **Class Body:** Body of the class consists of the methods or properties related to the class. It is enclosed by the curly braces.

The following is an example of declaring a class in Kotlin:

Example:

```
class people{
    // class property
    var name:String = ""
    var age:Int = 0
    var gender:String = ""
    // class methods or function
    fun name(){
        //fun body
    }
    fun age(){
        //fun body
    }
    fun gender(){
        //fun body
    }
}
```

Objects

In Kotlin programming, objects are a real-life entity and have some properties and methods. We can access properties and methods using objects. We can create multiple objects of the same class. Objects consist of identity, attributes, and behavior.

- **Identity:** Object's identity is a unique name, which we can assign to each and every object. Objects can also interact with other objects using identity.

- **Attribute:** This refers to the state of an object. It is also known as a property of the object. It can have more than one.
- **Behavior:** This is generally represented as the methods of an object. It can also show the response from one object to another object.

Creating an Object

We can create an object using the name of the class and the following syntax:

Syntax:

```
var obj = className()
```

Access the property of the class

We can access the properties of the class using objects. For that, first we need to create an object and then use that object to access the properties.

Syntax:

```
Obj.nameOfProperty
```

Access the Member Function of the Class

We can access the member function of the class using an object. First we need to create an object and then use that object to access the member functions.

Syntax:

```
Obj.functionName(parameters)
```

Let's see an example of creating a Kotlin object and accessing properties as well as member functions.

Example:

```
fun main() {
    val people1 = people()
    val people2 = people()
    people1.printValues("John",23,"Male")
    people2.name("Jacob")
    people2.age(25)
    people2.gender("Male")
    println("Name: ${people2.name}")
```

```kotlin
    println("Age: ${people2.age}")
    println("Gender: ${people2.gender}")
}
class people{
    // class property
    var name:String = ""
    var age:Int = 0
    var gender:String = ""
    // class methods or function
    fun name(n:String){
        this.name=n
    }
    fun age(a:Int){
        this.age=a
    }
    fun gender(g:String){
        this.gender=g
    }
    fun printValues(n:String,a:Int,g:String){
        println("Name:$n")
        println("Age:$a")
        println("Gender:$g")
    }
}
```

Output:

```
Name: John
Age: 23
Gender: Male
Name: Jacob
Age: 25
Gender: Male
```

CHAPTER 4 OBJECT-ORIENTED PROGRAMMING WITH KOTLIN

Nested Classes

Nested classes are defined as classes inside other classes. In Kotlin, we can define one class in another class. Nested classes can't access properties or methods from outer classes, but outer classes can access properties and methods from nested classes. The following is the syntax of nested classesa.

Syntax:

```
class outerClass{
    //outer class properties or functions
    class nestedClass{
        // nested class properties or functions
    }
}
```

Let's see an example of a nested class. This example declares the nested class and accesses the value of the nested class from the outer class.

Example:

```
class outerClassHere {
    var outerClassProperty = "property of outer class"
    // nested class declaration
    class nestedClassHere {
        val nestedClassProperty1  = "property 1 of nested class"
        val nestedClassProperty2 = "property 2 of nested class"
    }
}
fun main(args: Array<String>) {
    // accessing member of Nested class
    println(outerClassHere.nestedClassHere().nestedClassProperty1)
    println(outerClassHere.nestedClassHere().nestedClassProperty2)
}
```

Output:

```
property 1 of nested class
property 2 of nested class
```

Inner Classes

We have seen that nested classes cannot access properties or methods from outer classes. In inner classes this limitation is overcome because an inner class can access the properties and methods from outer classes. Like nested classes, inner classes also are declared inside the outer class but using the `inner` keyword. Following is the syntax of using an inner class.

Syntax:

```
class outerClass{
    //outer class properties or functions
    inner class innerClass{
        // inner class properties or functions
    }
}
```

Let's see an example of an inner class. The following example declares the inner class and accesses the value of an outer class property from inside the inner class.

Example:

```
class outerClassHere {
    var outerClassProperty = "property of outer class"
    // inner class declaration
    inner class innerClassHere {
        val innerClassProperty1  = "property 1 of inner class"
        val innerClassProperty2 = "property 2 of inner class"
        fun accessOuterClassProperty(){
            println("Accessing property of outer class from inner class:
            $outerClassProperty")
        }
    }
}
fun main(args: Array<String>) {
    // accessing member of inner class
    println(outerClassHere().innerClassHere().innerClassProperty1)
    println(outerClassHere().innerClassHere().innerClassProperty2)
    outerClassHere().innerClassHere().accessOuterClassProperty()
}
```

Accessing property of outer class from inner class: property of outer class

Output:

```
property 1 of inner class
property 2 of inner class
```

1. **Advantages of Using Nested and Inner Classes**

    a. **Provides Encapsulation:** Nested and inner classes allow you to keep certain functionality separate from the rest of the code; hence, it provides encapsulation.

    b. **Improves Accessibility:** Inner classes can access the properties of outer classes, which improves accessibility.

    c. **Code Reuse:** Nested and inner classes can be reused within multiple classes or the same class, which reduces code repetition.

2. **Disadvantages of Using Nested and Inner Classes**

    a. If multiple nested or inner classes are used in a class, then it will be difficult for one to debug the program.

    b. Using multiple levels of nested and inner classes can slow down the performance of the program.

    c. Using deep nested and inner classes will make the program more complex, less readable, and harder to understand.

In conclusion, we can use nested and inner classes in our program but they must be used in the proper way, which will be more advantageous.

4.2 Constructors

A constructor is a method used for initializing objects. It is called when the object of the class is created. If we do not create a constructor, then the compiler creates the default constructor. There are two types of constructors available in Kotlin.

1. **Primary Constructor**
2. **Secondary Constructor**

Kotlin classes can contain one primary constructor and multiple secondary constructors. Generally, a primary constructor is used for initializing the class and the secondary constructor is used to initialize as well as add extra functionality.

Primary Constructor

Primary constructors can be initialized in the class header using the `constructor` keyword. We can also use parameters in primary constructors if required. Following is an example of using a primary constructor.

Example:

```
class person constructor(val name:String){
    //class body
}
```

Writing the `constructor` keyword is not necessary if no annotations or modifiers are used. Hence, we can omit it.

```
class person(val name:String){
    //class body
}
```

Let's see a program for Kotlin that has a primary constructor with output.

Example:

```
class person constructor(val first_name:String, val last_name:String) {
    val full_name = first_name+last_name
}
fun main(args: Array<String>) {
    val person = person("Mark", "Brown")
    println("Full Name: ${person.full_name}")
}
```

Output:

```
Full Name: MarkBrown
```

The following is the same example without using the constructor keyword.

CHAPTER 4   OBJECT-ORIENTED PROGRAMMING WITH KOTLIN

Example:

```
class person(val first_name:String, val last_name:String) {
    val full_name = first_name+last_name
}
fun main(args: Array<String>) {
    val person = person("Mark", "Brown")
    println("Full Name: ${person.full_name}")
}
```

Output:

Full Name: MarkBrown

Init Block

This is used to initialize member variables. It is called when the object of the class is created. There can be multiple init blocks inside one class. Init blocks get called before the constructor of the class is called. The following is an example of using an init block inside a class.

Example:

```
class person(val first_name:String, val last_name:String) {
    val full_name = first_name+last_name
    init{
        println("Inside first init block")
    }
    init{
        println("Inside second init block")
    }
    init{
        println("Inside third init block")
    }
    init{
        println("Full Name: $full_name")
    }
}
```

82

```
fun main(args: Array<String>) {
    val person = person("Mark", "Brown")
}
```

Output:

```
Inside first init block
Inside second init block
Inside third init block
Full Name: MarkBrown
```

Using Default Value in Primary Constructor

Similar to the use of default values in functions, we can also use them with constructors, as follows.

Example:

```
class person(first_name:String = "Mark", last_name:String = "Brown") {
    val full_name = first_name+last_name
    init{
        println("Full Name: $full_name")
    }
}
fun main(args: Array<String>) {
    val person1 = person()
    val person2 = person(last_name="Bell")
    val person3 = person("Evan")
}
```

Output:

```
Full Name: MarkBrown
Full Name: MarkBell
Full Name: EvanBrown
```

Using Secondary Constructors

Kotlin secondary constructors can be used for initialization as well as to add more functionality. Kotlin programs can have more than one secondary constructor. Secondary constructors are prefixed by the keyword constructor. Following is an example of using a secondary constructor.

Example:

```
class person{
    constructor(first_name:String,last_name:String){
            val full_name = first_name+last_name
            println("Full Name: $full_name")
    }
}
fun main(args: Array<String>) {
    person("Mark", "Brown")
}
```

Output:

Full Name: MarkBrown

Using Multiple Secondary Constructors Inside the Same Class

In the following example we declare three constructors: one for name, one for age, and one for gender. We create the object of the class according to the required constructor.

Example:

```
class person{
    constructor(first_name:String,last_name:String){
            val full_name = first_name+last_name
            println("Full Name: $full_name")
    }
    constructor(age:Int){
            println("Age: $age")
    }
```

```
        constructor(gender:String){
                println("Gender: $gender")
        }
}
fun main(args: Array<String>) {
    person("Mark", "Brown")
    person(24)
    person("Male")
}
```

Output:

```
Full Name: MarkBrown
Age: 24
Gender: Male
```

Calling One Secondary Constructor from Another

We can call one constructor from another constructor using the this() function. We are calling the full name constructor from the age constructor in the following example.

Example:

```
class person{
    constructor(first_name:String,last_name:String){
            val full_name = first_name+last_name
            println("Full Name: $full_name")
    }
    constructor(age:Int):this("Mark", "Brown"){
            println("Age: $age")
    }
}
fun main(args: Array<String>) {
    person(24)
}
```

Output:

```
Full Name: MarkBrown
Age: 24
```

4.3 Inheritance

Inheritance is one of the most important OOP concepts. Kotlin supports inheritance. It enables the code reuse feature. Inheritance is defined as using properties or features from a parent class in a child class. The parent class is also called the super class or base class, and the child class also called the subclass or derived class. A subclass can also add new properties or methods if required. Following is the syntax of using inheritance in Kotlin. The open keyword is used in the base class to enable it to use a base class for the derived class.

Syntax:

```
open class baseClass(a:Int){
    // class body
}
class derivedClass(a:Int):baseClass(a){
    // class body
}
```

Following is an example of using inheritance in Kotlin. This example declares the base class Fruits and inherits it in derived classes Apple and Banana.

Example:

```
open class Fruits{
    fun run(){
            println("Fruits are good for health")
        }
}
class Apple:Fruits(){
    fun color(){
        println("Apples have red color")
    }
}
class Banana:Fruits(){
    fun color(){
        println("Bananas have yellow color")
    }
}
```

```kotlin
fun main(args: Array<String>) {
    val apple = Apple()
    println("For Apple Subclass")
    apple.run()
    apple.color()
    println()
    val banana = Banana()
    println("For Banana Subclass")
    banana.run()
    banana.color()
}
```

Output:

```
For Apple Subclass
Fruits are good for health
Apples have red color

For Banana Subclass
Fruits are good for health
Bananas have yellow color
```

Kotlin Override Property

If the base class and the derived class both have the same name property or function, then we can override the base class property or function using the override keyword. Let's see an example where the apple class has the same function run and so we need to use the override keyword in the apple class and make the base class function run in order to open.

Example:

```kotlin
open class Fruits{
    open fun run(){
        println("Fruits are good for health")
    }
}
```

```
class Apple:Fruits(){
    override fun run(){
        println("Apples are good for health")
    }
    fun color(){
        println("Apples have red color")
    }
}
fun main(args: Array<String>) {
    val apple = Apple()
    apple.run()
    apple.color()
}
```

Output:

```
Apples are good for health
Apples have red color
```

Kotlin Inheritance with Primary Constructor

Inheritance and primary constructors can also be used together.

Example:

```
open class baseClass(first_name:String,last_name:String){
        val full_name = first_name+last_name
}
class derivedClass(first_name:String,last_name:String,age:Int):baseClass(first_name,last_name){
    init{
            println("Full Name: $full_name")
            println("Age: $age")
    }
}
fun main(args: Array<String>) {
    derivedClass("Mark","Brown",24)
}
```

Output:

```
Full Name: MarkBrown
Age: 24
```

Kotlin Inheritance with Secondary Constructor

Inheritance and secondary constructors can also be used together. When a derived class object is created it uses and initializes the base class too. We also need to add all the parameters of the secondary constructor in the derived class, as shown in this example.

Example:

```
open class baseClass{
    constructor(first_name:String,last_name:String){
            val full_name = first_name+last_name
            println("Full Name: $full_name")
    }
}
class derivedClass(first_name:String,last_name:String,age:Int):baseClass
(first_name,last_name){
    init{
            println("Age: $age")
    }
}
fun main(args: Array<String>) {
    derivedClass("Mark","Brown",24)
}
```

Output:

```
Full Name: MarkBrown
Age: 24
```

Calling Base Class Secondary Constructor from Derived Class Secondary Constructor

We can call a secondary constructor of a base class from the secondary constructor of a derived class using the super keyword.

Example:

```
open class baseClass{
    constructor(first_name:String,last_name:String){
        val full_name = first_name+last_name
        println("From Base Class")
        println("Full Name:$full_name")
    }
}
class derivedClass:baseClass{
    constructor(first_name:String,last_name:String,age:Int):super(first_name,last_name){
        println("From Derived Class")
        println("Full Name: $first_name+$last_name")
        println("Age: $age")
    }
}
fun main(args: Array<String>) {
    derivedClass("Mark","Brown",24)
}
```

Output:

```
From Base Class
Full Name: MarkBrown

From Derived Class
Full Name: Mark+Brown
Age: 24
```

4.4 Interfaces

Interfaces are generally referred to as the blueprint of the class. An interface contains all the abstract methods and properties that are common for classes that implement that interface. Interfaces can be implemented by multiple classes. They help achieve OOP concepts like abstraction and polymorphism. Interface declaration in Kotlin starts with the keyword `interface` followed by name of that interface; after that goes the bracket for starting and ending the interface. The following is the syntax for this.

Syntax:
Declaration of interface

```
interface interface_name{
    //interface body
}
```

Implementing interface

```
class class_name : interface_name{
    //class body
}
```

The following is an example of an interface. It shows the interface calculator having two methods to implement and that the class that implements this interface will override these two methods and implement it.

Example:

```
interface calculator{
    fun add(a:Int,b:Int)
    fun subtract(a:Int,b:Int)
}
class myCalculator : calculator{
    override fun add(a:Int,b:Int){
        println("Addition of $a and $b is: "+(a+b))
    }
    override fun subtract(a:Int,b:Int){
        println("Subtraction of $a and $b is: "+(a-b))
    }
}
```

```kotlin
fun main(){
    val mycalc = myCalculator()
    mycalc.add(6,8)
    mycalc.subtract(9,6)
}
```

Output:

```
Addition of 6 and 8 is: 14
Subtraction of 9 and 6 is: 3
```

Default Values and Methods

We can use default values and methods in interfaces. Building on the preceding example, let's implement one default method and override it in another class and also add default values in the add and subtract methods.

Example:

```kotlin
interface calculator{
    fun add(a:Int,b:Int = 5)
    fun subtract(a:Int,b:Int = 3)
    fun defaultMethodPrint(){
        println("Default method run")
    }
}
class myCalculator : calculator{
    override fun add(a:Int,b:Int){
        println("Addition of $a and $b is: "+(a+b))
    }
    override fun subtract(a:Int,b:Int){
        println("Subtraction of $a and $b is: "+(a-b))
    }
    override fun defaultMethodPrint(){
        super.defaultMethodPrint() //interface default method run
        println("Default Method override")
    }
}
```

```
fun main(){
    val mycalc = myCalculator()
    mycalc.add(6)
    mycalc.subtract(9)
    mycalc.defaultMethodPrint()
}
```

Output:

```
Addition of 6 and 5 is: 11
Subtraction of 9 and 3 is: 6
Default Method run
Default Method override
```

Properties in Interfaces

Interfaces can also have properties. All the properties can be declared inside the interface either abstractly or by implementation. The following example shows the usage of interface properties.

Example

```
interface interfacePropertyDemo{
    val X:Int
    val Y:String
}
class propertyClass : interfacePropertyDemo{
    override val X : Int = 30
    override val Y : String = "Override Property"
}
fun main(){
    val obj = propertyClass()
    println("X = ${obj.X}")
    println("Y = ${obj.Y}")
}
```

Output:

```
X = 30
Y = Override Property
```

Inheritance in Interfaces

Interfaces can also inherit another interface. To do so, it gets the property and methods from the base interface, and also it can add its own methods and properties. The class that implements these interfaces has to implement all the methods from the base and derived interfaces. Interfaces can inherit multiple interfaces. Following is an example of inheritance in interfaces.

Example:

```
interface baseInterface{
    val a:Int
    val b:Int
}
interface derivedInterface : baseInterface{
    fun add()
    fun subtract()
}
class myCalculator : derivedInterface{
    override val a:Int = 10
    override val b:Int = 5
    override fun add(){
        println("Addition of $a and $b is: "+(a+b))
    }
    override fun subtract(){
        println("Subtraction of $a and $b is: "+(a-b))
    }
}
fun main(){
    val mycalc = myCalculator()
    mycalc.add()
    mycalc. Subtract()
}
```

Output:
Addition of 10 and 5 is: 15
Subtraction of 10 and 5 is: 5

Multiple Interfaces

In Kotlin one class can implement more than one interface. A class needs to implement all the methods from all implemented interfaces. The following example shows the usage of multiple interface implementation in a single class.

Example:

```
interface add{
    fun addition(a:Int,b:Int)
}
interface subtract {
    fun subtraction(a:Int,b:Int)
}
class myCalculator : add,subtract{
    override fun addition(a:Int,b:Int){
        println("Addition of $a and $b is: "+(a+b))
    }
    override fun subtraction(a:Int,b:Int){
        println("Subtraction of $a and $b is: "+(a-b))
    }
}
fun main(){
    val mycalc = myCalculator()
    mycalc.addition(10,6)
    mycalc.subtraction(8,6)
}
```

Output:

```
Addition of 10 and 6 is: 16
Subtraction of 8 and 6 is: 2
```

4.5 Visibility Modifiers

Visibility modifiers in Kotlin are used to control the visibility of things like class, methods, properties, and so on. Following are the visibility modifiers that are available in the Kotlin language.

1. **Public:** In Kotlin, public is the default visibility modifier. The public modifier makes the variables and methods visible to all the other variables and methods available in particular file. If we don't declare any modifier then by default it is public. If we declare top-level components like classes or methods, then all the code inside that class or method is public. Following is an example of using a public modifier.

   Example:

   ```
   //this class is by default public, because modifier is not
   declared
   class X{
       fun runX(){
           println("X class: Accessible everywhere")
       }
   }
   //public modifier declared
   class Y{
       fun runY(){
           println("Y class: Accessible everywhere")
       }
   }
   fun main(){
       val objX = X()
       val objY = Y()
       objX.runX()
       objY.runY()
   }
   ```

   Output:

   X class: Accessible everywhere

Y class: Accessible everywhere

2. **Private:** Private makes the modifier visible to only a particular class; outside that class, it is not visible. Following is an example of a private modifier.

   Example:

   ```
   // class X is accessible from same file
   private class X {
       private val num = 40
       fun run()
       {
           // we can access num here in same class
           println(num)
           println("Accessing num successful")
       }
   }
   fun main(args: Array<String>){
       var obj = X()
       obj.run()
       //we can't access num here, it is private in class X
       println(obj.num)
   }
   ```

   Output:

   ```
   Error: Cannot access 'val num: Int': it is private in '/X'.
   ```

3. **Internal:** An internal modifier makes the code visible to the particular module in which it is declared. A module is a set of Kotlin files that are compiled together. Following is an example of an internal modifier.

   Example:

   ```
   // class X is accessible from same module
   internal class X {
   ```

CHAPTER 4   OBJECT-ORIENTED PROGRAMMING WITH KOTLIN

```
    internal val num = 40
    fun run()
    {
        println("Accessing from same module")
    }
}
fun main(args: Array<String>){
    var obj = X()
    obj.run()
}
```

Output:

Accessing from same module

4. **Protected:** A protected modifier is related to inheritance. The modifier is visible to only the class it is declared in and its subclass. Following is an example of using a protected modifier.

Example:

```
open class X{
    val num = 30
}
class Y: X(){
    fun accessX(){
        println("Access from X: $num")
    }
}
fun main(){
    val objY = Y()
    objY.accessX()
}
```

Output:

Access from X: 30

4.6 Property

A property is declared the same way as variables are declared—by using the var and val keywords in classes or methods. A property declared using var can be changed, while one declared with val cannot be changed. Following is the syntax of declaring a property in a class.

Syntax:

Using var
```
var <propertyName>[: <PropertyType>] [= <property_initializer>]
    [<getter>]
    [<setter>]
```
Using val
```
val <propertyName>[: <PropertyType>] [= <property_initializer>]
    [<getter>]
```

Initializer, getter, and setter are optional. When using val, we can't use setter, because val properties cannot be changed—they are constant.

Example:

```
fun main() {
    var x:Int = 10
    val y:Int = 20
    x=30     //can be reassigned because it is var
    y=20     //cannot be reassigned because it is val
}
```

Output:

```
Error: 'val' cannot be reassigned.
```

Class Properties

In Kotlin, just as we declare properties in the main function, we can also declare them inside the class. The meanings of the val and var keywords is the same.

Example:

```
class X(
    val name:String,
    val age:Int
){
    //class body
}
fun main() {
    val obj = X("Mark",24)
    println("Name: ${obj.name}")
    println("Age: ${obj.age}")
}
```

Output:

```
Name: Mark
Age: 24
```

Setters and Getters

Setter, as its name suggests, is used to set the value, while getter is used to get the value. Getters and setters are generally auto-generated in the code. Let's take an example of a person class. Define the property name in that class and assign the value Mark to it.

Example:

```
class person{
    var name:String = "Mark"
}
```

The preceding code is equivalent to the following code.

```
class person {
    var name: String = "Mark"
        get() = field                        // getter
        set(value) { field = value }         // setter
}
```

Access Getter and Setter

```
fun main(){
    val obj = person()
    obj.name="Evan" //setter
    println("Name: ${obj.name}")    //getter
}
```

Where value and field are used in the preceding program, value is assigned to field and field is assigned to get().

Custom Setter and Getter

We can create custom getters and setters in the program, as shown in the following code.

Example:

```
class X(age:Int){
    var age:Int = age    //custom
        set(value) {
            field = if(value > 18 ) value else 0
        }
    var isEligible:Boolean = false    //custom
        get(){
            return age>18
        }
}
fun main() {
    val obj = X(19)
    obj.age = 10
    println("isEligible:${obj.isEligible}")
    println("Age: ${obj.age}")
}
```

Output:

```
isEligible:false
Age: 0
```

4.7 Abstract Class

An abstract class is used to define a template for the class, methods, and properties inside this class that cannot be instantiated. An abstract class can be declared using the abstract keyword. Following is the syntax for declaring an abstract class.

Syntax:

```
abstract class class_name{
    //code
}
```

Objects cannot be created for an abstract class. Methods and properties declared inside an abstract class are not abstract unless they are declared as abstract. The following is an example.

```
abstract class class_name{
    abstract var a:Int      //abstract
    abstract fun run()      //abstract
    fun run2(){
        println("Non abstract")
    }
}
```

The following is an example of using abstract and non-abstract properties as well as methods in abstract classes.

Example:

```
//abstract class
abstract class People(val name: String) {    // Non-Abstract Property
    // Abstract Property (Must be overridden by Subclasses)
    abstract var age: Int

    // Abstract Methods (Must be implemented by Subclasses)
    abstract fun birthDate(date:String)

    // Non-Abstract Method
    fun peopleDisplay() {
        println("Name: $name")
    }
}
```

```
// derived class
class person(name: String) : People(name) {
    override var age = 34
    override fun birthDate(date:String){
        println("Date of Birth is: $date")
    }
}
fun main(args: Array<String>) {
    val obj = person("Mark")
    obj.peopleDisplay()
    obj.birthDate("12 January 1992")
}
```

Output:

```
Name: Mark
Date of Birth is: 12 January 1992
```

Overriding Non-abstract Open Member with the Abstract

In Kotlin, we can override a non-abstract method or property from an open class to an abstract class and use it in a different class, as follows.

Example:

```
open class MainClass(){
    open fun run(){
        println("Animals can run")
    }
}
abstract class Animal:MainClass(){
    override abstract fun run()
}
class Lion:Animal(){
    override fun run(){
        println("Lions can run")
    }
}
```

CHAPTER 4   OBJECT-ORIENTED PROGRAMMING WITH KOTLIN

```
fun main(){
    val objmain = MainClass()
    objmain.run()
    val objLion = Lion()
    objLion.run()
}
```

Output:

```
Animals can run
Lions can run
```

Multiple Derived Classes

We can use an abstract member of an abstract class in multiple classes that derive the abstract class. Following is an example. The abstract class animal with the abstract method run can be derived by the Tiger, Lion, and Dog classes.

Example:

```
abstract class Animal{
    abstract fun run()
}
class Lion:Animal(){
    override fun run(){
        println("Lions can run")
    }
}
class Tiger:Animal(){
    override fun run(){
        println("Tigers can run")
    }
}
class Dog:Animal(){
    override fun run(){
        println("Dogs can run")
    }
}
```

```
fun main(){
    val objLion = Lion()
    objLion.run()
    val objTiger = Tiger()
    objTiger.run()
    val objDog = Dog()
    objDog.run()
}
```

Output:

```
Lions can run
Tigers can run
Dogs can run
```

4.8 Data Class

In Kotlin, we can create data classes to seize data inside them. There are some derivable functions available for that data that are automatically derived from the data class. To create a data class, the keyword data is required. Following is an example of a data class.

Example:

data class Person(val name: String, val age: Int)

There are some rules for creating a data class, as follows:

- Primary constructor must have at least one parameter.
- Data classes cannot be abstract class, sealed class, or inner class.
- It may implement interfaces.
- Primary constructor must be declared using either val or var.

Functions that are automatically derived by the compiler are as follows:

1. **toString():** This function creates a string of all parameters available in the class. The following is an example of that.

    Example:

    ```
    fun main(){
        data class people(val name:String, val age:Int)
    ```

```
        val obj = people("Mark",23)
        println(obj.toString())
}
```

Output:

people(name=Mark, age=23)

2. **hashCode():** This function returns the hashcode of the object. The following is an example of using this function.

Example:

```
fun main(){
    data class people(val name:String, val age:Int)
    val obj = people("Mark",23)
    println("Hashcode: "+obj.hashCode())
}
```

Output:

Hashcode: 74113738

3. **equals():** This method is used to compare two objects, and if both are similar it returns true. The following is an example.

Example:

```
fun main(){
    data class people(val name:String, val age:Int)
    val obj1 = people("Mark",23)
    val obj2 = people("Mark",23)
    val obj3 = people("Evan",25)
    println("Compare obj1 and obj2: "+obj1.equals(obj2))
    println("Compare obj1 and obj3: "+obj1.equals(obj3))
}
```

Output:

Compare obj1 and obj2: true
Compare obj1 and obj3: false

4. **copy():** Using this, we can copy all the parameters defined in the primary constructor. Sometimes we need this function to copy an object to another object. The following is an example.

Example:

```
fun main(){
    data class people(val name:String, val age:Int)
    val obj = people("Mark",23)
    println(obj.toString())
    val obj2 = obj.copy()              //copy all parameters
    val obj3 = obj.copy(age=24)        //copy only name
    println(obj2.toString())
    println(obj3.toString())
}
```

Output:

```
people(name=Mark, age=23)
people(name=Mark, age=23)
people(name=Mark, age=24)
```

4.9 Sealed Class

As their name suggests, sealed classes are used for bounded hierarchies. A sealed class defines a set of subclasses within it. It restricts that type to be matched at compile time rather than at runtime. Sealed classes are by default abstract, so they cannot be instantiated. All subclasses of the sealed class need to be declared in the same file. To declare a sealed class use the following syntax.

Syntax:

```
sealed class class_name
```
Following is an example of its usage.

Example:

```
sealed class Animal(){
    class Dog:Animal(){
        fun display(){
            println("Subclass Dog of Sealed class Animal ")
        }
    }
    class Cat:Animal(){
        fun display(){
            println("Subclass Cat of sealed class Animal")
        }
    }
}
fun main(){
    val obj =Animal.Dog()
    obj.display()
    val obj1=Animal.Cat()
    obj1.display()
}
```

Output:

```
Subclass Dog of sealed class Animal
Subclass Cat of sealed class Animal
```

4.10 Enum Class

In Kotlin programming there will sometimes be the need for constants, and for that, enumeration is used. Enum is nothing but a named list of constants, and it has its own type. Following are some important points related to enum in Kotlin:

- An enum can have methods and properties.
- It acts as a separate instance of a class and is separated by comma.
- It increases readability.
- An instance of the enum class cannot be created using constructors.

The following is an example of using the enum class.

Example:

```
Enum class Months{
January,
February,
March,
April,
May,
June,
July,
August,
September,
October,
November,
December
}
```

An enum class can have constructor. It is initialized by passing some value to the primary constructor, as follows:

```
enum class colors(val name:String){
    color1("Red"),
    color2("Green")
}
```

To access these colors we need to write the following line in code:

```
val color = colors.color1.name
```

Enum Properties and Methods

Let's look at several enum properties and methods.

Properties:

- Ordinal: This property stores the value of constants.
- Name: This property stores the name of the constants.

Methods:

- values: This method returns the list of all constants defined in that enum.
- valueOf: This method returns the value of enum defined in the class, and if it is not available then it returns an IllegalArgumentException error.

The following is an example of using enum with functions and properties.

Example:

```kotlin
enum class Colors(val isPrimarycolor: Boolean = false){
    Red(true),
    Green(true),
    Blue(true),
    Orange,
    Purple;
    companion object{
        public fun check(obj: Colors): Boolean {
            return obj.name.compareTo("Red") == 0 || obj.name.
            compareTo("Green") == 0
        }
    }
}
fun main(){
    for(color in Colors.values()) {
        println("${color.ordinal} = ${color.name} and is primary ${color.isPrimarycolor}")
    }
    val objColor = Colors.Orange
    println("$objColor Is Primary Color ${Colors.check(objColor)}")
}
```

Output:

```
0 = Red and is primary true
1 = Green and is primary true
2 = Blue and is primary true
```

3 = Orange and is primary false
4 = Purple and is primary false
Orange Is Primary Color false

4.11 Practical Programming Exercises

1. **Create a banking management system that can manage different types of accounts, such as savings, current, and fixed deposit.** Each account must have parameters—account holder name, account number, balance. Each account type can do the following:

   - **Savings Account:** Allows you to withdraw and deposit money. Offers calculating interest rate on balance.

   - **Fixed Deposit Account:** It offers a higher interest rate, and in this type of account money cannot be withdrawn until fixed deposit period ends.

   - **Current Account:** Allows deposit and withdrawal of money but does not offer interest.

   Solution:

```
open class classBankAccount(
    val accountHolderName: String,
    val accountNo: String,
    protected var balanceAvailable: Double
){
    open fun depositMoney(money: Double) {
        if (money > 0) {
            balanceAvailable += money
            println("Deposit $$money. New balance available:
            $$balanceAvailable")
        } else {
            println("Invalid Money.")
        }
```

CHAPTER 4   OBJECT-ORIENTED PROGRAMMING WITH KOTLIN

```kotlin
    }
    open fun withdrawMoney(money: Double) {
        if (money <= balanceAvailable && money > 0) {
            balanceAvailable -= money
            println("withdraw $$money. New balance available:
            $$balanceAvailable")
        } else {
            println("Insufficient balance or invalid money.")
        }
    }
    fun accountDetails() {
        println("Account Holder Name: $accountHolderName")
        println("Account Number: $accountNo")
        println("Available Balance: $$balanceAvailable")
    }
    open fun calculateInterestRate(): Double {
        return 0.0
    }
}
class classSavingsAccount(
    accountHolderName: String,
    accountNo: String,
    balanceAvailable: Double,
    val interest: Double
) : classBankAccount(accountHolderName, accountNo,
balanceAvailable) {
    override fun depositMoney(money: Double) {
        super.depositMoney(money)
        println("Deposit into Savings Account with interest of
        $interest%")
    }
    override fun calculateInterestRate(): Double {
        return balanceAvailable * (interest / 100)
    }
}
```

```kotlin
class classCurrentAccount(
    accountHolderName: String,
    accountNo: String,
    balanceAvailable: Double
) : classBankAccount(accountHolderName, accountNo,
balanceAvailable) {
    override fun depositMoney(money: Double) {
        super.depositMoney(money)
        println("Deposit into Current Account without interest")
    }
    override fun calculateInterestRate(): Double {
        return 0.0
    }
}
class classFixedDepositAccount(
    accountHolderName: String,
    accountNo: String,
    balanceAvailable: Double,
    val fixedDepositPeriod: Int, // In months
    val interest: Double
) : classBankAccount(accountHolderName, accountNo,
balanceAvailable) {
    override fun depositMoney(money: Double) {
        if (fixedDepositPeriod > 0) {
            println("Deposit into Fixed Deposit Account is not
            allowed until the period ends.")
        } else {
            super.depositMoney(money)
        }
    }
    override fun calculateInterestRate(): Double {
        if (fixedDepositPeriod > 0) {
            return balanceAvailable * (interest / 100)
```

```kotlin
        } else {
            println("Interest cannot be calculated until the
            deposit period ends.")
            return 0.0
        }
    }
}
fun main() {
    val savingsAccount = classSavingsAccount("Mark", "SA234788",
    3000.0, 4.0)
    val currentAccount = classCurrentAccount("Evan",
    "CA340099", 1000.0)
    val fixedDepositAccount = classFixedDepositAccount("Alice",
    "FD343434", 5000.0, 12, 6.0)
    savingsAccount.accountDetails()
    savingsAccount.depositMoney(500.0)
    savingsAccount.withdrawMoney(500.0)
    println("Interest Savings Account: ${savingsAccount.
    calculateInterestRate()}")
    println()
    currentAccount.accountDetails()
    currentAccount.depositMoney(200.0)
    currentAccount.withdrawMoney(100.0)
    println("Interest Current Account: ${currentAccount.
    calculateInterestRate()}")
    println()
    fixedDepositAccount.accountDetails()
    fixedDepositAccount.depositMoney(400.0)
    fixedDepositAccount.withdrawMoney(300.0)
    println("Interest Fixed Deposit Account:
    ${fixedDepositAccount.calculateInterestRate()}")
}
```

Output:

Account Holder Name: Mark
Account Number: SA234788
Available Balance: $3000.0
Deposit $500.0. New balance available: $3500.0
Deposit into Savings Account with interest of 4.0%
withdraw $500.0. New balance available: $3000.0
Interest Savings Account: 120.0

Account Holder Name: Evan
Account Number: CA340099
Available Balance: $1000.0
Deposit $200.0. New balance available: $1200.0
Deposit into Current Account without interest
withdraw $100.0. New balance available: $1100.0
Interest Current Account: 0.0

Account Holder Name: Alice
Account Number: FD343434
Available Balance: $5000.0
Deposit into Fixed Deposit Account is not allowed until the period ends.
withdraw $300.0. New balance available: $4700.0
Interest Fixed Deposit Account: 282.0

Develop a library management system that is able to manage various books, track their details, and calculate late fees for overdue book. Book should have attributes like title, author, ISBN, availability. Include functionality to borrow book, return book, display book details, calculate overdue book fees, and check availability.

Solution:

```
import java.time.LocalDate
import java.time.temporal.ChronoUnit
class Book(
    val booktitle: String,
```

```kotlin
        val author: String,
        val isbn: String,
        var isAvailable: Boolean = true,
        val dueDate: LocalDate,
        val lateFeePerDay: Double = 1.0
) {
    fun checkAvailability() {
        if (isAvailable) {
            println("The book '$booktitle' is available")
        } else {
            println("The book '$booktitle' is borrowed.")
        }
    }
    fun borrowBook() {
        if (isAvailable) {
            isAvailable = false
            println("You have borrowed the book '$booktitle'.")
        } else {
            println("Sorry, the book '$booktitle' is currently
            unavailable.")
        }
    }
    fun returnBook(returnDate: LocalDate): Double {
        if (!isAvailable) {
            isAvailable = true
            val lateFee = calculateLateFee(returnDate)
            println("You have returned the book '$booktitle'.")
            if (lateFee > 0) {
                println("Late fee: $$lateFee")
            }else{
                println("Late fee: $0.0")
            }
            return lateFee
        } else {
            println("The book '$booktitle' was not borrowed.")
            return 0.0
```

```kotlin
        }
    }
    private fun calculateLateFee(returnDate: LocalDate): Double {
        if (returnDate.isAfter(dueDate)) {
            val daysLate = ChronoUnit.DAYS.between(dueDate,
            returnDate)
            return daysLate * lateFeePerDay
        }
        return 0.0
    }
    fun displayDetails() {
        println("Book Title: $booktitle")
        println("Author: $author")
        println("ISBN: $isbn")
        println("Available: ${if (isAvailable) "Yes" else "No"}")
        println("Due Date: $dueDate")
    }
}
fun main() {
    val book1 = Book(
        booktitle = "The Great Gatsby",
        author = "F. Scott Fitzgerald",
        isbn = "9780743273565",
        dueDate = LocalDate.of(2024, 11, 10)
    )
    book1.displayDetails()
    println()
    book1.checkAvailability()
    println()
    book1.borrowBook()
    println()
    val returnDateLate = LocalDate.of(2024, 11, 15)
    book1.returnBook(returnDateLate)
    book1.displayDetails()
    println()
```

```
book1.borrowBook()
println()
val returnDateOnTime = LocalDate.of(2024, 11, 10)
book1.returnBook(returnDateOnTime)
println()
}
```

Output:

```
Book Title: The Great Gatsby
Author: F. Scott Fitzgerald
ISBN: 9780743273565
Available: Yes
Due Date: 2024-11-10

The book 'The Great Gatsby' is available

You have borrowed the book 'The Great Gatsby'.

You have returned the book 'The Great Gatsby'.
Late fee: $5.0
Book Title: The Great Gatsby
Author: F. Scott Fitzgerald
ISBN: 9780743273565
Available: Yes
Due Date: 2024-11-10

You have borrowed the book 'The Great Gatsby'.

You have returned the book 'The Great Gatsby'.
Late fee: $0.0
```

2. **Create a geometric shape management system that has different types of shapes, like rectangle, triangle, and circle.** Calculate area of all the shapes.

   Solution:

   ```
   abstract class Shape {
       abstract fun calculateAreaOfShape(): Double
   }
   ```

```kotlin
class classCircle(val radius: Double) : Shape() {
    override fun calculateAreaOfShape(): Double {
        return Math.PI * radius * radius
    }
}
class classRectangle(val width: Double, val height: Double) : Shape() {
    override fun calculateAreaOfShape(): Double {
        return width * height
    }
}
class classTriangle(val base: Double, val height: Double) : Shape() {
    override fun calculateAreaOfShape(): Double {
        return 0.5 * base * height
    }
}
fun displayAreaofShape(shape: Shape) {
    println("The area of the shape is: ${shape.calculateAreaOfShape()}")
}
fun main() {
    val circle = classCircle(6.0)
    val rectangle = classRectangle(4.0, 5.0)
    val triangle = classTriangle(4.0, 5.0)
    displayAreaofShape(circle)
    displayAreaofShape(rectangle)
    displayAreaofShape(triangle)
}
```

Output:

```
The area of the shape is: 113.09733552923255
The area of the shape is: 20.0
The area of the shape is: 10.0
```

3. **Create a student management system that displays and manages students.** Each student has a name, email, phone number, roll number, and department. Display information of students.

Solution:

```kotlin
data class student(val name: String, val roll_no:Int, val department: String, val email:String, val phone: String){
    fun displayStudentDetails(){
        println("Name: $name")
        println("Roll No: $roll_no")
        println("Department: $department")
        println("Email: $email")
        println("Phone Number: $phone")
    }
}
fun main(){
    val student1 = student("Mark",1,"Computer Engineering","mark123@gmail.com","9433434343")
    val student2 = student("Evan",2,"IT Engineering","evan123@gmail.com","9953433334")
    val student3 = student("bOB",2,"Automobile Engineering","evan123@gmail.com","9953433334")
    println()
    println("Student 1 Details")
    student1.displayStudentDetails()
    println()
    println("Student 2 Details")
    student2.displayStudentDetails()
    println()
    println("Student 3 Details")
    student3.displayStudentDetails()
    println()
    println("student1 == student2: "+student1.equals(student2))
    println()
```

```
    val student4 = student1.copy(name = "Alice", roll_no = 3)
    println("Updated student1")
    student4.displayStudentDetails()
}
```

Output:

```
Student 1 Details
Name: Mark
Roll No: 1
Department: Computer Engineering
Email: mark123@gmail.com
Phone Number: 9433434343

Student 2 Details
Name: Evan
Roll No: 2
Department: IT Engineering
Email: evan123@gmail.com
Phone Number: 9953433334

Student 3 Details
Name: bOB
Roll No: 2
Department: Automobile Engineering
Email: evan123@gmail.com
Phone Number: 9953433334

student1 == student2: false

Updated student1
Name: Alice
Roll No: 3
Department: Computer Engineering
Email: mark123@gmail.com
Phone Number: 9433434343
```

CHAPTER 4　OBJECT-ORIENTED PROGRAMMING WITH KOTLIN

4. **Create a cinema ticket calculation system that calculates ticket price according to the morning, evening, and afternoon show; ticket type needs to be basic, premium, or VIP.**

   Solution:

   ```
   enum class classTicketType(val basePrice: Double) {
       BASIC(15.0),
       PREMIUM(20.0),
       VIP(30.0);
       fun getDetails(): String {
           return when (this) {
               BASIC -> "Basic seat"
               PREMIUM -> "Premium seat"
               VIP -> "VIP seat"
           }
       }
   }
   enum class classShowTime(val showTimeValue: Double) {
       MORNING(5.0),
       AFTERNOON(4.0),
       EVENING(3.5);
       fun getDetails(): String {
           return when (this) {
               MORNING -> "Morning Show"
               AFTERNOON -> "Afternoon Show"
               EVENING -> "Evening Show"
           }
       }
   }
   class CinemaTicket(
       val ticketType: classTicketType,
       val showTime: classShowTime
   ) {
       fun calculatePrice(): Double {
           return ticketType.basePrice * showTime.showTimeValue
       }
   ```

```kotlin
    fun displayTicketInfo() {
        println("Ticket: ${ticketType.getDetails()}")
        println("Showtime: ${showTime.getDetails()}")
        println("Final Price: $${"%.2f".format(calculatePrice())}")
        println()
    }
}
fun main() {
    val basicEveningTicket = CinemaTicket(classTicketType.BASIC, classShowTime.EVENING)
    basicEveningTicket.displayTicketInfo()
    val premiumAfternoonTicket = CinemaTicket(classTicketType.PREMIUM, classShowTime.AFTERNOON)
    premiumAfternoonTicket.displayTicketInfo()
    val vipMorningTicket = CinemaTicket(classTicketType.VIP, classShowTime.MORNING)
    vipMorningTicket.displayTicketInfo()
}
```

Output:

```
Ticket: Basic seat
Showtime: Evening Show
Final Price: $52.50

Ticket: Premium seat
Showtime: Afternoon Show
Final Price: $80.00

Ticket: VIP seat
Showtime: Morning Show
Final Price: $150.00
```

CHAPTER 4   OBJECT-ORIENTED PROGRAMMING WITH KOTLIN

4.12 Summary

In this chapter we have learned various object-oriented programming concepts, like abstraction, encapsulation, and inheritance, along with some advanced options for using them. Each concept has its own syntax, libraries, methods, and hands-on exercises.

4.13 Test Your Knowledge

1. Which of the following is true about classes?

    a. Class must have constructors.

    b. Class only has constructors.

    c. Class is a blueprint for creating objects and contains properties and methods.

    d. Class only has methods and not properties.

2. Inner class can access the property of outer class.

    a. True

    b. False

3. Nested class can access property of outer class.

    a. True

    b. False

4. How many primary constructors can a Kotlin class have?

    a. one

    b. two

    c. three

    d. multiple

5. Which keyword is used in Kotlin to enable a class to be inherited by another class?

    a. inherit

    b. open

    c. super

    d. this

6. Select correct way to define an interface.

    a. class interfacename{}

    b. abstract class interfacename{}

    c. interface interfacename() {}

    d. interface interfacename{}

7. How do you declare an abstract property in Kotlin?

    a. abstract var propertyName: Type

    b. var propertyName: Type = value

    c. abstract property propertyName: Type

    d. propertyName: abstract Type

8. Which of the following function is derived in data classes in Kotlin?

    a. toString()

    b. equals()

    c. hashcode()

    d. All of the above

9. What is the default modifier for members in a Kotlin class?

    a. private

    b. public

    c. protected

    d. inner

10. Can an abstract class be instantiated in Kotlin?

    a. Yes, if it implements all abstract methods.

    b. Yes, if abstract class has a constructor.

    c. No, abstract class cannot be instantiated directly.

    d. Yes, if it is instantiated in a constructor.

4.14 Answers

1. c
2. a
3. b
4. a
5. b
6. d
7. a
8. d
9. b
10. c

CHAPTER 5

Error Handling and Exceptions

In programming, when a program behaves abnormally for any of the input from a user or experiences any event that causes a disturbance in the flow of the program, it is known as an error in the code. Errors occur in the program at the runtime. To handle errors that can disturb the flow of the program, an exception-handling mechanism is available in Kotlin.

5.1 Exception-Handling Basics

An exception is unwanted behavior by a program or any unexpected event that can occur at runtime of the program and cause a disturbance in the normal flow of the program. "Exception handling" means handling those events or exceptions that can cause error or disrupt the normal flow of a program.

There are **two** types of exceptions available in general:

1. **Checked Exception**: Exceptions that are set with methods and checked at compile time of the program, like `FileNotFoundException`.

2. **Unchecked Exception:** Exceptions that are checked at runtime and generally arise due to logical errors in programs, like `NullPointerException`.

In Kotlin, only unchecked exceptions are available. All unchecked exceptions can be caught at the runtime of a program. All the exception classes are derived from the `Throwable` class. The keyword throw is used for throwing an exception object.

CHAPTER 5   ERROR HANDLING AND EXCEPTIONS

Syntax:

```
throw Exception("throw statement")
```

Let's see the following example of an ArithmeticException:

```
fun main(){
    val num = 30/0      //throw an exception
    println(num)
}
```

Output:

```
Exception in thread "main" java.lang.ArithmeticException: / by zero
```

In the preceding program, we initialize the value of num to 30/0, but as we know from barithmetric division operations, we cannot divide any number by zero. That's why at runtime this program gives an error of divide by zero. To solve this problem, we can use a try-catch block.

In Kotlin, we use try-catch block for handling exceptions at runtime like in the preceding example. In a try block, we need to write code, which can throw an exception. This try block must be written inside the main method. Every try block is followed by either a catch block or a finally block or both. The following shows the syntax of a try-catch block.

Syntax:

```
try{
    //code that can throw an exception
}catch(e: ExceptionName){
    //statement that catch the exception and handle it
}
```

The following shows the Kotlin program that can handle arithmetic exceptions.

Example:

```
fun main(){
    try{
        val num = 20/0
        println(num)
    }catch(e: ArithmeticException){
```

```
        println("Divide by zero is not applicable")
    }
}
```

Output:

```
Divide by zero is not applicable
```

In the preceding example, the variable num is assigned the value of 10/0. In mathematics, dividing by zero is not available or not defined; that's why the variable num throws an exception, which is already written inside the try block. The exception thrown is handled by a catch block, which is written and prints the appropriate result or the warning message to alert the user that an exception occurred in the program.

The try-catch Block as an Expression

We can use a try-catch block as an expression in Kotlin. The expression evaluation result will be the last statement in the try block as well as in the catch block. If an exception occurs, then the catch block will return the value accordingly. The following shows this:

Example:

```
fun division(x: Int, y: Int) : Any {
    return try {
    x/y
    }
    catch(e:Exception){
        println(e)
        "Divide by zero not applicable"
    }
}
fun main(args: Array<String>) {
    // invoke division function
    var result1 = division(15,3)     //executes try block
    println(result1)
    var result2 = division(15,0)     // executes catch block
    println(result2)
}
```

CHAPTER 5 ERROR HANDLING AND EXCEPTIONS

Output:

```
5
java.lang.ArithmeticException: / by zero
Divide by zero not allowed
```

In the preceding example, we have created one function for division, which executes `try` and `catch` blocks according to the input provided inside the `main` function. In the main method we first gave 15 and 3 as an input, which executed the `try` block and gave the division result 5. Then in the next line we gave 15 and 0 as an input, which executed the try block for the result, but as input y = 0, an exception occurred, and it executes the `catch` block.

Finally Block

In Kotlin, the `finally` block is always executed, whether the `catch` block is executed or not. We use the `finally` block to execute some important code. We can use it with or without the `catch` block.

Syntax of `finally` block with `try` block:

```
try{
    //code which can throw exception
}
finally{
    //important code which always executes
}
```

The following shows the `finally` block without a `catch` block. First, it will execute the given `try` block, and then the `finally` block is executed. Here, an exception occurs and is not handled by the `catch` block, so it will throw an error with the name of the exception, as written in the output.

Example:

```
fun main(){
    try{
        val num = 30/0
        println(num)
    }
```

CHAPTER 5 ERROR HANDLING AND EXCEPTIONS

```
    finally{
        println("Inside finally block::this will run always")
    }
}
```

Output:

```
Inside finally block::this will run always
Exception in thread "main" java.lang.ArithmeticException: / by zero
```

Syntax of finally block with try-catch block:

```
try{
    //code which can throw exception
}catch(e:Exception){
    //code which can handle exception
}
finally{
    //important code which always executes
}
```

The following shows an example that handles the divide by zero exception seen in the previous example with the finally block, which always executes.

Example:

```
fun main(){
    try{
        val num = 30/0
        println(num)
    }catch(e: ArithmeticException){
        println("Divide by zero is not Applicable")
    }
    finally{
        println("Inside finally block::this will run always")
    }
}
```

CHAPTER 5   ERROR HANDLING AND EXCEPTIONS

Output:

```
Divide by zero is not Applicable
Inside finally block::this will run always
```

Throw Keyword

In Kotlin we use the throw keyword as name suggests, for throwing an exception. The exception thrown by the throw keyword can be explicit or custom. The following shows an example of throwing an exception.

Example:

```
fun main(args: Array<String>) {
    demo("kotlin programming")
    println("kotlin programming accepted")
    demo("k")
    println("k not accepted")
}
fun demo(name: String) {
    if (name.length < 6)
        throw ArithmeticException("Name is too short")
    else
        println("Accepted")
}
```

Output:

```
Accepted
kotlin programming accepted
Exception in thread "main" java.lang.ArithmeticException: Name is too short
```

In the preceding example, we check whether the name is of a length less than 6 or not. If it is less than 6, then it will throw a custom-generated exception; otherwise, it will print the line name accepted.

5.2 Nested try Block

In Kotlin we can implement one try block inside another try block, which is known as a nested try block. The following shows the syntax for a nested try block.

Syntax:

```
// try block 1
try
{
    // try block 2 inside try block 1
    try
    {
        // code which can throw exception
    }
    catch(e: Exception)
    {
        // catch the exception and handle it
    }
}
catch(e: Exception)
{
    // catch the exception and handle it
}
```

The following is an example of using a nested try block.

Example:

```
fun main(args: Array<String>) {
    val numArray = arrayOf(1,2,3,4,5,6,7,8)
    try {
        for (i in numArray.indices) {
            try {
                var r = (0..8).random()
                println(numArray[i+1]/r)
            } catch (e: ArithmeticException) {
                println(e)
            }
```

            }
        } catch (e: ArrayIndexOutOfBoundsException) {
            println(e)
        }
    }
}
```

**Output:**

```
2
1
2
java.lang.ArithmeticException: / by zero
2
7
1
java.lang.ArrayIndexOutOfBoundsException: Index 8 out of bounds for length 8
```

In the preceding example, numArray is assigned values from 0 to 8, and in the for loop there are two possibilities of exceptions. One is a dividing by zero exception and the other is an ArrayIndexOutOfBound exception. The first outer try block handles the ArrayIndexOutOfBound exception, and the inner try block handles the arithmetic exception (divide by zero).

Note Here the output will be different every time when you run the program because we are using a function to generate random numbers.

Multiple Catch Blocks

In Kotlin one try block can have multiple catch blocks. When we are not aware of which type of exception may occur in the program, then we can use multiple catch blocks to handle different types of exceptions that may occur in the program. The following shows the syntax of using multiple catch blocks with single try block.
```

CHAPTER 5　ERROR HANDLING AND EXCEPTIONS

Syntax:

```
try {
    // code that can throw exception
} catch(e: ExceptionOne) {
    // catch exception one and handle it
} catch(e: ExceptionTwo) {
    // catch exception two and handle it
}
```

Let's see an example of using multiple catch blocks.

Example:

```
fun main(args: Array<String>) {
    try {
        val numArray = arrayOf(1,2,3,4,5,6,7,8)
        for(i in numArray.indices){
        var r = (0..4).random()
        println(numArray[i+1]/r)
    }
    } catch (e: ArithmeticException) {
        println(e)
    } catch (e: ArrayIndexOutOfBoundsException) {
        println(e)
    }
}
```

Output:

```
2
1
4
1
java.lang.ArithmeticException: / by zero
```

This example handles exceptions for arithmetic and `ArrayIndexOutOfBound`. According to the exception that occurs, the appropriate `catch` block will run.

135

CHAPTER 5   ERROR HANDLING AND EXCEPTIONS

Note   Here the output will be different every time when you run the program because we are using a function to generate random numbers.

Using When in Catch Block

In Kotlin, instead of using multiple `catch` blocks, we can use the when keyword. The following shows an example of using the when expression.

Example:

```
fun main(args: Array<String>) {
    try {
        val numArray = arrayOf(1,2,3,4,5,6,7,8)
        for(i in numArray.indices){
            var r = (0..4).random()
            println(numArray[i+1]/r)
        }
    } catch (e: Exception) {
        when(e){
            is ArithmeticException -> {
                println(e)
            }
            is ArrayIndexOutOfBoundsException -> {
                println(e)
            }
        }
    }
}
```

Output:

```
0
3
java.lang.ArithmeticException: / by zero
```

In the preceding example we have replaced the previous example's two `catch` blocks with one single `catch` block and one when expression. Every time, the `catch` block will handle all types of exceptions and check inside the when expression, and print according to the type of exception.

Note Here the output will be different every time when you run the program because we are using a function to generate random numbers.

5.3 Custom Exceptions

In addition to the already available exceptions, you can build your own exceptions that can handle your own error cases in the program. When a user creates their own expression that is different from the built-in expression, it is known as a custom exception or user-defined exception. The following shows the syntax to create a custom exception.

Syntax:

```
class CustomException(message:String): Exception(message)
To throw the exception write below line:
throw CustomException("throw custom exception")
Let's take an example of custom exception.
```

Example:

```
class WrongPasswordException(message:String):Exception(message)
fun main(args: Array<String>) {
try {
val password = "hello1"
if(password.length<8){
throw WrongPasswordException("Password must be greater than length 8")
}
}catch (e: WrongPasswordException) {
println(e)
}
}
```

Output:

WrongPasswordException: Password must be greater than length 8

5.4 Real-Life Programming Practices

1. **Write a program for a payment-processing system and handle situations where the payment fails.**

   Code:

   ```
   fun tryPayment(payment:Double){
       try {
           if(payment <= 0){
               throw IllegalArgumentException("Payment must be
               greater than zero")
           }else if((1..10).random() <3){
               throw Exception("Payment Gateway Error")
           }else{
               println("Payment Successful")
           }
       }catch (e: IllegalArgumentException) {
           println(e)
       }catch(e:Exception){
           println(e)
       }
   }
   fun main(args: Array<String>) {
       tryPayment(0.0)
       tryPayment(200.0)
   }
   ```

   Output:

   java.lang.IllegalArgumentException: Payment must be greater than zero
   Payment Successful

2. **Write a program to handle invalid user data (name, password, age).**

   Code:

```kotlin
class InvalidDataException(message:String):Exception(message)
fun checkUserData(name:String,age:Int,password:String){
    try {
        if(password.length<8){
            throw InvalidDataException("Password must be greater
            than length 8")
        }
        if(name.isBlank()){
            throw InvalidDataException("Name must not be blank")
        }
        if(age<18){
            throw InvalidDataException("Age must be greater
            than 18")
        }
    }catch (e: InvalidDataException) {
        println(e)
    }
}
fun main(args: Array<String>) {
    checkUserData("",19,"123456789")
    checkUserData("kotlin",10,"123456789")
    checkUserData("kotlin",19,"1234")
}
```

   Output:

```
InvalidDataException: Name must not be blank
InvalidDataException: Age must be greater than 18
InvalidDataException: Password must be greater than length 8
```

3. **Write a program for connecting to a database and handle a situation when database connection fails.**

   Code:

   ```
   fun connectToDatabase(){
       var retryCount = 0
       var maxtryCount = 3
       while (retryCount < maxtryCount) {
           try {
               println("Attempt database query...")
               if ((1..10).random() < 7) throw Exception("Database query not successful")
               println("Query successful!")
               return
           } catch (e: Exception) {
               retryCount++
               println(e)
           }
       }
       println("Maximum retries reached.")
   }
   fun main(args: Array<String>) {
       connectToDatabase()
   }
   ```

   Output:

   ```
   Attempt database query...
   java.lang.Exception: Database query not successful
   Attempt database query...
   java.lang.Exception: Database query not successful
   Attempt database query...
   Query successful!
   ```

CHAPTER 5 ERROR HANDLING AND EXCEPTIONS

4. **Write a program for requesting network connection and handle a situation when connection is not available and request times out.**

    Code:

    ```
    fun tryNetworkRequest() {
        try {
            println("Trying network request...")
            val success = (1..10).random() > 2 // Random
            success/failure
            if (!success) throw Exception("Network timeout")
            println("Network request successful!")
        } catch (e: Exception) {
            println(e)
        }
    }
    fun main() {
        tryNetworkRequest()
    }
    ```

    Output:

    ```
    Trying network request...
    java.lang.Exception: Network timeout
    ```

5. **Write a program to find the square root of a number given by user and handle the cases when input is negative and not a usable number.**

    Code:

    ```
    import kotlin.math.sqrt
        fun squareRoot() {
        val input = -2

        try {
            val number = input?.toDouble() ?: throw
            IllegalArgumentException("Input cannot be null")
    ```

141

```
            if (number < 0) throw IllegalArgumentException("Number
            cannot be negative")
            println("Squareroot is ${sqrt(number)}")
        } catch (e: NumberFormatException) {
            println("Invalid input!")
        } catch (e: IllegalArgumentException) {
            println(e.message)
        } catch (e: Exception) {
            println(e)
        }
    }
    fun main() {
        squareRoot()
    }
```

Output:

Number cannot be negative

6. **Write a program that divides two numbers by zero and handles the case when dividing by zero.**

    Code:

```
fun division() {
    try {
        val input = 20/0
    }catch (e: Exception) {
        println(e)
    }
}
fun main() {
    division()
}
```

Output:

java.lang.ArithmeticException: / by zero

5.5 Summary

In this chapter we have learned about how the Kotlin program handles exceptions. We have also seen how to use `try`, `catch`, and `finally` blocks with their syntax, usage, and examples. We've also seen real-life programming exercises.

5.6 Test Your Knowledge

1. What is the benefit of using when inside a `catch` block?

    a. It allows handling multiple exceptions in a single block.

    b. It reduces code redundancy.

    c. Both a and b.

    d. None of the above.

2. How can you define a custom exception in Kotlin?

    a. by extending the `Throwable` class.

    b. by extending the `Exception` class.

    c. by implementing a `catch` block.

    d. None of the above

3. What is the advantage of using multiple `catch` blocks in Kotlin?

    a. It allows handling different types of exceptions separately.

    b. It reduces the need for nested `try` blocks.

    c. Both a and b

    d. None of the above

4. Why are nested `try` blocks used in Kotlin?

    a. to handle multiple types of exceptions hierarchically

    b. to optimize code performance

    c. to replace the finally block

    d. None of the above

CHAPTER 5 ERROR HANDLING AND EXCEPTIONS

5. What does the `throw` keyword do in Kotlin?

    a. It handles exceptions.

    b. It explicitly raises an exception.

    c. It terminates the program immediately.

    d. None of the above

6. In Kotlin, can a `finally` block exist without a `catch` block?

    a. Yes

    b. No

    c. Only if a `throw` statement is present

    d. None of the above

7. What is the role of a `finally` block in Kotlin?

    a. to handle exceptions

    b. to execute important code regardless of exception occurrence

    c. to replace the `catch` block

    d. None of the above

8. What is the purpose of a `try` block?

    a. to handle exceptions

    b. to close resources

    c. to write code that might throw exceptions

    d. None of the above

9. All exception classes in Kotlin inherit from which class?

    a. Exception

    b. RuntimeException

    c. Error

    d. Throwable

10. What is an exception in programming?

    a. a compile-time error

    b. an unwanted event disrupting the program flow at runtime

    c. a logical issue identified during debugging

    d. None of the above

5.7 Answers

1. c
2. b
3. c
4. a
5. b
6. a
7. b
8. c
9. d
10. b

CHAPTER 6

Collections and Generics

6.1 Collections

In Kotlin, collections are used to store and manipulate data or objects. Collections are used in real-world applications to efficiently store, retrieve, and update data. Some examples of real-world applications are shopping carts, game development, and social media feeds. There are many types of collections available in Kotlin, as follows:

- **Lists:** Lists are ordered collections that can have duplicate elements.
- **Set:** Sets are unordered collections that do not include duplicate elements.
- **Map:** Maps are collections with key–value pairs; in map the key cannot be duplicated but the value can be the same.
- **Arrays:** Arrays are fixed-size collections with the same type of elements inside it. We have already covered arrays in Chapter 2.

Kotlin collections are similar to Java collections. A collection generally contains a number of objects or data of the same type, which are known as items or elements. The Kotlin standard library provides a wide set of tools for managing **collections.** There are two types of Kotlin collections:

- **Immutable Collections:** "Immutable" means that it supports read-only functions and cannot modify its elements. Immutable collections are as follows:
  - **Immutable List**
  - **Immutable Set**
  - **Immutable Map**

- **Mutable Collections:** Mutable collections support both read and write access. You can add as well as remove elements from mutable collections. The following are the types of mutable collections:

  - **Mutable List**
  - **Mutable Set**
  - **Mutable Map**

Let's learn all the collections—list, set, and map—in detail.

6.2 List

- **Immutable List:** This is an ordered collection with duplicate values. Values inside an immutable list can be repeated multiple times. We can access elements or items by using indices or integer numbers, which give the position of the elements. Immutable lists can be created by using the `listOf()` method. As this is an immutable list we can only access the elements and cannot perform add or remove operations. The following is an example of an immutable list that prints the elements present in the list `immutableNameList`.

  Example:

  ```
  fun main() {
      val immutableNameList = listOf("Bob","Alice","Jacob","Alice")
      for(item in immutableNameList){
          println(item)
      }
  }
  ```

  Output:

  ```
  Bob
  Alice
  Jacob
  Alice
  ```

- **Mutable List:** As it is mutable we can update or add elements to the list. To create a mutable list, functions like mutableListOf(), arrayListOf(), and ArrayList are used. The following shows an example of using a mutable list.

Example:

```kotlin
fun main() {
    var mutableNameList = mutableListOf("Bob","Alice","Jacob","Alice")
    println("Before Add Operation...")
    for(item in mutableNameList){
        println(item)
    }
    mutableNameList.add("Mark")     //add
    println("After Add Operation...")
    for(item in mutableNameList){
        println(item)
    }
    mutableNameList[3]="George"     //update
    println("After updating 4th Element...")
    for(item in mutableNameList){
        println(item)
    }
}
```

Output:

```
Before Add Operation...
Bob
Alice
Jacob
Alice
After Add Operation...
Bob
Alice
Jacob
Alice
```

```
Mark
After updating 4th Element...
Bob
Alice
Jacob
George
Mark
```

In this example, first we created a mutable list with four elements. After that we added one element and updated one element in the list.

- **Accessing First and Last Elements in List**

    We can access or retrieve the first and last elements of a list using the methods `first()` and `last()`. The following shows an example of accessing both elements.

    Example:

    ```
    fun main() {
        val numList = listOf(1,2,3,4,5)
        println(numList.first())
        println(numList.last())
    }
    ```

    Output:

    ```
    1
    5
    ```

- **List-Traversing Methods**

    In Kotlin, we can access a list using multiple methods. The following shows the different methods, with an example of accessing elements of a list one after another.

    Example:

    ```
    fun main() {
        val numList = listOf(1,2,3,4,5)
        // method 1
        println("Method 1")
    ```

```kotlin
    for (name in numList) {
        print("$name, ")
    }
    // method 2
    println()
    println("Method 2")
    for (i in 0 until numList.size) {
        print("${numList[i]} ")
    }
    // method 3
    println()
    println("Method 3")
    numList.forEachIndexed({i, j -> println("numList[$i] = $j")})
    // method 4
    println("Method 4")
    val it: ListIterator<Int> = numList.listIterator()
    while (it.hasNext()) {
        val i = it.next()
        print("$i ")
    }
}
```

Output:

```
Method 1
1, 2, 3, 4, 5,
Method 2
1 2 3 4 5
Method 3
numList[0] = 1
numList[1] = 2
numList[2] = 3
numList[3] = 4
numList[4] = 5
Method 4
1 2 3 4 5
```

Method 1: In this method we used for loop to traverse each and every element one by one and print it

Method 2: In this method we used again for loop but using position of element we print the value of that element.

Method 3: In this method a forEach loop is used to print elements of the list with position access and value.

Methods 4: In this method we used iterator function to iterate through the list until its last element and print its elements.

- **Sorting List**

    In Kotlin we can sort a list in ascending or descending order using functions sorted() and sortedDescending(). The following example shows that.

    Example:

    ```
    fun main() {
        val list = listOf(8, 4, 7, 1, 2, 3, 0, 5, 6 )
        println("List")
        println(list)
        val asc = list.sorted()
        println("Ascending Order")
        println(asc)
        val desc = list.sortedDescending()
        println("Descending Order")
        println(desc)
    }
    ```

    Output:

    ```
    List
    [8, 4, 7, 1, 2, 3, 0, 5, 6]
    Ascending Order
    [0, 1, 2, 3, 4, 5, 6, 7, 8]
    Descending Order
    [8, 7, 6, 5, 4, 3, 2, 1, 0]
    ```

- **Advantages and Disadvantages of Lists**

    - **Immutable:** The listOf() function creates an immutable list, which means that the data cannot be changed after list creation. It can be a disadvantage if your program needs to change the list at runtime.

    - **Type Safety:** The listOf() function provides type safety because it allows only the same type of elements inside it.

    - **Convenience:** Without writing multiple lines of code, list creation is simple and easy in Kotlin.

    - **Performance Overhead:** Immutable lists can have some performance overhead when you need to perform multiple operations in the list. Due to immutability, each new operation will require creating a new list, thus making it expensive in terms of memory.

    - The advantage of using a list is immutability, type safety, and convenience, while disadvantages are performance overhead and again immutability if multiple operations are required on the list. According to the need of the program, we need to decide whether list can be used or not.

6.3 Set

- **Immutable Set:** An immutable set is an unordered collection of elements without duplication. As it is an immutable set, we cannot perform add or remove operations. Immutable sets can be created using the setOf() method. The following shows an example of creating and using sets in Kotlin. In the example, we can see that though we gave values of 9, 0, and Alice multiple times, in the set it will only print the unique values.

CHAPTER 6 COLLECTIONS AND GENERICS

Example:

```
fun main(args: Array<String>) {
    var immutableSet = setOf(6,9,9,0,0,"Alice","Bob","Alice")
    for(item in immutableSet){
        println(item)
    }
}
```

Output:

```
6
9
0
Alice
Bob
```

- **Mutable Set:** In a mutable set we can read or write elements to or from the set. To create a mutable set, the mutableSetOf() function is used. The following shows an example of a mutable set.

Example:

```
fun main() {
    var mutableNameSet = mutableSetOf("Bob","Alice","Jacob")
    println("Before Add Operation...")
    for(item in mutableNameSet){
        println(item)
    }
    mutableNameSet.add("Mark")      //add
    println("After Add Operation...")
    for(item in mutableNameSet){
        println(item)
    }
}
```

Output:

```
Before Add Operation...
Bob
Alice
Jacob
After Add Operation...
Bob
Alice
Jacob
Mark
```

- **Set First and Last Elements**

  In Kotlin we can get the first as well as last elements of the set. The following example shows that. Functions first() and last() are used for accessing first and last elements, respectively.

  Example:

  ```
  fun main(args: Array<String>){
      val names = setOf(1,2,3,4,"mark","Jacob","Paulo","Smith")
      println("The first element of the set is: "+names.first())
      println("The last element of the set is: "+names.last())
  }
  ```

  Output:

  ```
  The first element of the set is: 1
  The last element of the set is: Smith
  ```

- **Set Indexing**

  In Kotlin, a set can be created using the setOf() function. To traverse through the index we can use the indexOf() and lastIndexOf() functions. Also, to find elements at a specific position we can use a function like elementAt(). The following shows an example.

Example:

```
fun main(args: Array<String>){
    val names = setOf(1,2,3,4,"mark","Jacob","Paulo","Smith")
    println("The element at index 2 is: "+names.elementAt(2))
    println("The index of element is : "+names.indexOf("Paulo"))
    println("The last index of element is: "+names.lastIndexOf("Paulo"))
}
```

Output:

```
The element at index 2 is: 3
The index of element is : 6
The last index of element is: 6
```

- **Set Basic Functions**

    In a Kotlin set, there are some basic functions available that can be used for multiple operations on the set. The following shows the list of functions:

    - **count():** It is used to count the number of elements in the set.
    - **max():** It is used to find out the maximum element from the set.
    - **min():** It is used to find out the minimum element from the set.
    - **sum():** It is used for finding the sum of all elements in the set.
    - **average():** It is used to find out the average of the elements of the set.
    - **contains():** This method is used to check if the set contains a particular element or not.
    - **containsAll():** This method is used to check if a set contains all the elements of given set or not.
    - **isEmpty():** This function is used to check if a given set is empty or not.

The following shows the example of using all the functions in the Kotlin program.

Example:

```
fun main(args: Array<String>){
    val numSet = setOf(5 ,7, 6, 4, 10, 3, 2, 8, 9, 1, 0)
    val emptySetDemo = setOf<String>()
    println("The number of element in the set is: "+numSet.count())
    println("The maximum element in the set is: "+numSet.max())
    println("The minimum element in the set is: "+numSet.min())
    println("The sum of the elements in the set is: "+numSet.sum())
    println("The average of elements in the set is: "+numSet.average())
    println("The set contains the element 6 or not?" +" "+numSet.contains(6))
    println("The set contains the given elements or not?" +" "+numSet.containsAll(setOf(1,3,4)))
    println("The set emptySetDemo is empty? "+emptySetDemo.isEmpty())
}
```

Output:

```
The number of element in the set is: 11
The maximum element in the set is: 10
The minimum element in the set is: 0
The sum of the elements in the set is: 55
The average of elements in the set is: 5.0
The set contains the element 6 or not?    true
The set contains the given elements or not?    true
The set emptySetDemo is empty? true
```

CHAPTER 6   COLLECTIONS AND GENERICS

Advantages and Disadvantages of Sets

- Creating and using a set is very easy and a simple method. Since the set we use is immutable it offers no updates in the set, which can be used when multi-threading.

- If you want to change elements of the set, and an immutable set is used at that time, it is a disadvantage. According to the requirement of the program, the set can be made either mutable or immutable.

6.4 Maps

- **Immutable Map:** Maps are key–value pairs, where the key must be unique, or unable to be duplicated, and the value can be repeated. Each key in a map has one value available. As it is an immutable map, we can only read the values. We cannot add to or remove from immutable maps. An immutable map can be created using the mapOf() method. The following shows an example of creating and using immutable maps. It prints the value of each and every key, and we can see that the values of keys 1 and 3 are the same.

Example:

```
fun main() {
    var immutableMap = mapOf(1 to "Alice",2 to "Bob",3 to "Alice")
    for(key in immutableMap.keys){
        println(immutableMap[key])
    }
}
```

Output:

```
Alice
Bob
Alice
```

- **Mutable Map:** It consists of key-value pairs and has functionalities like put, remove, clear, and so on. The following shows an example of using a mutable map.

Example:

```
fun main() {
    var mutableMap = mutableMapOf(1 to "Alice",2 to "Bob",3 to "Alice")
    println("Before Add Operation...")
    for(key in mutableMap.keys){
        println(mutableMap[key])
    }
    println("After Add Operation...")
    mutableMap.put(4,"Mark")     //add value
    for(key in mutableMap.keys){
        println(mutableMap[key])
    }
    println("After Updating 1st value...")
    mutableMap.put(1,"George")    //update value
    for(key in mutableMap.keys){
        println(mutableMap[key])
    }
}
```

Output:

```
Before Add Operation...
Alice
Bob
Alice
After Add Operation...
Alice
Bob
Alice
Mark
After Updating 1st value...
George
```

Bob
Alice
Mark

- **Map Keys, Values, and Entries:**

We can iterate through the keys, values, and entries of the map. The following example shows this.

Example:

```
fun main(args: Array<String>){
    val map = mapOf(1 to "Mark", 2 to "Jacob" , 3 to "Bob", 4 to "Iris")
    println("Map Entries : "+map)
    println("Map Keys: "+map.keys )
    println("Map Values: "+map.values )
}
```

Output:

```
Map Entries : {1=Mark, 2=Jacob, 3=Bob, 4=Iris}
Map Keys: [1, 2, 3, 4]
Map Values: [Mark, Jacob, Bob, Iris]
```

- **Map Size:**

Two methods are available for determining the size of the map: size and count. The following demonstrates the usage of both.

Example:

```
fun main(args: Array<String>){
    val map = mapOf(1 to "Mark", 2 to "Jacob" , 3 to "Bob", 4 to "Iris")
    println("Map Size: "+map.size)
    println("Map Size: "+map.count())
}
```

CHAPTER 6 COLLECTIONS AND GENERICS

Output:

```
Map Size: 4
Map Size: 4
```

- **Empty Map:**

We can create an empty, serializable map using the `mapOf()` function. The following shows an example.

Example:

```
fun main(args: Array<String>){
    val map = mapOf<String , Int>()
    println("Entries: " + map.entries)  //entries of map
    println("Keys: " + map.keys)  //keys of map
    println("Values: " + map.values)  //values of map
}
```

Output:

```
Entries: []
Keys: []
Values: []
```

- **Traversing Through the Map Values Using Different Methods:**

We can access values from the map using multiple methods, as is demonstrated in the following program. In method one, we directly access values using the name of the map and the position required. In the second method, we use the `getValue()` function to retrieve the particular value. In the third method, we use the `getOrDefault()` function, which will retrieve the value if available; otherwise it will return the default value. In the fourth method, we use the method `getOrElse()`, which will return the value if available; otherwise, it will return an `else` value.

Example:

```
fun main(args: Array<String>){
    val map = mapOf(1 to "Mark", 2 to "Jacob" , 3 to "Bob", 4 to "Iris")
    //method 1
```

161

```kotlin
    println("Element 1 is: "+map[1])
    //method 2
    println("Element 3 is: "+map.getValue(3))
    //method 3
    println("Element 4 is: "+map.getOrDefault(4, 0))
    // method  4
    val newMap = map.getOrElse(2 ,{ 0 })
    println(newMap)
}
```

Output:

```
Element 1 is: Mark
Element 3 is: Bob
Element 4 is: Iris
Jacob
```

- **Map Contains Key or Value:**

    We can check if the given map contains a particular key or value using functions like containsKey() and containsValue(). The following shows the use of both functions.

    Example:

```kotlin
fun main(args: Array<String>){
    val map = mapOf(1 to "Mark", 2 to "Jacob" , 3 to "Bob", 4 to "Iris")
    if (map.containsKey(3)) {
        println("Yes, it contains key 3")
    } else {
        println("No, it does not contain key 3")
    }
    if (map.containsValue("Iris")) {
        println("Yes, it contains value Iris")
    } else {
        println("No, it does not contain value Iris")
    }
}
```

Output:

```
Yes, it contains key 3
Yes, it contains value Iris
```

- **Two Values and Same Key:**

   We can assign two different values to the same key, but the map will consider only the last value of the key.

   Example:

   ```
   fun main(args: Array<String>){
       val map = mapOf(1 to "Mark", 2 to "Jacob", 3 to "Bob", 1 
       to "Iris")
       println("Entries of map : " + map.entries)
   }
   ```

   Output:

   ```
   Entries of map : [1=Iris, 2=Jacob, 3=Bob]
   ```

- **Advantages and Disadvantages of Maps**

    - The mapOf() function is easy and simple to use and it creates a read-
      only map, which is advantageous in multi-thread programming.

    - It uses a key–value pair structure, which helps in storing and organizing data.

    - Due to its read-only nature, we cannot add or remove elements in an immutable map.

    - If the data store is large, then the map will become insufficient.

6.5 Generics
Basics of Generics

In Kotlin, generics allow users to define type-safe classes, methods, and properties. It assures compile-time type safety. Using generics, we can create a parameterized class. To create it we use (< >) angle brackets. The following shows the syntax of declaring a generic class.

Syntax:

```
class myClass<T>(text: T){
     var name = text
}
```

The following shows the line of code creating an instance of a generic type class by providing type arguments:

```
val myClass1 : myClass<String> = myClass<String>("Hello World")
```

If a type can be inferred from the constructor, then we can omit the type while declaring the instance:

```
val myClass1 = muClass("Hello World")
```

The following shows why we need to use generics in Kotlin programs.

Example:

```
class People (text: String) {
    var x = text
    init{
        println(x)
    }
}
fun main(args: Array<String>){
    var name: People = People("Hello World")
    var rank: People = People(23)// compile time error
}
```

Output:
Argument type mismatch: actual type is 'kotlin.Int', but 'kotlin.String' was expected.

The preceding program will give a compile-time error if we pass the integer argument to the people class. To solve this problem we need to use generics. The following shows how this is done.

Example:

```
class People<T> (text: T) {
    var x = text
    init{
        println(x)
    }
}
fun main(args: Array<String>){
    var name: People<String> = People<String>("Hello World")
    var rank: People<Int> = People<Int>(23)// compile time error
}
```

Output:

```
Hello World
23
```

- **Variance:**

    Invariance is defined as when functions or methods are defined using one data type and thus cannot accept or return another data type. "Any" is the super type of all the other data types. In Kotlin, arrays are invariant by default. Extended generic types are invariant in Kotlin, which can be managed using in and out keywords. Variance is of two types:

    1. **Declaration-site variance**: In and out keywords
    2. **Use-site Variance**: Type projections

- **Kotlin In and Out Keywords**

  - **Out Keyword:** Using the out keyword in a generic class means that we can assign the reference to any of its super type. An out value can only be produced by and not consumed by the given class.

    Example:

    ```
    class OutClassDemo<out T>(val value: T) {
        fun getVal(): T {
            return value
        }
    }
    fun main(args: Array<String>){
        val out = OutClassDemo("string")
        val ref: OutClassDemo<Any> = out
        println(ref.getVal())
    }
    ```

    Output:

    String

    In the preceding program we have created `OutClassDemo`, which can produce the values of type T. If we do not use the out keyword, it will give a compile-time error.

  - **In Keyword:** Using the in keyword in a generic class means that we can assign a reference to any of its subtypes. The in keyword can only be used for a parameter type that is consumed and not produced. The following shows an example of using it in a program.

    Example:

    ```
    class InClass<in T> {
        fun toString(value: T): String {
            return value.toString()
    ```

```
        }
    }
    fun main(args: Array<String>){
        val inClassObject: InClass<Number> = InClass()
        val ref: InClass<Int> = inClassObject
        println(ref.toString(23))
    }
```

Output:

23

In the preceding example, we have declared a function named `toString()`, which can consume value with the type of T only. After that we can assign a number to the reference of its subtype: `Int`.

- **Covariance:**

In Kotlin, covariance is defined as being able to substitute subtypes but not supertypes. For example, a generic class can accept a subtype of data type that is already defined; i.e., a class that is defined for `Number` can accept `Int`, but a class that is defined for `Int` cannot accept `Number`. The following shows the implementation of covariance in a program.

Example:

```
fun main(args: Array<String>) {
        val y: MyClass<Any> = MyClass<String>() // Compiles
        without error
}
class MyClass<out T>
```

- **Contracovariance:**

In Kotlin, contracovariance is exactly opposite of covariance. It is defined as being able to substitute a supertype value in the subtypes. For example, a generic class can accept a supertype of the data type that is already defined; e.g., a generic class that is defined for Int can accept Number, but a generic class that is defined for Number cannot accept Int. The following shows the implementation of contracovariance in a Kotlin program.

Example:

```
fun main(args: Array<String>) {
        var a: Container<Ford> = Container<Car>() //compiles
        without error
//      var b: Container<Car> = Container<Ford>() //gives
        compilation error
}
open class Car
class Ford : Car()
class Container<in T>
```

- **Type Projections:**

Using type projections we can copy one type of element to the Any type of element. For example, if we want to copy elements of one array of some type to another array of Any type, then it is possible. The following shows this.

Example:

```
fun copy(mainArray: Array<out Any>, copyArray: Array<Any>) {
    assert(mainArray.size == copyArray.size)
    println("printing elements of main array...")
    for (i in mainArray.indices) {
    println(mainArray[i])
    }
    // copying (mainArray) array to (copyArray) array
    for (i in mainArray.indices)
        copyArray[i] = mainArray[i]
    println("printing elements of copied array...")
    for (i in copyArray.indices) {
```

```
        println(copyArray[i])
    }
}
fun main(args :Array<String>) {
    val intsArray: Array<Int> = arrayOf(1, 2, 3)
    val anyArray :Array<Any> = Array<Any>(3) { "" }
    copy(intsArray, anyArray)
}
```

Output:

```
printing elements of main array...
1
2
3
printing elements of copied array...
1
2
3
```

- **Star Projections(*):**

    When we want to print an element of an array whose type is not known by us, then we can use star(*) projection. The following shows an example.

    Example:

    ```
    fun printArray(array: Array<*>) {
        array.forEach { print(it) }
    }

    fun main(args :Array<String>) {
        val name = arrayOf("Mark","Jacob","Aries")
        println("printing String array...")
        printArray(name)
        println()
        val age = arrayOf(20,23,24)
    ```

```
        println("printing Int array...")
        printArray(age)
}
```

Output:

```
printing String array...
MarkJacobAries
printing Int array...
202324
```

6.6 Real-Life Programming Practices

1. **Create an online shopping platform that can manage various types of products, such as electronics, clothing, and books.**
   Each product has unique attributes, and the platform should be able to handle them efficiently while ensuring type safety and reusability. Additionally, the system should keep track of customer orders, which may contain a list of products with varying categories.

   Solution:

   ```
   // Generic class to represent a Product of any type
   class Product<T>(val id: Int, val name: String, val price: Double,
   val category: T) {
       fun getProductInfo() {
           println("ID: $id, Name: $name, Price: $$price, Category:
           $category")
       }
   }

   // Enum representing different product categories
   enum class Category {
       ELECTRONICS, CLOTHING, BOOKS
   }
   ```

```kotlin
// Data class to represent an Order containing a list of products
data class Order(val orderId: Int, val productList:
List<Product<*>>, val totalAmount: Double)

// Repository to manage orders using a MutableList collection
class OrderRepository {
    private val orders: MutableList<Order> = mutableListOf()

    fun addOrder(order: Order) {
        orders.add(order)
        println("Order with ID ${order.orderId} added
        successfully.")
    }

    fun listOrders() {
        for (order in orders) {
            println("Order ID: ${order.orderId}, Total Amount:
            $${order.totalAmount}")
            order.productList.forEach { it.getProductInfo() }
        }
    }
}

// Main function demonstrating the usage of generics and
collections
fun main() {
    // Creating products of different types using generics
    val laptop = Product(101, "Laptop", 1200.0, Category.
    ELECTRONICS)
    val tShirt = Product(102, "T-Shirt", 25.0, Category.CLOTHING)
    val book = Product(103, "Kotlin Programming", 40.0,
    Category.BOOKS)

    // Adding products to a list
    val productList = listOf(laptop, tShirt, book)

    // Creating an order with a list of products
    val order1 = Order(1, productList, productList.sumOf {
    it.price })
```

```kotlin
    // Creating an order repository and adding the order
    val orderRepo = OrderRepository()
    orderRepo.addOrder(order1)

    // Listing all orders
    println("\nAll Orders:")
    orderRepo.listOrders()
}
```

Output:

Order with ID 1 added successfully.

All Orders:
Order ID: 1, Total Amount: $1265.0
ID: 101, Name: Laptop, Price: $1200.0, Category: ELECTRONICS
ID: 102, Name: T-Shirt, Price: $25.0, Category: CLOTHING
ID: 103, Name: Kotlin Programming, Price: $40.0, Category: BOOKS

6.7 Summary

In this chapter, we have learned about collections and generics in Kotlin. We have seen that collections are used for storing, manipulating, and retrieving data, and that generics enable code reusability, clear structure, and null safety. Both are useful for writing code that is robust, flexible, and scalable.

6.8 Test Your Knowledge

1. Which of the following collections in Kotlin allows duplicate elements?

    a. Set

b. Map

   c. List

   d. None of the above

2. Which function is used to create an immutable list in Kotlin?

   a. list()

   b. listOf()

   c. arrayListOf()

   d. mutableListOf()

3. What will happen if you try to add elements to an immutable list in Kotlin?

   a. The elements will be added successfully.

   b. A runtime error will occur.

   c. A compile-time error will occur.

   d. The elements will be replaced.

4. Which of the following methods can be used to access the first element of a list in Kotlin?

   a. first()

   b. getFirst()

   c. accessFirst()

   d. fetchFirst()

5. Which function is used to create an immutable set in Kotlin?

   a. hashSetOf()

   b. listOf()

   c. mutableSetOf()

   d. setOf()

CHAPTER 6 COLLECTIONS AND GENERICS

6. In Kotlin maps, can keys be duplicated?

    a. Yes

    b. No

7. Which of the following is not a valid function for traversing a list in Kotlin?

    a. forEach()

    b. forEachIndexed()

    c. iterator()

    d. getElement()

8. Which function is used to check if a list is empty in Kotlin?

    a. isNull()

    b. hasElements()

    c. isEmpty()

    d. isBlank()

9. Which method is used to remove an element from a mutable map?

    a. remove()

    b. delete()

    c. discard()

    d. pop()

10. What is the advantage of using immutable collections in Kotlin?

    a. better performance

b. thread safety

c. can modify elements easily

d. less memory consumption

6.9 Answers

1. c
2. b
3. c
4. a
5. d
6. b
7. d
8. c
9. a
10. b

CHAPTER 7

Kotlin Coroutines

7.1 Introduction

Over the years while developing applications, all programmers have worried about one classical problem: how to stop our applications from blocking. Irrespective of the type of application, whether it is a website, mobile application, or server-side application, everyone wants to minimize the user's wait time, due to asynchronous programming blocking is the main reason that prevents applications from scaling.

There are many approaches to solve this problem, like threading, callbacks, futures, promises, reactive extensions, and coroutines. Following are the advantages of using coroutines for asynchronous programming in Kotlin.

Lightweight: Coroutines are lightweight, so you can run many coroutines on single threads, which does not block the thread where the coroutine is running. You can suspend the running thread at any time, which can prevent memory blocking.

Fewer Memory Leaks: To avoid memory leaks use structured concurrency to run operations.

Built-in Cancellation: Provides built-in cancellation support.

Kotlin provides a minimal, low-level API, **kotlinx.coroutines**, which is a library for coroutines in Kotlin and is developed by Jetbrains.

7.2 Creating Coroutines

Kotlin Coroutines are conceptually similar to threads, as it runs the block of assigned code concurrently with the rest of the code. However, it is not bound to a particular thread, so it can suspend its execution from one thread and start running another thread.

The following shows the usage of coroutines in Kotlin.

Example:

```
import kotlinx.coroutines.*
fun main() = runBlocking { // this: CoroutineScope
    launch { // launch new coroutine
        delay(1000L) // delay for 1 second which is non-blocking
        println("World!") // print after delay
    }
    println("Hello") // main continues while a previous one is delayed,
    printed first
}
```

The following is the explanation of the preceding program.

launch: This is used as the builder for the coroutine. It launches the new coroutine concurrently with the rest of the code, which works continuously—that's why *Hello* will be printed first.

delay: This is a function that is used to suspend a coroutine for a specific time period. Suspension of the particular coroutine will not block the thread; rather, it allows the running of another block of code.

runBlocking: This is also a builder function. It is used as a bridge between non-coroutine code and coroutine code. If we try to remove runBlocking from the preceding program, then an error will be generated—i.e., *unresolved reference launch*—because a launch can't be declared without a coroutine scope.

7.3 Structured Concurrency

Coroutines follow structured concurrency, meaning that we can declare new coroutines only inside the scope of a coroutine. In the preceding example, we saw that the runBlocking function is used for setting the scope of coroutines in the program and that is why the program waits until work gets printed after the delay and then exits.

In real-world applications, there will be multiple coroutines to launch and run in a single application, hence structured concurrency ensures that coroutines are not lost, nor are there memory leaks.

Structured concurrency avoids leaking, offers a clear structure with better error handling, and cancels the child coroutines automatically.

7.4 Extract Function Refactoring

In coroutines we can extract whatever is written inside the launch {...} and make a separate function for that. When we perform this, a new function will be created that is a suspend function. Suspend functions are the same as normal functions, but they can in turn use other suspending functions to suspend execution of coroutines.

Example:

```
import kotlinx.coroutines.*
fun main() = runBlocking { // this: CoroutineScope
    launch {
        printWorld()
    }
    println("Hello")
}
suspend fun printWorld(){
    delay(1000L)
    println("World!") // print after delay
}
```

Output:

```
Hello
World!
```

7.5 Scope Builder and Concurrency
Scope Builder

It is possible for coroutines to declare their own scope instead of having it defined by scope builders. It creates its scope and lets all its children complete. There are two types of scope builders available: runBlocking and coroutineScope. They are similar because they both let every child complete its task, and after that they exit. The difference is only that runBlocking blocks the current thread for other usage and coroutineScope only suspends the thread. That is why runBlocking is a regular function and coroutineScope is a suspending function.

The following shows both scope builders being used in a program.

Example:

```kotlin
import kotlinx.coroutines.*
fun main() = runBlocking {
    printWorld()
}
suspend fun printWorld() = coroutineScope {  // this: CoroutineScope
    launch {
        delay(1000L)
        println("World!")
    }
    println("Hello")
}
```

Output:

```
Hello
World!
```

Concurrency

We can launch multiple concurrent coroutine scopes inside a suspending function, as follows. This example runs two launch blocks continuously, which is why first `world 1` will be printed and after that `world 2`.

Example:

```kotlin
import kotlinx.coroutines.*
// Sequentially executes doWorld followed by "Done"
fun main() = runBlocking {
    printWorld()
    println("Done")
}
// Concurrently executes both sections
suspend fun printWorld() = coroutineScope { // this: CoroutineScope
    launch {
        delay(2000L)
        println("World 2")
    }
```

```
    launch {
        delay(1000L)
        println("World 1")
    }
    println("Hello")
}
```

Output:

```
Hello
World 1
World 2
Done
```

7.6 An Explicit Job

At launch the coroutine scope builder returns a job object that is a handle to launched operations and can be used for waiting for a child coroutine to run, after which it will print a Done string. The following is an example.

Example:

```
import kotlinx.coroutines.*
val job = launch { // launch a new coroutine and keep a reference
to its Job
    delay(1000L)
    println("World!")
}
println("Hello")
job.join() // wait until child coroutine completes
println("Done")
```

Output:

```
Hello
World!
Done
```

7.7 Coroutines Are Lightweight

Coroutines are lightweight, and they take less memory than threads do. The following is an example of a coroutine launching 60,000 different coroutines. Each waits for five seconds and then prints Done, and it consumes very little memory.

If we create the same example using threads, it will consume a lot of memory depending upon the version of JDK and the operating system on which it was developed. It may throw an out-of-memory exception.

Example:

```
import kotlinx.coroutines.*
fun main() = runBlocking {
    repeat(60_000) { // launch a lot of coroutines
        launch {
            delay(5000L)
            println("done")
        }
    }
}
```

7.8 Coroutine Exception Handling

A cancelled coroutine throws an exception named CancellationException. Coroutine exceptions can be thrown automatically or by exposing them to users. When coroutine builders throw an exception from the root coroutine, which is not part of any other exception, it is treated as an uncaught exception. All other exceptions rely on the users to consume the exception via await or receive. The following is an example of the root coroutine using the GlobalScope API.

Example:

```
import kotlinx.coroutines.*
@OptIn(DelicateCoroutinesApi::class)
fun main() = runBlocking {
    val job = GlobalScope.launch { // root coroutine with launch
        println("Throwing exception from launch")
        throw ExceptionInInitializerError() // printed by Thread.
        defaultUncaughtExceptionHandler
```

```
    }
    job.join()
    println("Joined failed job")
    val deferred = GlobalScope.async { // root coroutine with async
        println("Throwing exception from async")
        throw ArrayIndexOutOfBoundsException() //user to call await nothing
        is printed
    }
    try {
        deferred.await()
        println("Unreached")
    } catch (e: ArrayIndexOutOfBoundsException) {
        println("Caught ArrayIndexOutOfBoundsException")
    }
}
```

Output:

```
Throwing exception from launch
Exception in thread "DefaultDispatcher-worker-1 @coroutine#2" java.lang.
ExceptionInInitializerError
Joined failed job
Throwing exception from async
Caught ArrayIndexOutOfBoundsException
```

7.9 Coroutine Exception Handler

We can customize the way of printing uncaught exceptions. CoroutineExceptionHandler can be used as a generic catch block to handle all the coroutines of the parent and all its children. We can not recover from CoroutineExceptionHandler.

CoroutineExceptionHandler is generally used for all the uncaught exceptions that were not handled in the program. The following is an example of using it.

CHAPTER 7 KOTLIN COROUTINES

Example:

```
import kotlinx.coroutines.*
@OptIn(DelicateCoroutinesApi::class)
fun main() = runBlocking {
    val handler = CoroutineExceptionHandler { _, exception ->
        println("CoroutineExceptionHandler got $exception")
    }
    val job = GlobalScope.launch(handler) { // root coroutine
        throw ExceptionInInitializerError()
    }
    val deferred = GlobalScope.async(handler) { // also root, but async
    instead of launch
        throw ArrayIndexOutOfBoundsException() // nothing printed, user to
        call deferred.await()
    }
    joinAll(job, deferred)
}
```

Output:

```
CoroutineExceptionHandler got java.lang.ExceptionInInitializerError
```

7.10 Cancellation and Exceptions

Cancellation and exceptions are related to each other. For the exceptions that are ignored by handlers, which are only used for additional information, the coroutine uses CancellationException to cancel them. It will not affect the parent coroutine. In the following example we use the yield() function, which is generally used to temporarily suspend one coroutine and allow another coroutine to run.

Example:

```
import kotlinx.coroutines.*
fun main() = runBlocking {
    val job = launch {
        val child = launch {
            try {
```

```
                delay(Long.MAX_VALUE)
            } finally {
                println("Child is cancelled")
            }
        }
        yield()
        println("Cancelling child soon...")
        child.cancel()
        child.join()
        yield()
        println("Parent is running, not cancelled")
    }
    job.join()
}
```

Output:

```
Cancelling child soon...
Child is cancelled
Parent is running, not cancelled
```

7.11 Exception Aggregation

This is generally used when a program fails with multiple exceptions. When this situation occurs, the exception that is first will win and be handled. All the other exceptions are aggregated with the first one. The following example shows that.

Example:

```
import kotlinx.coroutines.*
@OptIn(DelicateCoroutinesApi::class)
fun main() = runBlocking {
    val handler = CoroutineExceptionHandler { _, exception ->
        println("CoroutineExceptionHandler got $exception with ${exception.
        suppressed.contentToString()}")
    }
    val job = GlobalScope.launch(handler) {
```

```
    launch {
        try {
            delay(Long.MAX_VALUE)
        } finally {
            throw ArrayIndexOutOfBoundsException() // the second
            exception
        }
    }
    launch {
        delay(100)
        throw IllegalArgumentException() // the first exception
    }
    delay(Long.MAX_VALUE)
  }
  job.join()
}
```

Output:

CoroutineExceptionHandler got java.lang.IllegalArgumentException with [java.lang.ArrayIndexOutOfBoundsException]

7.12 Real-Life Programming Practices

1. **A food delivery application needs to perform several asynchronous tasks, such as the following:**

    - Fetching restaurant details from a remote API.

    - Calculating estimated delivery time based on live traffic.

    - Processing user's order and updating the UI without blocking the main thread.

    Since these operations can take time, running them on the main UI thread could lead to laggy and unresponsive UI.

Solution:

```kotlin
import kotlinx.coroutines.*
suspend fun fetchRestaurantDetails(): String {
    delay(2000)  // Simulating network delay
    return "Restaurant: Foodie's Delight, Rating: 4.5"
}
suspend fun calculateDeliveryTime(): String {
    delay(1500)  // Simulating calculation
    return "Estimated Delivery Time: 30 mins"
}
suspend fun processOrder(): String {
    delay(3000)  // Simulating order processing
    return "Order Confirmed! Tracking ID: #12345XYZ"
}
fun placeOrder() {
    println("Placing your order...")
    // Using Dispatchers.Default instead of Main/IO for Kotlin
        Playground compatibility
    runBlocking {
        val restaurantDetails = async(Dispatchers.Default) {
        fetchRestaurantDetails() }
        val deliveryTime = async(Dispatchers.Default) {
        calculateDeliveryTime() }
        val orderConfirmation = async(Dispatchers.Default) {
        processOrder() }
        println(restaurantDetails.await())
        println(deliveryTime.await())
        println(orderConfirmation.await())
        println("Thank you for ordering with us!")
    }
}
// Entry point
fun main() {
    placeOrder()
}
```

Output:

```
Placing your order...
Restaurant: Foodie's Delight, Rating: 4.5
Estimated Delivery Time: 30 mins
Order Confirmed! Tracking ID: #12345XYZ
Thank you for ordering with us!
```

7.13 Summary

In this chapter, we have learned about Kotlin coroutines, which allow developers to write asynchronous and non-blocking code in a structured manner. They also allow developers to suspend and resume without blocking threads. Using coroutines, developers can write cleaner, safer, and more efficient code without a complex chain of threads.

7.14 Test Your Knowledge

1. **Which of the following is NOT an advantage of using coroutines for asynchronous programming in Kotlin?**

   a. lightweight

   b. built-in cancellation

   c. high memory consumption

   d. fewer memory leaks

2. **What is the purpose of the launch builder in Kotlin coroutines?**

   a. to block the main thread

   b. to launch a new coroutine concurrently with the rest of the code

   c. to handle exceptions

   d. to create a new thread

CHAPTER 7　KOTLIN COROUTINES

3. **What happens if runBlocking is removed from the given program?**

    a. The program runs faster.

    b. An unresolved reference error occurs.

    c. The launch function works without issues.

    d. Nothing changes.

4. **Which statement about structured concurrency is TRUE?**

    a. Coroutines can run independently without scope.

    b. Coroutines are always bound to a single thread.

    c. New coroutines must be declared inside the scope of another coroutine.

    d. Structured concurrency increases memory leaks.

5. **What is a suspend function in Kotlin coroutines?**

    a. a function that can suspend execution without blocking the thread

    b. a function that blocks the main thread

    c. a function that never returns

    d. a normal function without any difference

6. **Which function is used to delay a coroutine without blocking the thread?**

    a. sleep()

    b. wait()

    c. pause()

    d. delay()

189

7. **Why are coroutines considered lightweight compared to threads?**

    a. Thousands of coroutines can run on a few threads without blocking them.

    b. They require complex hardware resources.

    c. They use more CPU resources.

    d. They consume more memory.

8. **What is the role of** `CoroutineExceptionHandler`**?**

    a. It blocks the main thread.

    b. It handles uncaught exceptions in coroutines.

    c. It cancels running coroutines.

    d. It stops the coroutine from executing further.

9. **What does the** `yield()` **function do in a coroutine?**

    a. completely stops the coroutine

    b. immediately cancels the coroutine

    c. blocks the thread permanently

    d. temporarily suspends the coroutine to allow others to run

10. **What does the** `job.join()` **function do in Kotlin coroutines?**

    a. pauses the main thread indefinitely

    b. cancels the coroutine

    c. starts a new coroutine

    d. waits for the coroutine to complete

7.15 Answers

1. c
2. b
3. b
4. c
5. a
6. d
7. a
8. b
9. d
10. d

CHAPTER 8

Kotlin Domain-Specific Language (DSL)

8.1 Introduction to Kotlin DSLs

Domain-specific languages are in contrast to the general-purpose languages—for example, Java or Kotlin—which can be used to develop an application and can be written in multiple parts of an application. DSL is more concise and readable, as it mostly reads like an English statement. An example of DSL is the SQL language, which is readable and expressive rather than another general-purpose language.

Kotlin as a modern programming language supports DSL, or domain-specific language. It gives the customer the ease of writing Kotlin code. It will be easier for developers to read the code as it increases the readability. DSL can be divided into two parts; i.e., internal or external. Internal DSLs are part of the host language, and external DSLs are standalone language.

When we develop DSLs with existing general-purpose language, it is termed as using internal DSLs because we will not create a whole new language; we will define some way to use a language that is already available, like Kotlin.

We should not make or use DSLs everywhere we create classes, instead only doing so where a configuration class or library interface is used in the code.

Advantages of DSLs

Following are the advantages of using DSLs in kotlin. Increase Readability: Using DSLs with Kotlin will increase the code's readability, mostly for those who are non-technical investors.

More Expressive: By reducing the boilerplate code, DSLs allow you to write code that is more expressive and concise.

CHAPTER 8   KOTLIN DOMAIN-SPECIFIC LANGUAGE (DSL)

Specific to Domain: Rather than writing a whole application and creating a whole language, in Kotlin we use DSLs that are internal and used only in the specific part of an application.

Type Safe: DSLs can provide type safety by ensuring that no error or bug will be there during compilation time.

8.2 Writing Our First DSL

In this part we will be using three Kotlin features:

1. Lambdas outside of method parentheses

2. Lambdas with receivers

3. Extension functions

Let's create a simple DSL with which we will instantiate an object of a Student class.

```
val student = Student {
    name = "Jacob"
    age = 20
    class = "Engineering"
    address {
        street = "Street 3"
        number = 21
        city = "New York"
    }
}
```

Let's take a deep dive into the code. The code is self-descriptive, so people who are non-technical can understand what we are trying to write or are able to make changes in the code. To create this code, first we must create a new file for the Student class. We will put our DSLs in different files and the code in another file. Let's look at how we create a Student class separately.

```
data class Student(var name: String? = null,
                   var age: Int? = null,
                   var class:String = null,
                   var address: Address? = null){}
```

CHAPTER 8   KOTLIN DOMAIN-SPECIFIC LANGUAGE (DSL)

```
data class Address(var street: String? = null,
                   var number: Int? = null,
                   var city: String? = null){}
```

Looking at the preceding code, we can see that properties of the Student class are defined within the curly brackets, and these curly brackets are nothing but the lambdas. Here we **use lambdas outside the method parentheses.**

When the last parameter in the function is lambda, we can simply put it outside of the function parentheses and remove the parentheses completely. In our example, we can describe that Student{} is equal to Student({}). This creates a structure with less syntax. The following is the first way to write our student function.

```
fun student(block: (Student) -> Unit): Student {
    val s = Student()
    block(s)
    return s
}
```

This is a function that creates the Student object. It requires lambda, which we create in the second line, and before execution we want the object to get its properties. The following shows the usage of the function.

```
val student = student {
    it.name = "Jacob"
    it.age = 20
    it.class = "Engineering"
}
```

The lambda receives only one argument, and we can call the student object with it. Using it in our DSL is not good enough, so another feature comes into the picture—i.e., **lambdas with receivers.**

For this feature, we add a receiver function'()' to the lambda. When the function is in the scope of the receiver, we can execute the lambda on the receiver without providing it as an argument, as follows:

```
fun student(block: Student.() -> Unit): Student {
    val s = Student()
    s.block()
    return s
}
```

CHAPTER 8   KOTLIN DOMAIN-SPECIFIC LANGUAGE (DSL)

We can rewrite the preceding code in one line using Kotlin's `apply` function:

```
fun student(block: Student.() -> Unit): Student = Student().apply(block)
```

Hence, we can now remove it from our DSL:

```
val student = student {
    name = "Jacob"
    age = 20
class = "Engineering"
}
```

We want to leave one thing: the `Address` class. It is almost the same as the `Student` class, but is given as an argument to the `Student` class. To do this, we will use the last feature of Kotlin—the extension function.

Extension functions allow you to add classes of the function without accessing the source code. The following is the final DSL class:

```
fun student(block: Student.() -> Unit): Student = Student().apply(block)

fun Student.address(block: Address.() -> Unit) {
    address = Address().apply(block)
}
```

In the preceding code we have added an `Address` class that accepts the address in the `Student` class without a receiver. Now, finally, we have created DSL.

```
val student = Student {
    name = "Jacob"
    age = 20
    class = "Engineering"
    address {
        street = "Street 3"
        number = 21
        city = "New York"
    }
}
```

This is how we write simple Kotlin DSLs. In the following sections we will see how we can add collections and use the `@DslMarker` annotation.

8.3 DSL by Applying Builder Pattern

In the previous example, we saw a basic model for starting purposes. Those classes had mutable variables, which are very easy to change the properties of whenever it's required. If we use or change it to immutable values, then we will get a compile-time error saying that Val cannot be reassigned. To avoid this, we need to use builder classes. The following is our model.

```
data class Student(val name: String,
                   val dateOfBirth: Date,
                   var address: Address?)

data class Address(val street: String,
                   val number: Int,
                   val city: String)
```

If we want to create this object, we need to create constructors along with their property values. The builders will collect the data and call the build function that will create the object using its constructor. The following code shows that.

Code:

```
fun student(block: StudentBuilder.() -> Unit): Student = StudentBuilder().apply(block).build()
class StudentBuilder {
    var name: String = ""
    private var dob: Date = Date()
    var dateOfBirth: String = ""
        set(value) {
            dob = SimpleDateFormat("yyyy-MM-dd").parse(value)
        }
    private var address: Address? = null
    fun address(block: AddressBuilder.() -> Unit) {
        address = AddressBuilder().apply(block).build()
    }
    fun build(): Student = Student(name, dob, address)
}
```

CHAPTER 8 KOTLIN DOMAIN-SPECIFIC LANGUAGE (DSL)

```kotlin
class AddressBuilder {
    var street: String = ""
    var number: Int = 0
    var city: String = ""
    fun build() : Address = Address(street, number, city)
}
```

In this example, we have created another string, which uses a `setter` function to set the date value, so the date will be available in a format that is simple to read.

```kotlin
val student = student {
    name = "Jacob"
    dateOfBirth = "2002-09-02"
    address {
        street = "Street 3"
        number = 21
        city = "New York"
    }
}
```

8.4 DSL with Collections

Now that we have added builders to our DSL, we next turn to the use of collections in DSLs. Let's assume that one particular student has multiple addresses. To store the addresses, we will use a collection. We will convert the `Address` property mentioned in the builder class to `MutableList<Address>`, add multiple addresses to the `address` function, and pass the list of addresses to the constructor. The following are the changes.

Code:

```kotlin
data class Student(val name: String,
                   val dateOfBirth: Date,
                   val addresses: List<Address>)
class StudentBuilder {
  // ... other properties
  private val addresses = mutableListOf<Address>()
```

```kotlin
    fun address(block: AddressBuilder.() -> Unit) {
        addresses.add(AddressBuilder().apply(block).build())
    }
    fun build(): Student = Student(name, dob, addresses)
}
// result
val student = student {
    name = "Jacob"
    dateOfBirth = "2002-09-02"
    address {
        street = "Street 3"
        number = 21
        city = "New York"
    }
    address {
        street = "Street 5"
        number = 22
        city = "London"
    }
}
```

From this example we can see that there are multiple blocks for addresses, and we don't want to see multiple blocks of the same content. The way to solve this problem is to use a helper class with the address method and add the receiver with lambda in the class StudentBuilder.

Code:

```kotlin
fun student(block: StudentBuilder.() -> Unit): Student = StudentBuilder().apply(block).build()
class StudentBuilder {
    var name: String = ""
    private var dob: Date = Date()
    var dateOfBirth: String = ""
        set(value) { dob = SimpleDateFormat("yyyy-MM-dd").parse(value) }
    private val addresses = mutableListOf<Address>()
```

```kotlin
    fun addresses(block: ADDRESSES.() -> Unit) {
        addresses.addAll(ADDRESSES().apply(block))
    }
    fun build(): Student = Student(name, dob, addresses)
}
class ADDRESSES: ArrayList<Address>() {
    fun address(block: AddressBuilder.() -> Unit) {
        add(AddressBuilder().apply(block).build())
    }
}
class AddressBuilder {
    var street: String = ""
    var number: Int = 0
    var city: String = ""
    fun build() : Address = Address(street, number, city)
}
```

In this code the helper class is created using capital letters so that it can be identified easily. Now the following is the structured result:

```kotlin
val student = student {
    name = "Jacob"
    dateOfBirth = "2002-09-02"
    addresses {
            address {
            street = "Street 3"
            number = 21
            city = "New York"
        }
        address {
            street = "Street 5"
            number = 22
            city = "London"
        }
    }
}
```

8.5 DSL with @DslMarker Annotation

The preceding code is simple, easy, readable, and safe. But there is one issue with this code: as we can see we are creating lambdas inside lambdas; thus, we can access the receiver of the outer lambdas. Though the following code will change the name from Jacob to Mark, it will run without any compilation errors.

Code:

```
val student = student {
    name = "Jacob"
    dateOfBirth = "2002-09-02"
    addresses {
        address {
            addresses {
                name = "Mark"
            }
            street = "Street 5"
            number = 22
            city = "London"
        }
    }
}
```

To avoid name changing, we can use @DslMarker annotation in Kotlin 1.1 or later. This will be added in a custom annotation class, and after that it will be used inside your DSL class. The following shows how to create and use @DslMarker annotation.

Code:

```
@DslMarker
annotation class StudentDsl

@ StudentDsl
class StudentBuilder {
  //...
}
```

CHAPTER 8   KOTLIN DOMAIN-SPECIFIC LANGUAGE (DSL)

```kotlin
@ StudentDsl
class ADDRESSES: ArrayList<Address>() {
  //...
}

@ StudentDsl
class AddressBuilder {
  //...
}
```

Now, in the previous example where we use name inside the address block, it will give the error "name and addresses can't be called in this context by implicit receiver."

8.6 Real-Life Programming Practices

1. **Create a custom HTML builder in Kotlin without using string concatenation.**

   Code:

   ```kotlin
   @DslMarker
   annotation class HtmlDsl

   @HtmlDsl
   class Html {
       private val elements = mutableListOf<String>()

       fun body(init: Body.() -> Unit) {
           val body = Body().apply(init)
           elements.add("<body>${body.render()}</body>")
       }

       fun render(): String = "<html>${elements.joinToString("")}</html>"
   }

   @HtmlDsl
   class Body {
       private val elements = mutableListOf<String>()
   ```

```kotlin
    fun h1(text: String) {
        elements.add("<h1>$text</h1>")
    }

    fun p(text: String) {
        elements.add("<p>$text</p>")
    }

    fun render(): String = elements.joinToString("")
}

fun html(init: Html.() -> Unit): String {
    val html = Html().apply(init)
    return html.render()
}
//using above dsl to generate html
fun main() {
    val page = html {
        body {
            h1("Welcome to Kotlin DSL!")
            p("This is an example of a Kotlin DSL for
            generating HTML.")
        }
    }
    println(page)
}
```

Output:

```
<html>
    <body>
        <h1>Welcome to Kotlin DSL!</h1>
        <p>This is an example of a Kotlin DSL for generating
HTML.</p>
    </body>
</html>
```

2. **Create a Kotlin DSL for generating a database query.**

   Code:

```
@DslMarker
annotation class SqlDsl

// Base class for queries
abstract class SqlQuery {
    abstract fun build(): String
}

// SELECT Query Builder
@SqlDsl
class SelectQueryBuilder : SqlQuery() {
    private var table: String = ""
    private val columns = mutableListOf<String>()
    private var whereClause: String? = null

    fun select(vararg cols: String) {
        columns.addAll(cols)
    }

    fun from(tableName: String) {
        table = tableName
    }

    fun where(condition: String) {
        whereClause = condition
    }

    override fun build(): String {
        val columnPart = if (columns.isEmpty()) "*" else columns.joinToString(", ")
        val wherePart = whereClause?.let { " WHERE $it" } ?: ""
        return "SELECT $columnPart FROM $table$wherePart;"
    }
}
```

```kotlin
// INSERT Query Builder
@SqlDsl
class InsertQueryBuilder : SqlQuery() {
    private var table: String = ""
    private val values = mutableMapOf<String, Any>()

    fun into(tableName: String) {
        table = tableName
    }

    fun values(init: ValuesBuilder.() -> Unit) {
        values.putAll(ValuesBuilder().apply(init).build())
    }

    override fun build(): String {
        val columns = values.keys.joinToString(", ")
        val vals = values.values.joinToString(", ") { "'$it'" }
        return "INSERT INTO $table ($columns) VALUES ($vals);"
    }
}

// UPDATE Query Builder
@SqlDsl
class UpdateQueryBuilder : SqlQuery() {
    private var table: String = ""
    private val updates = mutableMapOf<String, Any>()
    private var whereClause: String? = null

    fun table(tableName: String) {
        table = tableName
    }

    fun set(init: ValuesBuilder.() -> Unit) {
        updates.putAll(ValuesBuilder().apply(init).build())
    }

    fun where(condition: String) {
        whereClause = condition
    }
```

CHAPTER 8   KOTLIN DOMAIN-SPECIFIC LANGUAGE (DSL)

```kotlin
        override fun build(): String {
            val setPart = updates.entries.joinToString(", ")
            { "${it.key} = '${it.value}'" }
            val wherePart = whereClause?.let { " WHERE $it" } ?: ""
            return "UPDATE $table SET $setPart$wherePart;"
        }
    }

    // Helper class for inserting/updating values
    @SqlDsl
    class ValuesBuilder {
        private val values = mutableMapOf<String, Any>()

        infix fun String.to(value: Any) {
            values[this] = value
        }

        fun build(): Map<String, Any> = values
    }

    // DSL Wrapper Functions
    fun selectQuery(init: SelectQueryBuilder.() -> Unit): String {
        return SelectQueryBuilder().apply(init).build()
    }

    fun insertQuery(init: InsertQueryBuilder.() -> Unit): String {
        return InsertQueryBuilder().apply(init).build()
    }

    fun updateQuery(init: UpdateQueryBuilder.() -> Unit): String {
        return UpdateQueryBuilder().apply(init).build()
    }
    //using above dsl to generate query
    fun main() {
        // SELECT Query Example
        val selectSQL = selectQuery {
            select("id", "name", "email")
            from("users")
```

```kotlin
        where("age > 18")
    }
}
println(selectSQL) // Output: SELECT id, name, email FROM
users WHERE age > 18;
// INSERT Query Example
val insertSQL = insertQuery {
    into("users")
    values {
        "name" to "John Doe"
        "email" to "john@example.com"
        "age" to 30
    }
}
println(insertSQL) // Output: INSERT INTO users (name, email,
age) VALUES ('John Doe', 'john@example.com', '30');
// UPDATE Query Example
val updateSQL = updateQuery {
    table("users")
    set {
        "email" to "newemail@example.com"
        "age" to 31
    }
    where("id = 1")
}
println(updateSQL) // Output: UPDATE users SET email =
'newemail@example.com', age = '31' WHERE id = 1;
}
```

Output:

SELECT id, name, email FROM users WHERE age > 18;
INSERT INTO users (name, email, age) VALUES ('John Doe', 'john@example.com', '30');
UPDATE users SET email = 'newemail@example.com', age = '31' WHERE id = 1;

8.7 Summary

In this chapter, we have learned about Kotlin DSL, which is commonly used by developers to create expressive, concise, and clear code. DSLs create more-descriptive code. Overall, it increases readability by adding domain-focused mini-languages inside Kotlin.

8.8 Test Your Knowledge

1. **What is the primary advantage of using DSLs in Kotlin?**

    a. They reduce the size of the compiled application.

    b. They improve code readability and expressiveness.

    c. They replace the need for general-purpose languages.

    d. They are faster than all general-purpose languages.

2. **How is an internal DSL different from an external DSL?**

    a. Internal DSLs are separate programming languages, while external DSLs are embedded in a host language.

    b. Internal DSLs are part of a host language, while external DSLs are standalone languages.

    c. Internal DSLs require a separate compiler, while external DSLs do not.

    d. Internal DSLs must be interpreted, while external DSLs are compiled.

3. **Which of the following is NOT an advantage of DSLs?**

    a. increased readability

    b. more expressiveness

    c. universal applicability across all domains

    d. type safety

4. **What is the purpose of the `@DslMarker` annotation in Kotlin DSLs?**

    a. It allows external DSLs to work within Kotlin.

    b. It prevents accidental access to outer lambda receivers in nested DSL blocks.

    c. It helps in compiling the DSL faster.

    d. It converts Kotlin DSLs into external DSLs.

5. **What Kotlin feature allows functions to execute within the scope of a receiver?**

    a. lambda expressions

    b. extension functions

    c. higher-order functions

    d. lambdas with receivers

6. **What Kotlin function simplifies DSL object creation by applying configuration inside its scope?**

    a. apply

    b. with

    c. let

    d. run

7. **Why do we use builder classes in Kotlin DSLs?**

    a. to allow mutable variables to be reassigned dynamically

    b. to support immutable objects and avoid reassigning `val` properties

    c. to replace the need for Kotlin's default constructors

    d. to prevent objects from being instantiated

CHAPTER 8   KOTLIN DOMAIN-SPECIFIC LANGUAGE (DSL)

8. **What happens if we don't use `@DslMarker` in a nested DSL structure?**

    a. The code will not compile.

    b. The DSL will run, but it might modify unintended properties due to implicit receivers.

    c. It will automatically prevent outer lambda access.

    d. The DSL will be slower in execution.

9. **What is a key characteristic of Kotlin DSLs that makes them different from general-purpose Kotlin code?**

    a. They use special syntax that Kotlin does not support normally.

    b. They are executed using an external Kotlin compiler.

    c. They allow domain-specific configurations using a structured format.

    d. They can only be used in Android development.

10. **Which of the following Kotlin DSL features helps in creating structured domain-specific configurations?**

    a. infix functions

    b. named parameters

    c. extension functions

    d. reflection

11. **What is the primary benefit of using lambdas with receivers in Kotlin DSLs?**

    a. They improve performance by reducing memory allocation.

    b. They allow functions to be called on a receiver object without explicitly passing it.

    c. They replace constructors in class instantiation.

    d. They make Kotlin DSLs work faster in Android applications.

12. **What is the main reason for using the builder pattern in Kotlin DSLs?**

    a. to enforce immutability while constructing objects

    b. to eliminate the need for object creation

    c. to allow runtime modifications of objects

    d. to simplify function overloading

13. **What does the following Kotlin DSL block represent?**

    ```
    val student = student {
        name = "Alice"
        dateOfBirth = "1998-04-15"
        addresses {
            address {
                street = "Park Avenue"
                number = 10
                city = "New York"
            }
            address {
                street = "Baker Street"
                number = 221
                city = "London"
            }
        }
    }
    ```

    a. a Kotlin class that cannot be modified

    b. a structured DSL configuration for a Student object with multiple addresses

    c. a function that initializes two address objects separately

    d. a Kotlin singleton instance

CHAPTER 8   KOTLIN DOMAIN-SPECIFIC LANGUAGE (DSL)

8.9 Answers

1. b
2. b
3. c
4. b
5. d
6. a
7. b
8. b
9. c
10. c
11. b
12. a
13. b

CHAPTER 9

Kotlin Standard Library

9.1 Introduction to the Kotlin Standard Library

The Kotlin standard library is a very rich set of functions and extensions that help simplify complex programming problems or tasks. These functions are very easy to understand because they were built in the Kotlin language and provide easy access to multiple functions.

By using standard library functions, developers can write easy, readable, clean, and concise code that will be more efficient than normal code. In the following sections we will see some of the categories provided by the Kotlin standard library.

9.2 Collection Functions

Collections are a powerful feature that provides numerous functions to work with, like lists, sets, and maps. Some common operations that we can perform on collection functions are sorting, filtering, and transforming. Following are several examples.

Sorting

When working with certain collections, the order of an element may play a pivotal role. For example, if we create two lists with the same elements but one has elements sorted in ascending order and the other has the elements sorted in descending order, both lists will be considered different because the order of elements is different in each list. There are four ways in which we can use sorting: natural sorting, custom sorting, reverse sorting, and random sorting.

Natural Sorting

In natural sorting, we will either sort the given collection in ascending order or in descending order using the sorted() and sortedDescending() functions, respectively.

The following example shows sorting in ascending and descending order.

Example:

```
fun main() {
    val numbers = listOf(3,5,2,6,1,8,7,4)
    println("Sorted ascending: ${numbers.sorted()}")
    println("Sorted descending: ${numbers.sortedDescending()}")
}
```

Output:

```
Sorted ascending: [1, 2, 3, 4, 5, 6, 7, 8]
Sorted descending: [8, 7, 6, 5, 4, 3, 2, 1]
```

Custom Sorting

To use custom sorting, we use comparators. Collections will be sorted according to the given conditions either in ascending order using the sortedBy() function or in descending order using the sortedDescending() function.

The following shows both functions, which sort the list of names, first by length in ascending order and then by length in descending order.

Example:

```
fun main() {
    val names = listOf("Aly", "Mark", "Jacob", "Bob","Lee")
    val sortedNamesAscending = names.sortedBy { it.length }
    println("Sorted by length ascending: $sortedNamesAscending")
    val sortedNamesDescending = names.sortedByDescending { it.length }
    println("Sorted by length descending: $sortedNamesDescending")
}
```

Output:

```
Sorted by length ascending: [Aly, Bob, Lee, Mark, Jacob]
Sorted by length descending: [Jacob, Mark, Aly, Bob, Lee]
```

Reverse Sorting

Reverse sorting sorts the whole collection in reverse order. We can use the function `reversed()` to sort the collection in reverse order. It returns a new collection with copies of the elements, so if we change the original collection there will not be any effect on previously obtained reversed collections. The following is an example of using `reverserd()`. We can see both the output before and after adding an element.

Example:

```
fun main() {
    val numbers = mutableListOf(3,5,2,6,1,8,7,4)
        val reverse = numbers.reversed()
    println("Before Adding Element: "+reverse)
        numbers.add(0)
        println("After Adding Element: "+reverse)
}
```

Output:

```
Before Adding Element: [4, 7, 8, 1, 6, 2, 5, 3]
After Adding Element: [4, 7, 8, 1, 6, 2, 5, 3]
```

Now if we want to change the collection after reversing it, we can use the `asReversed()` function. This function will create a reversed view of the same collection. If we change the collection after reversing it, then it will be added to the reversed list also.

The following example shows this. First it will print the list of elements in reversed order with the original list. After that, '0' is added to the list. When we check the reversed list, we can see that the new element just added inside the original list is added in the reversed list as well. Using `asReversed()` instead of `reversed()` is advantageous because it's lightweight and dynamic.

Example:

```
fun main() {
    val numbers = mutableListOf(3,5,2,6,1,8,7,4)
    val reverse = numbers.asReversed()
    println("Before Adding Element: "+reverse)
        numbers.add(0)
        println("After Adding Element: "+reverse)
}
```

CHAPTER 9 KOTLIN STANDARD LIBRARY

Output:

```
Before Adding Element: [4, 7, 8, 1, 6, 2, 5, 3]
After Adding Element: [0, 4, 7, 8, 1, 6, 2, 5, 3]
```

Random Sorting

At last, we have the function shuffled(), which will print the collection in a random order every time you call it.

The following example shows that it will give a different output every time you run it.

Example:

```
fun main() {
    val numbers = listOf(3,5,2,6,1,8,7,4)
    println(numbers.shuffled())
}
```

Output:

```
[5, 7, 1, 6, 3, 4, 2, 8]
```

Filtering

Filtering will return the list of elements that match the condition given. It uses the filter() function. There are several types by which to filter the collections.

The first one is **filter by predicate**, which filters collections according to the given condition.

Example:

```
fun main() {
    val numbers = listOf(1, 2, 3, 4, 5)
    val evenNumbers = numbers.filter { it % 2 == 0 }
    println("Even Numbers: "+evenNumbers)
}
```

Output:

```
Even Numbers: [2, 4]
```

CHAPTER 9 KOTLIN STANDARD LIBRARY

If we want to predicate the condition where collections fails to match, then we can use the function `filterNot()`, as in the following example.

Here we are printing all the elements that don't match the given condition. Hence, it will print a list of odd numbers, as displayed in the output.

Example:

```
fun main() {
    val numbers = listOf(1, 2, 3, 4, 5)
    val oddNumbers = numbers.filterNot { it % 2 == 0 }
    println("Odd Numbers: "+oddNumbers)
}
```

Output:

```
Odd Numbers: [1, 3, 5]
```

We can also filter values that are not null in the collection using the `filterNotNull()` function. It returns `List<T: Any>`. The following example prints the values that are not null from the list.

Example:

```
fun main() {
    val numbers = listOf(null, "Mark", "Jacob", null)
    numbers.filterNotNull().forEach {
        println(it)
    }
}
```

Output:

```
Mark
Jacob
```

The function `filterIsInstance()` returns the collection of elements of the given type. If we called a function on `List<Any>`, `filterIsInstance<T>()` returns a `List<T>`. The following example returns the list of type `string`.

CHAPTER 9 KOTLIN STANDARD LIBRARY

Example:

```
fun main() {
    val numbers = listOf(null, 1, "Mark", 2.0, "John","Jacob",3.44)
    numbers.filterIsInstance<String>().forEach {
    println(it)
    }
}
```

Output:

Mark
John
Jacob

Another type of filtering is done by using the function `partition()`, which filters the collection according to the given condition and also puts the remaining elements in a separate list.

Example:

```
fun main() {
    val names = listOf("John", "Mark", "Bob", "Aly","Lee")
    val (match, rest) = names.partition { it.length > 3 }
    println(match)
    println(rest)
}
```

Output:

[John, Mark]
[Bob, Aly, Lee]

The last type simply tests the predicate for all the elements available in the collection. `any()` returns true if any of the elements match the condition, `all()` returns true if all the elements match the condition, and `none()` returns true if none of the elements match the condition.

Example:

```
fun main() {
    val names = listOf("John", "Mark", "Bob", "Aly","Lee")
    val empty = emptyList<String>()
    println("Use with Predicate")
    println(names.any { it.endsWith("e") })
    println(names.none { it.endsWith("a") })
    println(names.all { it.endsWith("e") })
    println("Use without Predicate")
    println(names.any())
    println(empty.any())
    println(names.none())
    println(empty.none())
}
```

Output:

```
Use with predicate
true
true
false
Use without predicate
true
false
false
true
```

Transforming

The map() function will transform each element from a given collection into another form, which will be specified. In the following program we have declared one list and applied the mapping function to transform each element by multiplying it by 3.

Example:

```
fun main() {
    val numbers = listOf(1, 2, 3, 4, 5)
    val transformedNumbers = numbers.map{it*3}
    println("Transformed Numbers: "+transformedNumbers)
}
```

Output:

```
Transformed Numbers: [3, 6, 9, 12, 15]
```

These functions are called as the part of Kotlin's rich set of functional programming, which allows the developers to write some common operations concisely.

9.3 String Functions

Kotlin provides multiple string manipulation functions, which simplify common tasks. Let's revisit these. The following table shows the name and use of the function given.

Table 9-1. String Manipulation Functions

Function Name	Description
format()	This function is used to convert the given string in specific a certain format.
get(index: Int)	Used to get specified character at given index
substring(startIndex:Int, endIndex:Int)	Give substring from start index to end index
drop(i: Int)	It will remove the first 'i' characters
dropLast(i:Int)	It will remove the last 'i' characters
take(i:Int)	It will take the first 'i' characters
takeLast(i:Int)	It will take the last 'i' characters
uppercase()	It converts string to uppercase
lowercase()	It converts string to lowercase
capitalize()	It capitalizes the first character

(continued)

Table 9-1. (*continued*)

Function Name	Description
decapitalize()	It converts the first character to lowercase
replaceFirstChar{it.uppercaseChar()}	It capitalizes the first character
replace(oldValue:String, newValue:String)	It replaces the old string with new string
replace(oldChar:Char, newChar:Char)	It replaces the old character with new character
replaceFirst(oldValue:String, newValue:String)	It replaces only the first occurrence of old string to new string
replaceAfter(delimiter:String, newValue:String)	It replaces the string that comes after the first occurrence of the delimiter.
replaceBefore(delimiter:String, newValue:String)	It replaces the string that comes before the specified delimiter.
replaceAfterLast(delimiter:String, newValue:String)	It replaces the string after the last occurrence of the delimiter.
replaceBeforeLast(delimiter:String, newValue:String)	It replaces the string before the last occurrence of the delimiter.
trim()	It is used for removing leading and trailing whitespaces from the string.
trimStart()	It removes the starting or leading whitespace from the string.
trimEnd()	It removes the ending or trailing whitespace from the string.
trimIndent()	It removes leading whitespaces from each line.
trimMargin(prefix: String = "|")	It removes the specified margin prefix.
padStart(length:Int, charValue:Char = ' ')	It starts padding to the beginning until it reaches the length mentioned in parameter.
padEnd(length:Int, charValue:Char = ' ')	It starts padding to the ending until it reaches to the length mentioned in the parameter.

(*continued*)

Table 9-1. (*continued*)

Function Name	Description
split(delimiter:String, ignoreCase:Boolean, limit:Int = 0)	It is used to divide a string into multiple substring based on delimeter within a given limit and taking case in consideration.
split(delimiter:Char, limit:Int = 0)	It is used to divide a string into multiple substring based on delimeter within given limit.
lines()	It is used to split the string into lines based on line breaks.
chunked(size:int)	It splits the string into equal-size chunks.
windowed(size:Int, steps:Int, partialWindow:Boolean = false)	It splits the string into equal-size chunks, but with overlapping and given step size.
joinToString(separator: String = ",")	It converts the given collection into string with given separator.
contains(substring:String, ignoreCase: Boolean = false)	It checks if the given substring exists or not, with considering case if it is false.
startsWith(prefix:String, ignoreCase: Boolean = false)	It checks if given string starts with specified substring or not.
endsWith(suffix:String, ignoreCase: Boolean = false)	It checks if given string ends with specified substring or not.
indexOf(substring:string, startIndex: Int = 0, ignoreCase:Boolean = false	It finds the occurrence of a substring from start index.
indexOf(charValue:Char, startIndex: Int = 0, ignoreCase:Boolean = false)	It finds the occurrence of a character from start index.
lastIndexOf(substring:String, startIndex: Int = this.length, ignoreCase:Boolean = false)	It finds the last occurrence of a given substring from start index.
compareTo(stringValue:String, ignoreCase:Boolean = false)	It compares the two strings in dictionary order and returns the integer value indicating their order.
equals(stringValue:String, ignoreCase: Boolean = false)	It checks if the two strings are equal or not.

(*continued*)

Table 9-1. *(continued)*

Function Name	Description
matches(regex:Regex)	It checks if entire string matches the given regular expression or not.
contains(regex:Regex)	It checks if entire string contains a match for the given regular expression or not.
replace(regex:Regex, replacement:String)	It replaces all the matches of string with the replacement string.
replaceFirst(regex:Regex, replacement:String)	It replace only the first match of string with replacement string.
split(regex:Regex)	It splits the string based on given regular expression.
isEmpty()	It checks if the string is empty or not.
isNotEmpty()	It checks if the string is not empty.
isBlank()	It checks if the string is empty or if it contains only white space characters.
isNotBlank()	It checks if string is non-empty or does not contain whitespace characters.
toCharArray()	It converts the string into array of characters.
reversed()	It reverses the string.
toString()	It converts the object into string.
first()	It returns the first character of the string.
last()	It returns the last character of the string.
firstOrNull()	It returns the first character or null if the string is empty.
lastOrNull()	It returns the last character or null if the string is empty.
slice(IntRange)	It extracts the substring using a given range of integers.

9.4 Extension Functions

Kotlin extension functions add a rich set of functionalities to the already available classes without changing their source code.

These functions can be used to add methods to standard library types or classes, which greatly enhances code readability.

To add an extension function to a class, we need to define the new function appended to the class name, as shown in the following example.

Example:

```kotlin
// A sample class to demonstrate extension functions
class ArithmeticOperation (val a: Int, val b:Int){
    // member function of class
    fun add(): Int{
        return a+b;
    }
}
fun main(){
    // Extension function created for a class Circle
    fun ArithmeticOperation.subtraction(): Int{
        return a-b;
    }
    val arithmeticOperation = ArithmeticOperation(5,2);
    // invoke member function
    println("Addition is: ${arithmeticOperation.add()}")
    // invoke extension function
    println("Subtraction is ${arithmeticOperation.subtraction()}")
}
```

Output:

```
Addition is: 7
Subtraction is 3
```

Extended Library Classes

Kotlin also has some library classes that can be extended. Following is an example of doing so.

```
fun main(){
    // Extension function defined for Int type
    fun Int.Square() : Int{
        return this*this
    }
    println(4.Square())
}
```

Output:

16

9.5 Null Safety Functions

Kotlin provides null safety by overcoming the very common `NullPointerException`. The Kotlin compiler also throws a `NullPointerException` if it is found in the program. We can overcome these by using the `!!` operator or using the safe call operator (`?.`).

For example,

`name?.toString()`

is equal to

```
If(name!=null)
{
    name.toString()
}else{
    null
}
```

We will revisit null safety in detail in chapter 13.

CHAPTER 9   KOTLIN STANDARD LIBRARY

9.6 File and I/O Functions

Kotlin provides file handling using the library java.io.File and also the kotlin.io package. Let's see how we can create, read, and write files and also how to delete files.

Create File

The resolve() function is used to create a file if there is no such file or directory in the file object's path. If the file already exists, then it will open the file.

```
import java.io.File
var fileDirectiry = File(".") //get the root directory
val newFile = File(".").resolve("newFile.txt")
```

Writing to File

The writeText() function is used for writing inside the file. Following is an example:

```
newFile.writeText("Hello Kotlin...!!")
```

Reading from File

The readText() function is used for reading all the contents of the file. To read the large contents of the file, we can use the readLines() function. The following example shows that.

```
val newFileData:String = newFile.readText()
```

or

```
newFile.readLines().forEach { line ->
//do something with line
}
```

To handle big file-reading operations, we need to read lines into streams. The following example shows that.

```
newFile.bufferedReader().use { br ->
    br.lines().forEach{
        line->
        // do something with line
    }
}
```

Delete File

The `delete()` function is used for deleting a file or an empty directory. The following is an example.

```
val isDeleted:Boolean = newFile.delete()
```

The `deleteRecursively()` function deletes all the files and its sub-directories in a directory, as follows.

```
val isDeleted:Boolean = newFile.deleteRecursively()
```

9.7 Real-Life Programming Practices

1. **Scenario: Employee Management System**
   This program allows you to store employee details, sort them, filter based on conditions, manipulate names using string functions, and save the data to a file.

   Code:

   ```
   import java.io.File
   // Data class for Employee
   data class Employee(val id: Int, val name: String, val salary: Double)

   // Extension function to format employee details
   fun Employee.displayInfo(): String {
       return "ID: $id, Name: ${name.capitalize()}, Salary: $$salary"
   }
   ```

CHAPTER 9 KOTLIN STANDARD LIBRARY

```kotlin
fun main() {
    // Sample list of employees
    val employees = listOf(
        Employee(101, "alice", 50000.0),
        Employee(102, "bob", 60000.0),
        Employee(103, "charlie", 45000.0),
        Employee(104, "david", 70000.0),
        Employee(105, "eve", 55000.0)
    )

    // Sorting employees by salary (ascending)
    val sortedEmployees = employees.sortedBy { it.salary }
    println("Employees sorted by salary:")
    sortedEmployees.forEach { println(it.displayInfo()) }

    // Filtering employees with salary > 50000
    val highEarners = employees.filter { it.salary > 50000 }
    println("\nEmployees earning more than $50000:")
    highEarners.forEach { println(it.displayInfo()) }

    // Transforming names to uppercase
    val transformedNames = employees.map { it.name.uppercase() }
    println("\nEmployee names in uppercase: $transformedNames")

    // Save employees to a file
    val file = File("employees.txt")
    file.writeText("Employee Details:\n")
    employees.forEach { file.appendText(it.displayInfo() + "\n") }
    println("\nEmployee details saved to employees.txt")
}
```

Output:

```
Employees sorted by salary:
ID: 103, Name: Charlie, Salary: $45000.0
ID: 101, Name: Alice, Salary: $50000.0
ID: 105, Name: Eve, Salary: $55000.0
ID: 102, Name: Bob, Salary: $60000.0
```

```
ID: 104, Name: David, Salary: $70000.0
```

```
Employees earning more than $50000:
ID: 105, Name: Eve, Salary: $55000.0
ID: 102, Name: Bob, Salary: $60000.0
ID: 104, Name: David, Salary: $70000.0
```

```
Employee names in uppercase: [ALICE, BOB, CHARLIE, DAVID, EVE]
```

```
Employee details saved to employees.txt
```

9.8 Summary

In this chapter, we have learned about Kotlin standard library functions available, including syntax and examples. In short, Kotlin standard library functions enable developers to develop programs faster, cleaner, and more easily by providing some built-in functions.

9.9 Test Your Knowledge

1. **Which function is used to sort a list in ascending order?**

   a. sortedDescending()

   b. sortBy()

   c. sorted()

   d. reverse()

2. **What function is used for filtering elements that do not match a given condition?**

   a. filter()

   b. filterNot()

   c. filterIsInstance()

   d. filterNotNull()

CHAPTER 9   KOTLIN STANDARD LIBRARY

3. **Which function is used to check whether all elements of a collection satisfy a given condition?**

    a. all()

    b. any()

    c. none()

    d. filter()

4. **Which function is used to shuffle elements randomly in a list?**

    a. sorted()

    b. reversed()

    c. shuffled()

    d. sortBy()

5. **Which function can be used to safely access elements in a collection without throwing an exception?**

    a. getOrElse()

    b. get()

    c. getOrNull()

    d. both a and c

6. **What function is used to get the first character of a string safely?**

    a. first()

    b. firstOrNull()

    c. charAt(0)

    d. get(0)

7. **Which function is used to capitalize the first character of a string?**

    a. uppercase()

    b. capitalize()

c. toUpperCase()

d. replaceFirstChar { it.uppercaseChar() }

8. **Which function can be used to remove leading and trailing whitespaces from a string?**

    a. trimStart()

    b. trimEnd()

    c. trim()

    d. strip()

9. **What is the main advantage of using Kotlin standard library functions?**

    a. They make code less readable.

    b. They provide easy access to multiple functions.

    c. They make the code more complex.

    d. They slow down execution.

10. **Which function is used to sort a list in natural ascending order?**

    a. sortAscending()

    b. sortList()

    c. sorted()

    d. sortByAscending()

11. **What does asReversed() do in Kotlin?**

    a. reverses the collection and creates a new list

    b. modifies the original collection

    c. creates a reversed view of the original collection

    d. removes the last element of the list

12. **Which function is used to shuffle a list randomly?**

    a. randomSort()

    b. shuffleList()

CHAPTER 9   KOTLIN STANDARD LIBRARY

      c. shuffled()

      d. randomize()

13. **Which function returns a new string with leading and trailing whitespaces removed?**

    a. trimSpaces()

    b. removeSpaces()

    c. trim()

    d. clean()

14. **What is the correct function to check if a string is empty in Kotlin?**

    a. isBlank()

    b. isNullOrEmpty()

    c. length == 0

    d. All of the above

15. **Which function is used to write data into a file?**

    a. writeFile()

    b. writeText()

    c. write()

    d. appendText()

16. **What function reads all the content of a file as a single string?**

    a. readFile()

    b. readText()

    c. getFileContent()

    d. readLines()

17. **Which function is used to delete a file in Kotlin?**

    a. deleteFile()

    b. removeFile()

CHAPTER 9   KOTLIN STANDARD LIBRARY

    c. delete()

    d. deleteNow()

18. **What does the function** partition() **return?**

    a. a list of elements matching the condition

    b. a single element that matches the condition

    c. a pair of lists, one matching and one not matching the condition

    d. an empty list

19. **What does** !! **(double exclamation mark) do in Kotlin?**

    a. forces a nullable variable to be non-null

    b. converts a string to uppercase

    c. checks if a variable is null

    d. throws an exception if the variable is null

20. **What does** filterNotNull() **do?**

    a. removes all null values from a list

    b. returns only null values

    c. filters elements that match a given condition

    d. converts null values to empty strings

9.10 Answers

1. c
2. b
3. a
4. c
5. d
6. b

CHAPTER 9   KOTLIN STANDARD LIBRARY

7. d
8. c
9. b
10. c
11. c
12. c
13. c
14. d
15. b
16. b
17. c
18. c
19. a
20. a

CHAPTER 10

Testing in Kotlin

Testing is one of the key parts of the software development process. This ensures the correctness, reliability, and maintenance of the code. The Kotlin language supports all the major testing frameworks, as this language is interoperable with the Java language.

10.1 Unit Testing

Unit testing is an essential component of Android application development that guarantees code stability, minimizes defects, and facilitates maintenance. This chapter will examine the principles of unit testing on Android utilizing Kotlin. It offers a comprehensive foundation for both novices and those seeking to enhance their unit testing abilities, enabling the creation of effective and robust unit tests for Android Kotlin applications.

The Significance of Unit Testing

Unit testing is essential in software development. It enables developers to evaluate discrete pieces, such as procedures or functions, in isolation to ascertain their accuracy. The following are some key advantages of unit testing:

- Proactive Bug Identification: Unit tests facilitate the early detection of coding flaws, averting their escalation into more substantial difficulties.

- Enhanced Code Quality: The practice of writing unit tests promotes modular and loosely connected code, resulting in superior code quality and maintainability.

- Accelerated Development Cycles: Through test automation, developers can swiftly detect regressions and confirm that new modifications do not compromise current functionality.

CHAPTER 10 TESTING IN KOTLIN

Establishing the Testing Environment

Prior to initiating the composition of unit tests, let us establish the testing environment within our Android Kotlin project, as follows:

- Launch your project in Android Studio.
- Access the project view and go to the app module.
- Right-click on the application module and choose "New" ➤ "Folder" ➤ "Java Folder."
- Select the "Test" source directory option and click "Finish."

Composing Your Initial Unit Test

We shall compose two straightforward tests: one for evaluating two numbers in a basic function and another for assessing strings in a different function.

Illustration 1

Let us compose the initial example of a straightforward unit test for a hypothetical class named `Calculator`, which possesses a function called `add` that sums two values. An illustration of the potential structure of the `Calculator` class is presented here:

```kotlin
class Calculator {
    fun add(a: Int, b: Int): Int {
        return a + b
    }
}
```

We will now construct a unit test class for the aforementioned example. To develop a comparable unit test class for the `Calculator` class, adhere to the following steps:

- Access the Java directory established for testing purposes.
- Right-click on the package in which you wish to create the test class.
- Choose "New" ➤ "Kotlin Class/File."
- Designate a name for the test class (e.g., `CalculatorTest`) and choose the "Class" type.

- Select "OK" to generate the test class.

```
import org.junit.jupiter.api.Assertions.assertEquals
import org.junit.jupiter.api.Test

class CalculatorTest {

    private val calculator = Calculator()

    @Test
    fun `add should return the sum of two numbers`() {
        val result = calculator.add(2, 3)
        assertEquals(5, result, "Expected 2 + 3 to equal 5")
    }
}
```

In the aforementioned example, we import the requisite classes from JUnit and compose a test method annotated with @Test. Within the test function, we instantiate the Calculator class, use the add method with test inputs, then employ the assertEquals method to validate the anticipated outcome.

Running Unit Tests

To run the unit tests, follow these steps:

1. Go to the toolbar in Android Studio.

2. Click on the "Build Variants" tab.

3. Choose the desired test configuration (e.g., app ➤ Unit Tests).

4. Click on the green play button or use the shortcut Shift + F10 to run the tests.

Illustration 2

We will now develop a simple class named StringUtils, which has a function called reverseString to invert a specified string. Here is an example implementation of the StringUtils class:

```kotlin
class StringUtils {
    fun reverseString(input: String): String {
        return input.reversed()
    }
}
```

Now, let's write a unit test inside the StringUtilsTest class. To write a corresponding unit test for the reverseString method, follow these steps:

1. Navigate to the Java directory you created for tests.

2. Right-click on the package where you want to create the test class.

3. Select "New" ➤ "Kotlin Class/File."

4. Provide a name for the test class (e.g., StringUtilsTest) and select the "Class" type.

5. Click "OK" to create the test class.

    ```kotlin
    import org.junit.jupiter.api.Assertions.assertEquals
    import org.junit.jupiter.api.Test

    class StringUtilsTest {
        private val stringUtils = StringUtils()

        @Test
        fun `reverseString should return the reversed string`() {
            val original = "hello"
            val expected = "olleh"
            val result = stringUtils.reverseString(original)
            assertEquals(expected, result, "Expected reverse of 'hello' to be 'olleh'")
        }
    ```

```kotlin
    @Test
    fun `reverseString should return empty string when input is
    empty`() {
        val result = stringUtils.reverseString("")
        assertEquals("", result, "Expected reverse of empty string
        to be empty")
    }

    @Test
    fun `reverseString should handle single-character strings`() {
        val result = stringUtils.reverseString("A")
        assertEquals("A", result, "Expected reverse of 'A' to
        be 'A'")
    }
}
```

Optimal Strategies for Unit Testing

To compose effective and sustainable unit tests, consider the following recommended practices:

- Test One Aspect at a Time: Each unit test must concentrate on a particular behavior or functionality, guaranteeing that tests are succinct and independent.

- Employ Descriptive Nomenclature: Assign descriptive names to your test methods and test classes to enhance comprehension of their objectives.

- Organize, Execute, Validate: Structure your tests utilizing the "Organize, Execute, Validate" framework. Initially, establish the requisite preconditions (setup), then execute the operation under examination (act), and ultimately validate the anticipated result (assert).

- Employ Mocking: When evaluating classes with dependencies, such as network queries or database activities, it is advisable to utilize mocking frameworks such as Mockito or MockK. Mocking facilitates the creation of simulated dependencies, permitting the isolation of the unit under examination and concentrating only on its behavior.

- Employ Assertions: Assertions are essential in unit tests as they facilitate the validation of anticipated outcomes. Employ assertion techniques offered by testing frameworks such as JUnit or Kotlin's native assert functions (e.g., `assertEquals`, `assertTrue`, etc.) to juxtapose actual values against predicted values.

- Maintain Independence and Order Insensitivity of Tests: Unit tests must remain autonomous, ensuring that the result of one test does not influence the result of another. Refrain from depending on a particular execution sequence or the exchange of state among tests. This guarantees that tests may be conducted independently or in any sequence, enhancing their robustness and maintainability.

- Utilize Test Coverage Instruments: Test coverage tools, such as JaCoCo, assess the proportion of code included by tests. Strive for extensive code coverage to guarantee that essential components of your codebase are comprehensively evaluated. Nonetheless, it is essential to recognize that complete coverage does not ensure the absence of bugs; hence, prioritize comprehensive testing of crucial and intricate components.

- Evaluate Edge Instances and Boundary Circumstances: It is important to assess not just standard situations but also edge instances and boundary circumstances. Examine inputs at both the lower and higher thresholds, null values, empty collections, or any other situations that may influence the behavior of the unit under evaluation. These assessments reveal possible problems and guarantee resilience.

- Preserve Test Suites: As your software expands, categorize your unit tests into coherent test suites. Test suites consolidate linked tests, facilitating the execution of specified test sets, optimizing test execution duration, and augmenting test maintenance.

- Conduct Tests Consistently: Establish continuous integration (CI) or continuous delivery (CD) pipelines to execute your unit tests automatically with each code commit or build. Consistent testing facilitates the early detection of regressions and instills trust in the stability of your software.

Testing Frameworks

Kotlin supports various testing frameworks, each catering to different use cases and preferences. Some of the most popular ones include the following:

1. JUnit: JUnit, especially JUnit 5, is the most prevalent testing framework in Kotlin. It offers a comprehensive API for executing and conducting tests.

   Features:

   - Annotation-driven test specifications (@Test, @BeforeEach, @AfterEach, etc.)
   - Assertions to validate anticipated outcomes
   - Parameterized tests for executing an identical test with various inputs
   - Assistance for test lifecycle management

   Example:

   ```
   import org.junit.jupiter.api.Assertions.*
   import org.junit.jupiter.api.Test

   class CalculatorTest {
       @Test
       fun testAddition() {
           val result = 2 + 3
           assertEquals(5, result, "Addition should be correct")
       }
   }
   ```

2. KotlinTest (Kotest): Kotest is a powerful and flexible testing framework for Kotlin, offering expressive DSLs and additional matchers.

   Features:

   - Concise syntax and expressive matchers
   - Property-based testing support
   - Test configuration and tagging
   - Custom assertions and matchers

Example:

```
import io.kotest.core.spec.style.StringSpec
import io.kotest.matchers.shouldBe
class SampleTest : StringSpec({
    "Addition should work correctly" {
        (2 + 3) shouldBe 5
    }
})
```

3. Spek

   Spek is a specification-based testing framework that encourages behavior-driven development (BDD).

   Features:

   - DSL for writing structured and readable tests
   - Nested test structures
   - Support for lifecycle hooks

   Example:

   ```
   import org.spekframework.spek2.Spek
   import org.spekframework.spek2.style.specification.describe
   import kotlin.test.assertEquals

   object CalculatorSpec : Spek({
       describe("Calculator") {
           it("should add two numbers correctly") {
               assertEquals(5, 2 + 3)
           }
       }
   })
   ```

10.2 Kotlin Unit Testing with MockK

One of the most intricate facets of constructing resilient test suites is guaranteeing the ability to simulate the data required and processed by your code. Numerous libraries provide straightforward and adaptable solutions for this demand, with MockK being one of the most prominent.

Mocking and MockK: mocking in kotlin behaves like external real dependencies and mockK is powerful and lightweight mocking library

Mocking refers to the process of creating an imitation of a real dependency (class, interface, or an external service, etc.) that behaves like a real dependency but allows you to control the behavior for the purpose of testing. The imitations we want to create may have specific (and different) return values, exceptions that we want to throw, or interactions that we want to verify.

MockK is a popular, powerful, lightweight API for mocking in Kotlin. MockK will work with most SQLite features (such as coroutines, extension functions, and object classes) which makes it easy to utilize.

- Mocking: In unit testing, mocking entails the creation of simulated objects (mocks) that replicate the behavior of actual dependents. This enables the segregation of the unit under examination (your code) from extraneous elements, facilitating independent functionality testing.

- MockK is a succinct and efficient mocking library explicitly tailored for Kotlin. It provides a seamless API for generating mocks, specifying their behavior, and validating interactions with them during testing.

Let us examine the distinctive features of the MockK library.

MockK Annotations

MockK annotations provide an efficient method for specifying mock objects and their interactions in Kotlin tests. They offer a declarative methodology, enhancing the conciseness and readability of your test code. Let's look at a few of them.

1. @MockK

    This annotation designates a property as a fake object. It is generally utilized for a property that signifies a dependence or collaborator we intend to simulate.

CHAPTER 10 TESTING IN KOTLIN

```
MockK
private lateinit var myInterface: MyInterface

@MockK
private lateinit var myClass: MyClass
```

2. @RelaxedMockK

   This annotation resembles @MockK; however, it generates a relaxed mock, implying that, by default, the relaxed mock will not raise exceptions when using methods that have not been explicitly stubbed. This is beneficial for testing when verification of interactions is not a priority.

   ```
   @RelaxedMockK
   private lateinit var myInterface: MyInterface
   ```

3. @Spyk

   The @SpyK annotation facilitates the creation of a partial mock, enabling the use of actual implementations for certain methods of a class while mocking others.

   ```
   @Spyk
   private lateinit var myRealObject: MyRealObject
   ```

4. @UnmockK

   This annotation serves to unmock a property or object that was previously designated as a mock using @MockK or other annotations. This is beneficial when we must restore a mock to its original functionality.

   ```
   @UnmockK
   lateinit var unmockedService: SomeService
   ```

5. @Test

   An annotation commonly employed in testing frameworks (such as JUnit) to signify that a method constitutes a test case.

```
@Test
fun everyExample() {
    val mock = mockk<MyClass>()
    every { mock.doSomething() } returns "Mocked result"
}
```

6. **@Before**

   An annotation commonly utilized in testing frameworks to indicate that a method should be performed before to each test case.

   ```
   @Before
   fun setUp() {
       MockKAnnotations.init(this)
       Dispatchers.setMain(Dispatchers.Unconfined)
       newsViewModel = NewsViewModel(newsUseCase)
   }
   ```

MockK Keywords

When using the MockK library for mocking and validating interactions in Kotlin tests, it is imperative to be acquainted with many fundamental keywords and methods. The following are a few frequently utilized keywords and functions in MockK:

Keyword	Description
mockk<T>()	Creates a mock of type T
mockk<T>(relaxed = true)	Creates a mock with default return values (no need to stub everything)
spyk(obj)	Creates a spy (partial mock) on a real object
slot<T>()	Captures arguments passed to mocked functions
mockkObject(MyObject)	Mocks a Kotlin object (singleton)
mockkClass(MyClass::class)	Mocks a class (useful for final classes)

10.3 Kotlin Integration Testing

Integration testing verifies that various components/modules of your program function cohesively, including services, repositories, controllers, and the database.

CHAPTER 10   TESTING IN KOTLIN

In contrast to unit tests, which utilize mocks, integration tests typically employ actual or in-memory databases and genuine HTTP queries.

- **Dependencies**

```
dependencies {
    testImplementation("org.springframework.boot:spring-boot-starter-test")
    testImplementation("io.mockk:mockk:1.13.5") // optional
    testImplementation("org.testcontainers:junit-jupiter:1.19.0")
    // for real DBs
}
```

- **Basic Setup**

```
@SpringBootTest
@AutoConfigureMockMvc
@TestInstance(TestInstance.Lifecycle.PER_CLASS)
class UserControllerIntegrationTest {

    @Autowired
    lateinit var mockMvc: MockMvc

    @Test
    fun `should return user by id`() {
        mockMvc.perform(get("/users/1"))
            .andExpect(status().isOk)
            .andExpect(jsonPath("$.name").value("John"))
    }
}
```

- **Using a Real DB with Testcontainers**

```
@Testcontainers

@SpringBootTest
@AutoConfigureTestDatabase(replace = AutoConfigureTestDatabase.Replace.NONE)
class UserServiceIT {
    companion object {
```

```kotlin
    @Container
    val postgresContainer = PostgreSQLContainer("postgres:
    14-alpine")
        .apply {
            withDatabaseName("testdb")
            withUsername("test")
            withPassword("test")
        }
}

@DynamicPropertySource
fun datasourceConfig(registry: DynamicPropertyRegistry) {
    registry.add("spring.datasource.url",
    postgresContainer::getJdbcUrl)
    registry.add("spring.datasource.username", postgres
    Container::getUsername)
    registry.add("spring.datasource.password", postgres
    Container::getPassword)
}

@Autowired
lateinit var userRepository: UserRepository

@Test
fun `should fetch user from real PostgreSQL DB`() {
    userRepository.save(User(name = "Alice"))
    val user = userRepository.findByName("Alice")
    assertEquals("Alice", user?.name)
}
}
```

CHAPTER 10   TESTING IN KOTLIN

Integration Testing in Kotlin with Ktor

Integration testing in Kotlin with Ktor focuses on testing your entire application flow, including routing, middleware (features), serialization, and sometimes even database or external service integration, rather than just isolated components (as in unit testing).

- **Dependencies**

  ```
  testImplementation("io.ktor:ktor-server-tests:2.3.2")
  testImplementation("org.jetbrains.kotlin:kotlin-test")
  }
  ```

- **Setup**

  ```
  fun Application.testModule() {
      configureRouting()
      configureDatabase()
  }
  ```

- **HTTP Integration Test**

  ```
  class UserRouteTest {
      @Test
      fun testGetUser() = testApplication {
          application {
              testModule()
          }
          val response = client.get("/users/1")
          assertEquals(HttpStatusCode.OK, response.status)
          assertTrue(response.bodyAsText().contains("John"))
      }
  }
  ```

10.4 Conclusion

This chapter examined the fundamental importance of testing in the Kotlin development environment, emphasizing the components of unit testing, mocking, and integration testing. As software systems grow in complexity, the significance of ensuring code dependability, maintainability, and correctness escalates, with testing serving as the cornerstone for achieving these objectives.

We started with the principles of unit testing, emphasizing its essential significance within the software development lifecycle. Unit testing is not a mere formality but rather a proactive strategy to identify defects early, reduce technical debt, and enforce clean, modular code. By unit-testing discrete components of functionality—typically methods or classes—we can verify their behavior in controlled settings. This degree of detail facilitates rapid feedback during development, allows for secure reworking, and accelerates the delivery pace.

We also examined the most prevalent testing libraries for Kotlin. Among them, JUnit 5 remains a preferred choice, including robust annotations, lifecycle management, and assertion capabilities. Kotlin's compatibility with Java enables developers to utilize JUnit while also capitalizing on Kotlin's expressive syntax and capabilities, such as extension functions and lambdas. Moreover, libraries like TestNG and Kotest offer distinctive capabilities for more expressive or behavior-driven testing methodologies, accommodating various team preferences.

Then, we discussed the methodology for developing effective unit tests. Merely composing exams is inadequate; the tests must also be of high quality. Effective unit tests are rapid, autonomous, repeatable, and meaningful. We addressed the establishment of tests using naming conventions that precisely convey purpose, ensuring effective setup and deconstruction of resources, and the use of assertions that evaluate not just anticipated outcomes but also edge cases. Kotlin facilitates the creation of unit tests that are both clear and succinct, allowing developers to focus on the test logic rather than excessive verbosity.

Subsequently, we proceeded to mocking, an essential technique for isolating dependencies and conducting unit tests in appropriate isolation. We were introduced to MockK, the idiomatic and robust mocking library for Kotlin. In contrast to traditional Java-based mocking libraries, MockK is designed for Kotlin, including capabilities like relaxed mocks, coroutine support, argument capture, and object mocking. We demonstrated the use of MockK to simulate database access, external service contacts, and other engagements through real-world situations, ensuring that tests remain isolated, predictable, and efficient.

Finally, we examined integration testing, which shifts the emphasis from isolation to cooperation. Integration tests validate that various components—such as services, repositories, and external systems—interact appropriately. While unit tests validate the functionality of individual components, integration tests verify the proper interaction between these components. We acquired knowledge on developing integration tests in Spring Boot, utilizing annotations like `@SpringBootTest` and tools such as MockMvc, as well as testing Ktor apps with `testApplication`. We highlighted the benefits of employing `Testcontainers` to initiate actual databases during testing, therefore bridging the divide between development and production environments.

Kotlin's testing is robust and focused on developers. Its modern language features enhance the expressiveness and conciseness of tests, while its robust array of supporting tools, including JUnit, MockK, and Testcontainers, equips developers with all the essentials to design solid test suites. Kotlin provides comprehensive support for testing, whether you are developing unit tests for business logic, mocking dependencies for isolated feature testing, or doing integration tests to ensure cohesive system operation.

Implementing a rigorous testing methodology enhances code quality, increases developer trust, and promotes project sustainability. As teams increasingly choose Kotlin for production-grade apps, testing should be regarded not as a burden but as an essential facilitator of sustained success. Utilizing appropriate tools and a conducive mentality, testing in Kotlin can be both effective and pleasurable.

10.5 Test Your Knowledge

1. **What is the main purpose of unit testing?**

    a. to test the entire application end-to-end

    b. to test the interactions between modules

    c. to validate the functionality of individual components in isolation

    d. to deploy the code to production

2. **Which testing framework is most commonly used with Kotlin for unit testing?**

    a. Mocha

    b. JUnit

    c. Jasmine

    d. Cucumber

CHAPTER 10 TESTING IN KOTLIN

3. **What does the @SpringBootTest annotation do in a Spring Boot application?**

    a. runs a single unit test

    b. disables dependency injection

    c. boots the full application context for integration testing

    d. automatically mocks all dependencies

4. **In MockK, what does the `relaxed = true` parameter do when creating a mock?**

    a. enables random behavior

    b. automatically throws exceptions for unstubbed methods

    c. provides default values for all functions

    d. disables mocking

5. **Which function in MockK is used to define a behavior for a mocked function?**

    a. define {}

    b. when {}

    c. every { } returns

    d. doReturn {}

6. **What is the purpose of integration testing?**

    a. to mock external services

    b. to verify a single class behaves as expected

    c. to ensure multiple components work together correctly

    d. to test UI behavior

7. **Which keyword in MockK verifies that a mocked method was called?**

    a. check { }

    b. verify { }

    c. call { }

    d. assertCalled { }

8. **Which Kotlin test library is specifically designed with native coroutine support and idiomatic syntax?**

    a. Mockito

    b. TestNG

    c. MockK

    d. JUnit 4

9. **What is the advantage of using Testcontainers in integration tests?**

    a. mocks all network calls

    b. enables mocking of private methods

    c. spins up real databases or services in containers for realistic testing

    d. speeds up compilation time

10. **In Ktor testing, which function is used to simulate a test environment for integration tests?**

    a. simulateApp()

    b. testServer()

    c. testApplication()

    d. mockServer()

10.6 Answers

1. c
2. b
3. c
4. c
5. c
6. c
7. b
8. c
9. c
10. c

CHAPTER 11

Kotlin Reactive Extension

11.1 Introduction to RxKotlin

RxKotlin is a Kotlin-specific wrapper and extension for RxJava, making it easier to use reactive programming in Kotlin applications. It provides Kotlin-friendly APIs, extension functions, and utilities for working with reactive streams in a more idiomatic manner. Based on extension function, null safety, and conciseness features, there are significant differences between RxJava and RxKotlin, as shown in Table 11-1. Kotlin can be integrated and tested with existing Java. Kotlin's strong interoperability with Java enables the use of RxJava and RxKotlin to write reactive programs. RxJava and RxKotlin libraries from the ReactiveX (Rx) project are used to add reactive capabilities [1]. Reactive libraries, such as Reactor, can also be used. At the same time, coroutines and suspension functions are used as a reactive extension in Kotlin [2]. RxJava serves as the backbone for other ReactiveX JVM ports, including RxScala and RxKotlin [3]. RxKotlin utilizes the majority of RxJava operators, as outlined on its GitHub page for Kotlin. RxAndroid is RxJava bindings for Android [4].

Table 11-1. *Features of RxJava and RxKotlin*

Feature	RxJava	RxKotlin
Language	Java	Kotlin
Extension Functions	No	Yes
Null Safety	No	Yes
Conciseness	Less	More

RxKotlin has an inbuilt API that makes RxJava easier to use in Kotlin. The idiomatic Kotlin API adds a Kotlin extension to make RxJava easier to use. Kotlin has an upper hand over Java because it features a unique null safety mechanism that reduces the potential null pointer exception issues associated with Java.

Another feature of Kotlin is the use of lambda expressions, which reduce boilerplate by allowing functions to be written in more concise code. RxKotlin is interoperable with RxJava, allowing developers to integrate RxJava code into their Kotlin code. RxKotlin is also compatible with Kotlin coroutines. Idiomatic Kotlin API, null safety, more concise code, interoperability, and coroutine compatibility are five key features of RxKotlin, as shown in Figure 11-1.

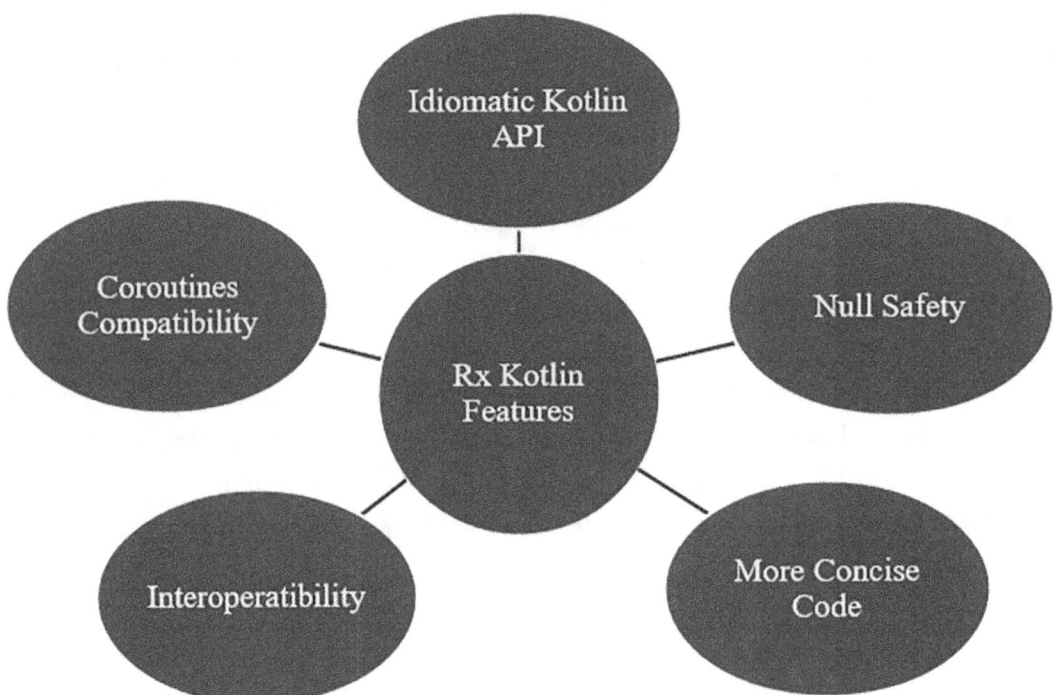

Figure 11-1. Features of RxKotlin

11.2 Core Rx Concepts

Reactive programming in Kotlin, primarily seen in asynchronous Kotlin applications, is designed and developed with Android, RxKotlin, Reactor Kotlin, and Spring [5]. Reactive programming changes how apps interact with data in software development. It enables systems to manage data flows and respond to changes promptly. It's centered around asynchronous programming, which boosts app adaptability and efficiency. At its core, reactive programming is about data flow and change propagation. It relies on data streams for handling real-time data. This method allows apps to automatically adjust to data or behavior changes, enhancing response times. Reactive programming is crucial, especially in Android apps developed with Kotlin. It's built on streams in reactive programming, the observer pattern, and knowing the difference between cold streams and hot streams. Understanding these helps improve app responsiveness and data management.

Streams: The Heart of Reactive Programming

Streams send sequences of data that can be handled asynchronously. Streams in Kotlin enable developers to manage changing data, such as user input or network data. Using the RxJava library's observable, single, and flowable makes managing these streams in reactive programming easier. For instance, an observable might send out items each second. This lets apps respond quickly to what's happening.

Hot and Cold Observables

Hot observables have no side effects during a subscription, regardless of the context. The context taken under consideration is usually neither usable to RxSwift nor capable of determining either scheduler or thread-based information on its own. In contrast to hot observables, cold observables have many side effects and do not produce any events until a subscriber establishes a valid subscription. That's why cold observables have no provision for threading or scheduling [6].

Flow of Hot and Cold Streams

Understanding the concepts of cold streams and hot streams is crucial for effective data management. Cold streams, like Kotlin Flow, start sending data only when activated. This ensures all data is received. Hot streams, however, send data regardless of whether observers are ready, meeting real-time needs, but requiring careful management, as shown in Table 11-2.

Table 11-2. Stream Type

Stream Type	Emission Timing	Use Cases
Cold Streams	Emit data on time for collection	Data fetching, UI updates, and so on
Hot Streams	Emit data regularly	Real-time updates, event notification, and so on

Kotlin flows offer a straightforward approach to handling asynchronous data management. Kotlin is used to create a data stream that sends out values over time. This makes managing asynchronous tasks simpler, improving app performance and response times. Defining flows in Kotlin involves setting up a cold data stream. This stream starts only when there is a collector. This differs from hot streams, which emit values without requiring a collector. Flows are ideal for tasks such as network calls and database queries, making apps faster and more responsive. Kotlin flows include the flow builder, operators, and collectors. The flow builder enables developers to create data streams easily. Operators change data and manage execution threads. Collectors then gather and process this data. This process improves memory use and app performance. Consider using Kotlin flows for real-time data updates. This helps keep the user interface responsive by managing state with flows. For example, a flow could send out user interactions or server data. Flows can be adjusted through operations like filtering and mapping to meet specific needs.

11.3 Usage of Rx

RxKotlin is a Kotlin wrapper for RxJava, providing extension functions and enhanced idiomatic support for reactive programming.

Basic RxKotlin Usage

The Kotlin code shown in Figure 11-2 demonstrates how to convert a Kotlin list into an observable using the `toObservable()` method. The `subscribeBy` extension function is used for handling emitted items, errors, and completion. The `onNext` callback prints each emitted item, and the `onComplete` callback prints a message when the stream finishes, as shown in Figure 11-2.

CHAPTER 11   KOTLIN REACTIVE EXTENSION

```
import io.reactivex.rxjava3.core.Observable
import io.reactivex.rxjava3.kotlin.subscribeBy
import io.reactivex.rxjava3.kotlin.toObservable

fun main() {
    // Creating an Observable from a list using RxKotlin extension
    val items = listOf("Apple", "Banana", "Cherry", "Date")

    val observable: Observable<String> = items.toObservable()

    // Subscribing to the observable
    observable.subscribeBy(
        onNext = { println("Received: $it") },
        onError = { println("Error: $it") },
        onComplete = { println("Completed!") }
    )
}
```

Figure 11-2. Creating an observable in Kotlin

Using filter and distinct

This Kotlin code in Figure 11-3 creates an observable from a list of numbers. The filter is used to retain only even numbers. Distinct removes duplicate values to ensure each emitted item is unique. The filtered and different values are printed as shown in Figure 11-3.

```kotlin
fun main() {
    val observable = listOf(1, 2, 2, 3, 4, 4, 5).toObservable()
        .filter { it % 2 == 0 }  // Keep only even numbers
        .distinct()  // Remove duplicates

    observable.subscribeBy(
        onNext = { println(it) },
        onComplete = { println("Filtered stream complete!") }
    )
}
```

Figure 11-3. Usage of filter and distinct in Kotlin

Observable.Interval for Periodic Emissions

Observable.interval() emits numbers at regular time intervals (one second, in this case). Take(5) ensures that only the first five emissions are processed before completion. Thread.sleep(6000) keeps the program running long enough to observe all emissions, as shown in Figure 11-4.

```kotlin
import io.reactivex.rxjava3.core.Observable
import java.util.concurrent.TimeUnit

fun main() {
    Observable.interval(1, TimeUnit.SECONDS)
        .take(5)   // Emit 5 items
        .subscribeBy(
            onNext = { println("Tick: $it") },
            onComplete = { println("Timer finished!") }
        )

    Thread.sleep(6000) // Keep the main thread alive
}
```

Figure 11-4. Usage of observable interval in Kotlin

11.4 Kotlin Coroutines

Researchers found that 87 out of 90 Android applications (96%) used Kotlin coroutines [7]. Kotlin coroutines represent a significant leap forward in asynchronous programming in Kotlin. The coroutines in Kotlin make it simpler to write code that doesn't block. This means developers can create apps that do tasks more effectively. This chapter explores what coroutines are and how Kotlin coroutines help with reactive programming. Kotlin coroutines enable developers to perform asynchronous tasks clearly and concisely. This section outlines how coroutines in Kotlin make writing code easier than the old callback methods. Coroutines can run multiple tasks concurrently without consuming excessive memory. Knowing how to use Kotlin effectively, especially with extension functions and lambdas, is crucial. Coroutines enhance reactive programming by simplifying asynchronous task handling and aligning perfectly with reactive programming, resulting in improved data handling and app performance. The coroutine scope concept helps manage the lifecycles of coroutines, allowing tasks to be stopped when needed. This helps apps run more efficiently and use resources more wisely. Table 11-3 demonstrates that Kotlin coroutines outperform traditional methods in terms of features such as memory usage, code reusability, lifecycle management, and error handling.

Table 11-3. Kotlin Coroutines and Traditional Threads

Feature	Kotlin Coroutines	Traditional Threads
Memory Usage	Low	High
Support	Thousands of coroutines	A few concurrent threads
Code Readability	Easier to read	Not easy to read
Lifecycle	Can cancel easily	Difficult to manage
Error Handling	Structures with easy-to-manage exceptions	Complex procedures

Understanding Kotlin coroutines helps developers handle the challenges of asynchronous programming. This enhances their ability to utilize reactive programming effectively.

11.5 Reactive Programming Patterns

Exploring reactive programming patterns is crucial for creating responsive apps. Through these patterns, developers can handle data wisely and boost user interaction. Using subjects, observables, and event streams demonstrates how reactive ideas work in practice. The following three approaches shine when using reactive programming patterns: *subjects* work as both observers and observables, providing multicast capabilities. *Observables* emit values over time and are crucial in real-world reactive apps. *Event streams* help manage event streams, which are key for reacting to user and data changes. These patterns often use libraries like RxJava. It makes defining observables, changing items, and handling threads easier. Shifting from traditional to reactive programming enables developers to respond more effectively to changes. This improves app quality and user happiness. Reactive programming patterns are used in many apps for real-time updates. Chat and social media apps use real-time updates to show data changes to users instantly. Interactive user interfaces make interfaces smooth and responsive to user actions and data updates. Data management apps efficiently manage extensive data flows, remaining responsive even under heavy load. These patterns not only enhance app design but also facilitate scaling across various platforms. Kotlin sequences, for example, work significantly better than traditional lists in terms of resource conservation. As more developers adopt these methods, the future of reactive apps appears promising, with improved performance and enhanced user experiences. Subjects, observables, and event streams are popular Kotlin patterns, as shown in Table 11-4.

Table 11-4. Usage of Kotlin Pattern

Pattern	Description	Usage Example
Subjects	Act as both observer and observable	Sending notification to multiple subscribers
Observables	Asynchronous data streams	Fetching data from repositories and update UI
Event Streams	Generating reactive responses	Managing button clicks or UI interactions smoothly

11.6 Best Practices for Testing Reactive Code

Using best practices for testing improves app quality. Key strategies include the following five steps: utilizing JUnit, applying unit testing, using integration testing, leveraging Kotlin features, and utilizing testing techniques from reactive libraries. The developer needs to utilize JUnit or Mockito for testing, supporting async operations and reactive programming tools. The developer must apply unit testing to coroutines and flows, ensuring that async tasks are thoroughly covered. They must ensure that integration tests verify the seamless integration of components, providing a smooth user experience. Developers use Kotlin coroutines' `try-catch` blocks for better error handling and debugging. The developer has to utilize testing utilities from reactive libraries to simplify testing and identify issues early. Adequate verification in debugging reactive code ensures that applications are robust and reliable. Developers should ensure that all flows and UI elements function correctly under various conditions. Testing practices encompass unit testing, integration testing, error handling, mocking and stubbing, and performance testing, as outlined in Table 11-5.

Table 11-5. Testing Practices for Reactive Code

Testing	Description
Unit Testing	Tests the individual component to ensure the working of a specific unit
Integration Testing	Check whether a group of units is working together or not
Error Handling	Handle exceptions of reactive code
Mocking and Stubbing	Simulate external dependencies
Performance Testing	Test reliability and scalability

By following the testing practices outlined in Table 11-5, developers ensure their testing is thorough and adequate. This leads to reliable and efficient reactive apps.

11.7 Conclusion

Reactive programming has significantly improved Android development, thanks to Kotlin. It enables apps to respond faster and makes them easier to maintain. This approach is now key in creating smooth user experiences. Kotlin's rise as the go-to language for Android shows a move toward advanced programming. Developers are getting behind live data and flow. These tools help manage data and app life cycles efficiently. This represents a significant step forward in Android's development, with Kotlin at its core. Tools like RxJava and ReactiveX improve teamwork in big projects. Yet it's essential to use reactive methods wisely so that reactive programming will make things simpler, not more complex.

11.8 Real-Life Programming Practices

1. **Scenario: Live Stock Price Updater**

   This program simulates fetching stock prices from an API and updates them every two seconds using RxKotlin. The program leverages:

   ✅ **Observables (RxKotlin) for real-time updates**

   ✅ **Kotlin coroutines for async operations**

CHAPTER 11 KOTLIN REACTIVE EXTENSION

✅ **Flow and cold streams for better efficiency**

Code:

```
import io.reactivex.rxjava3.core.Observable
import kotlinx.coroutines.*
import kotlinx.coroutines.flow.*
import kotlin.random.Random

// Simulating an API call that fetches stock prices
fun getStockPrice(stock: String): Observable<Double> {
    return Observable.create { emitter ->
        while (!emitter.isDisposed) {
            val price = Random.nextDouble(100.0, 500.0)  // 
            Simulated stock price
            emitter.onNext(price)  // Emit new stock price
            Thread.sleep(2000)  // Wait for 2 seconds before
            next update
        }
    }
}

// Using Kotlin Flow (Cold Stream) to fetch stock data when needed
fun getStockFlow(stock: String): Flow<Double> = flow {
    while (true) {
        val price = Random.nextDouble(100.0, 500.0)
        emit(price)
        delay(2000) // Emit new price every 2 seconds
    }
}

fun main() = runBlocking {
    println("Stock Price Updater Started!")

    // Example using RxKotlin Observable
    val stockObservable = getStockPrice("AAPL")
    stockObservable.subscribe { price -> println("RxKotlin: AAPL Stock Price: $$price") }
```

```
// Example using Kotlin Flow
launch {
    getStockFlow("GOOGL").collect { price ->
        println("Flow: GOOGL Stock Price: $$price")
    }
}

// Keep the main thread alive for demo purposes
delay(10000)
}
```

Output:

```
Stock Price Updater Started!
RxKotlin: AAPL Stock Price: $250.45
Flow: GOOGL Stock Price: $320.12
RxKotlin: AAPL Stock Price: $265.78
Flow: GOOGL Stock Price: $299.99
RxKotlin: AAPL Stock Price: $275.63
Flow: GOOGL Stock Price: $310.45
...
```

11.9 Test Your Knowledge

1. **What is the main goal of reactive programming in Android development?**

    a. to create static user interfaces

    b. to handle data flows and changes efficiently

    c. to avoid using multithreading

    d. to write only synchronous code

2. **How does Kotlin support reactive programming?**

    a. by using Java callbacks

    b. by providing libraries like RxJava and coroutines

    c. by enforcing single-thread execution

    d. by disabling asynchronous operations

3. **What is the key difference between hot and cold streams in reactive programming?**

    a. Hot streams always wait for an observer before emitting data, while cold streams do not.

    b. Hot streams emit data regardless of observers, while cold streams start only when an observer subscribes.

    c. Cold streams emit data continuously, while hot streams only emit on demand.

    d. Both function the same way and emit data randomly.

4. **What is the primary use of Kotlin flows in reactive programming?**

    a. to handle blocking operations in the UI thread

    b. to convert synchronous functions into asynchronous ones

    c. to replace all LiveData instances

    d. to manage asynchronous data streams in a cold manner

5. **Which of the following are common patterns in reactive programming?**

    a. using subjects, observables, and event streams

    b. writing only synchronous code

    c. avoiding any event-based programming

    d. using only Java's default threading model

6. **How can developers ensure reliability in reactive applications?**

   a. by avoiding testing since streams are automatically reliable

   b. by limiting the use of observables and subjects

   c. by using proper testing and debugging frameworks for reactive programming

   d. by writing only single-threaded synchronous code

7. **What is the advantage of reactive programming in Android app development?**

   a. It reduces the need for user interaction.

   b. It simplifies UI design but limits responsiveness.

   c. It enhances performance and user experience by handling data efficiently.

   d. It completely removes the need for threading.

11.10 Answers

1. b
2. b
3. b
4. d
5. a
6. c
7. c

CHAPTER 12

Working with API and Networking

12.1 Introduction to Kotlin APIs

In Kotlin, we can use over a hundred APIs depending on the domain we are working in. We can categorize all Kotlin APIs into the following families: Android, networking, database, graphical, machine learning, multimedia, and cloud. The Android API provides core functionality for building Android applications using Jetpack components, such as ViewModel, LiveData, Navigation, and WorkManager. It also includes permission handling, lifecycle management, and UI components.

The networking API is used to manage network communication using libraries such as Retrofit (for RESTful APIs), OkHttp (a low-level HTTP client), Ktor (an asynchronous HTTP client), and WebSockets (for real-time communication). For handling HTTP requests, two popular options are Retrofit and Ktor. Retrofit simplifies network requests in Kotlin, with `GsonConverterFactory` converting JSON into Kotlin objects. The `enqueue()` method is used for asynchronous calls, while coroutines (suspend functions) provide a modern approach to handling API requests efficiently. Ktor Client is a lightweight and coroutine-friendly networking library. HTTP requests are managed using `client.get()` and `client.post()`, with `gson()` handling serialization. While `runBlocking {}` can be used in `main()` for simplicity, real applications should rely on suspend functions for better performance. In Kotlin, we typically need a dependency known as `com.squareup.retrofit2:retrofit` to use Retrofit. Ktor is preferable to Retrofit because Ktor supports WebSocket communication.

The database API provides broad support for data storage using Room (SQLite ORM), Realm (NoSQL), and Firebase Firestore (Cloud NoSQL). Room simplifies database interactions, while Firebase enables cloud-based data storage and management.

CHAPTER 12   WORKING WITH API AND NETWORKING

The graphical API enables UI development for a better user experience (UX) with Jetpack Compose (declarative UI), Canvas API (custom drawing), and MotionLayout (advanced animations). These tools facilitate the creation of modern and dynamic user interfaces.

Machine learning APIs typically integrate AI/ML using ML Kit (Google's AI tools), TensorFlow Lite (on-device ML models), and Hugging Face (NLP models). These APIs enable features such as face detection, object recognition, and sentiment analysis. The multimedia API in Kotlin supports media handling through CameraX (camera integration), MediaPlayer (audio and video playback), and ExoPlayer (advanced video streaming). These enable multimedia-rich applications. The Kotlin-based cloud API facilitates cloud computing and storage with Firebase Authentication, Firebase Cloud Storage, AWS SDK for Kotlin, and Google Cloud Functions.

These APIs provide authentication, data storage, and serverless computing. Each of these APIs plays a crucial role in Android app development, enabling efficient networking, data handling, graphics, AI, multimedia, and cloud integrations. Dagger Hilt and Koin are both dependency injection (DI) frameworks for Kotlin and Android. Dagger Hilt is an officially recommended DI framework for Android, built on top of Dagger 2. Koin is a lightweight DI framework for Kotlin that utilizes runtime injection. Kotlin coroutines and flow API are both used for asynchronous programming, but they serve different purposes. The Kotlin coroutines API is a way to handle asynchronous tasks efficiently using suspend functions. Flow is a cold stream that emits multiple values over time. In Kotlin, Firebase, Outh and Encryption are application and security APIs. The Google Maps API, Fused Location API, and Geocoder API are geolocation APIs supported by Kotlin. The MQTT API, along with the Nearby API, is specifically designed to support Internet of Things (IoT) applications. For testing Kotlin-based development, there are various APIs available, including Espresso, JUnit, and Mockito.

12.2 Android Development APIs

The Android SDK APIs, including Jetpack Compose API, Room API, LiveData&ViewModel API, Navigation API, and WorkManager API, are fully supported by Kotlin and utilized in Android development with Kotlin, as shown in Table 12-1. The Android SDK APIs are a standard set of application programming interfaces (APIs) for developing Android applications. Jetpack Compose API is one of the most popular user interface (UI) APIs for modern Android UI development. Room API is a database persistence library that is part of Jetpack. The LiveData and ViewModel APIs are used

CHAPTER 12   WORKING WITH API AND NETWORKING

to manage UI-based data, enhancing the user experience (UX). Navigation API is used for handling app navigation. WorkManager API is used for background tasks and job scheduling.

Table 12-1. Android Development APIs Supported by Kotlin

Android Development API Name	Support with Kotlin
Android SDK APIs	Google officially supports Kotlin for Android development, and all Android SDK APIs work seamlessly with Kotlin. Developers are advised to merely use the public **APIs** released by the **AndroidSDK** for building apps [1].
Jetpack Compose API	Jetpack Compose is Kotlin-first, built entirely with Kotlin in mind for modern UI development. It replaces XML-based UI development with declarative programming. Jetpack Compose dramatically changes the way we write UIs on Android [2].
Room API	Jetpack library that provides a Kotlin-friendly API, simplifying database management [3]. It supports Kotlin coroutines and flow for reactive programming.
LiveData & ViewModel API [4]	Kotlin works perfectly with LiveData and ViewModel, ensuring lifecycle-aware data management and UI updates. It also supports StateFlow and SharedFlow as alternatives. **ViewModel** differentiates the business logic from the UI code [4]
Navigation API	Kotlin integrates seamlessly with the Navigation API, enabling type-safe navigation through Safe Args and the Kotlin DSL for defining navigation graphs.
WorkManager API	The WorkManager API is Kotlin-compatible and supports coroutines for scheduling background tasks and periodic tasks efficiently [3].

12.3 Networking APIs

Retrofit, OkHTTP, Ktor, and Volley are the most popular networking APIs usable with Kotlin, as shown in Table 12-2. Ktor or Retrofit are the best choices among these four popular networking APIs. Retrofit is the best for structured REST APIs with automatic parsing. OkHttp is a better choice if you need low-level HTTP handling, WebSockets, or custom network requests. Ktor is ideal for Kotlin-first applications and coroutines. Volley is suitable for small, quick network requests but is generally outdated. If you need maximum control, OkHttp is the most preferred API. Volley is mostly legacy at this point.

Table 12-2. Networking APIs Supported by Kotlin

Networking APIs Name	Support with Kotlin
Retrofit API	Retrofit is a type-safe HTTP client for REST API calls. This API is used for designing applications for both online digital libraries and data repositories [5].
OkHttp API	HTTP clients utilize this API to handle network requests.
Ktor API	This is an asynchronous framework for building web services and clients [6].
Volley API	Volley is Google's HTTP library for networking operations [7].

12.4 Database & Storage APIs

The SQLite API, Firebase Firestore Realtime Database API, and DataStore API are the most popular database and storage APIs, as shown in Table 12-3. We should use the SQLite API (with Room) when we need structured, relational data storage locally. Firebase Firestore is used when we need a cloud-based NoSQL database with flexible queries. It is the preferred API for ultra-fast, real-time syncing, such as in chat apps. If we need to store small user settings or preferences efficiently, then the DataStore API is the best fit. If you're working with Kotlin, Room (SQLite) and DataStore API integrate well with coroutines, while Firestore is the best option for cloud-based storage.

Table 12-3. Database APIs Supported by Kotlin

Database APIs Name	Support with Kotlin
SQLite API	This is the most standard Android database API [8].
Firebase Firestore & Realtime Database API	Kotlin also supports cloud-based NoSQL databases. Firestone is related to Firebase APIs and Firebase SDKs. These APIs offer various unique characteristics. [9]
DataStore API	Jetpack's alternative to SharedPreferences.

12.5 UI & Graphics APIs

The Jetpack Compose API, Canvas API, and Glide/Picasso API are the most popular UI and graphics APIs, as shown in Table 12-4. Jetpack Compose is the most popular UI API for building native Android UIs declaratively. This API uses Kotlin-based declarative syntax for the UI. It eliminates the need for XML layouts. The Jetpack Compose API is optimized for UI performance and compositing. Jetpack provides built-in support for animations, gestures, and theming. The Canvas API is used for low-level drawing operations in Jetpack Compose or the traditional Android View system. Both Glide and Picasso are widely used for loading and caching images in Android apps.

Table 12-4. UI & Graphics APIs Supported by Kotlin

Networking APIs Name	Support with Kotlin
Jetpack Compose API	The most popular UI toolkit for creating native UIs [10].
Canvas API	For drawing custom graphics.
Glide/Picasso API	Image loading and caching libraries [11].

12.6 Machine Learning & IoT APIs

The TensorFlow Lite API helps us to run machine learning algorithms on mobile, embedded, and IoT devices. It's optimized for on-device inference, meaning it can perform machine learning tasks directly on the device without needing a constant internet connection. This improves latency and privacy. The ML Kit API is a widely used mobile SDK. This API leverages the benefits of Google's machine-learning expertise for both Android and iOS developers. The ML Kit API provides ready-to-use APIs for machine learning functions, including image labelling in supervised learning, face detection, text recognition, and more. It simplifies the integration of machine learning into mobile apps. The MQTT (Message Queuing Telemetry Transport) API is a messaging protocol designed for IoT devices and networks with low bandwidth and high latency. The MQTT API enables devices to publish and subscribe to messages, making it an ideal choice for IoT applications that require efficient communication, as shown in Table 12-5.

Table 12-5. Machine Learning and IoT APIs Supported by Kotlin

Machine Learning and IoT APIs Name	Support with Kotlin
TensorFlow Lite API	Machine learning on Android devices. It is used for detecting leaf diseases [12].
ML Kit API	Google's machine learning APIs, including image labelling, face detection, etc.
MQTT API	This API is specially designed for IoT-based applications [14].

In [13], the researchers utilized Kotlin and Google's ML Kit to develop Android applications with optical character recognition capabilities.

12.7 Multimedia APIs

CameraX, MediaRecorder, and ExoPlayer are multimedia APIs available in Kotlin, as shown in Table 12-6. To achieve robust video playback capabilities, developers use **ExoPlayer** [17]. **CameraX** is a powerful tool for seamless photo capturing and editing [18].

This table highlights key multimedia APIs in Android with Kotlin support.

It includes ExoPlayer for advanced media playback, MediaRecorder for audio/video recording, and CameraX for easy camera integration.

Table 12-6. Multimedia APIs Supported by Kotlin

Multimedia APIs Name	Support with Kotlin
ExoPlayer API	Advanced media playback for Android.
MediaRecorder API	Recording audio and video.
CameraX API	Simplified camera integration.

12.8 Cloud & Backend APIs

Cloud-based APIs, such as Firebase Cloud Messaging (FCM) API, AWS SDK API, Google Cloud API, and Google Maps API, are shown in Table 12-7.

Table 12-7. Cloud APIs Supported by Kotlin

Cloud APIs Name	Support with Kotlin
Firebase Cloud Messaging (FCM) API	For push notifications.
AWS SDK for Kotlin	AWS services integration.
Google Cloud APIs	Various cloud services for computing, storage, and AI.
Google Map API	Integrating Google Maps in the Kotlin application.

12.9 CASE STUDY 1: Using Google Map API in Kotlin

To use Google Maps API in a **Kotlin** project (Android app), we need to go through the following steps.

STEP 1. Enable Google Maps API

1. Open https://console.cloud.google.com/.
2. Create a new project or select an existing one.
3. Navigate to **APIs & Services ➤ Library**.

CHAPTER 12   WORKING WITH API AND NETWORKING

4. Locate and enable **Google Maps SDK for Android**.
5. Go to **Credentials**, create an **API Key**, and restrict it to Android apps.

STEP 2. Add Dependencies

Open your app's build.Gradle.kt file and add the following before syncing our app:

```
dependencies {
    implementation("com.google.android.gms:play-services-maps:18.2.0")
    implementation("com.google.android.gms:play-services-location:21.0.1")
// For GPS & location updates
}
```

STEP 3. Add API Key to Manifest

In AndroidManifest.xml, add:

```
<manifest>
<uses-permission android:name="android.permission.ACCESS_FINE_LOCATION"/>
<uses-permission android:name="android.permission.ACCESS_COARSE_LOCATION"/>

<application>
<meta-data
Android:name="com.google.android.geo.API_KEY"
android:value="YOUR_API_KEY_HERE"/>
</application>
</manifest>
```

Replace "YOUR_API_KEY_HERE" with your actual **Google Maps API key**.

STEP 4. Add a Map Fragment

In res/layout/activity_main.xml, add:

```
<fragment
android:id="@+id/mapFragment"
android:name="com.google.android.gms.maps.SupportMapFragment"
android:layout_width="match_parent"
android:layout_height="match_parent"/>
```

STEP 5. Load the Map in Kotlin

Modify MainActivity.kt:

```kotlin
import android.os.Bundle
import androidx.appcompat.app.AppCompatActivity
import com.google.android.gms.maps.CameraUpdateFactory
import com.google.android.gms.maps.GoogleMap
import com.google.android.gms.maps.OnMapReadyCallback
import com.google.android.gms.maps.SupportMapFragment
import com.google.android.gms.maps.model.LatLng
import com.google.android.gms.maps.model.MarkerOptions

class MainActivity : AppCompatActivity(), OnMapReadyCallback {
    private lateinit var googleMap: GoogleMap

    override fun onCreate(savedInstanceState: Bundle?) {
super.onCreate(savedInstanceState)
setContentView(R.layout.activity_main)

        // Load the map
valmapFragment = supportFragmentManager
            .findFragmentById(R.id.mapFragment) as SupportMapFragment
mapFragment.getMapAsync(this)
    }

    override fun onMapReady(map: GoogleMap) {
googleMap = map

        // Set initial location (e.g., New York)
valnewYork = LatLng(40.7128, -74.0060)
googleMap.addMarker(MarkerOptions().position(newYork).title("New York"))
googleMap.moveCamera(CameraUpdateFactory.newLatLngZoom(newYork, 12f))
    }
}
```

STEP 6. Run the App

Run your app on an **emulator with Google Play services** or an actual Android device.

Extra Features

1. **Enable Location Tracking**

   a. Request **runtime permissions** (ACCESS_FINE_LOCATION).

   b. Use FusedLocationProviderClient to retrieve the user's location.

2. **Customize Markers & Polylines**

   a. Add custom marker icons.

   b. Draw routes using PolylineOptions.

3. **Google Places API**

   a. Get place details, autocomplete search, etc.

12.10 CASE STUDY 2: Using MQTT API in Kotlin

To use MQTT (Message Queuing Telemetry Transport) in a **Kotlin** application within **IntelliJ IDEA**, you can use the **Eclipse Paho MQTT** client.

STEP 1. Create a New Kotlin Project in IntelliJ IDEA

1. Open IntelliJ IDEA and create a **New Project**.

2. Select **Kotlin** (JVM) and click **Next**.

3. Name your project and choose a location.

4. Click **Finish**.

STEP 2. Add MQTT Dependency

Edit your build.gradle.kts file to include the **Paho MQTT** library:

```kotlin
CopyEdit
dependencies {
    implementation("org.eclipse.paho:org.eclipse.paho.client.mqttv3:1.2.5")
}
```

Sync the project to download dependencies.

STEP 3. Implement MQTT Client in Kotlin

Create a new Kotlin file, e.g., MqttClientExample.kt, and add the following:

```kotlin
CopyEdit
import org.eclipse.paho.client.mqttv3.*
import org.eclipse.paho.client.mqttv3.persist.MemoryPersistence

fun main() {
val broker = "tcp://broker.hivemq.com:1883" // Public broker for testing
valclientId = "KotlinMQTTClient"
val topic = "test/kotlin/mqtt"
val persistence = MemoryPersistence()

    try {
val client = MqttClient(broker, clientId, persistence)

        // MQTT Callback
client.setCallback(object : MqttCallback {
            override fun connectionLost(cause: Throwable?) {
println("Connection lost: ${cause?.message}")
            }

            override fun messageArrived(topic: String?, message:
            MqttMessage?) {
println("Message received: ${message.toString()} on topic: $topic")
            }
```

CHAPTER 12   WORKING WITH API AND NETWORKING

```kotlin
            override fun deliveryComplete(token: IMqttDeliveryToken?) {
                println("Message delivered")
            }
        })

        // MQTT Connection Options
        val options = MqttConnectOptions().apply {
            isCleanSession = true
        }

        println("Connecting to broker: $broker")
        client.connect(options)
        println("Connected!")

        // Subscribe to a Topic
        client.subscribe(topic, 1)

        // Publish a Message
        val message = MqttMessage("Hello from Kotlin!".toByteArray()).apply {
            qos = 1
        }
        println("Publishing message: ${message.toString()}")
        client.publish(topic, message)
        println("Message published")

        // Keep running to listen for messages
        Thread.sleep(5000)

        // Disconnect
        client.disconnect()
        println("Disconnected")
    } catch (e: MqttException) {
        e.printStackTrace()
    }
}
```

STEP 4. Run the MQTT Client

1. In IntelliJ IDEA, right-click the MqttClientExample.kt file.
2. Click Run 'MqttClientExampleKt'.
3. You should see logs confirming connection, message publishing, and subscription.

STEP 5. Explanation

1. Uses broker.hivemq.com:1883 (public broker) for testing.
2. Implements MqttCallback for handling incoming messages.
3. Connects, subscribes, publishes a message, and listens for responses.

STEP 6. Extra Features

Secure Connection (TLS/SSL): Use ssl://broker:8883.

User Authentication: Set username and password in MqttConnectOptions.

Keep Alive: Adjust setKeepAliveInterval() to maintain a connection.

12.11 Conclusion and Future Scope

There are over 100 APIs that are usable in the Kotlin programming language. We have discussed the most popular APIs in various categories, including Android API, networking API, database API, graphical API, machine learning API, multimedia API, IoT API, and cloud API, among others. We have illustrated two popular APIs: the MQTT API and the Google Location API. Retrofit simplifies HTTP requests in Kotlin. The APIs discussed are not the only APIs available for Kotlin. New APIs are being introduced at regular intervals. The next edition of this book will update the new APIs that will be released in or after 2025.

CHAPTER 12   WORKING WITH API AND NETWORKING

12.12 Test Your Knowledge

In order to test your knowledge for after reading this chapter, here are following 10 MCQ (Multiple Choice Questions) on Networking APIs in Kotlin, focusing on Ktor and Retrofit:

1. What is Retrofit used for in Kotlin?

    a. database management

    b. making network requests

    c. UI rendering dependency injection

2. Which dependency is required to use Retrofit in Kotlin?

    a. com.squareup.retrofit2:retrofit

    b. io.ktor:ktor-client-core

    c. androidx.lifecycle:lifecycle-viewmodel

    d. com.google.dagger:dagger

3. What does Retrofit use to convert JSON responses into Kotlin objects?

    a. Moshi

    b. Gson

    c. Kotlin Serialization

    d. All of the above

4. In Retrofit, which function makes an API request asynchronously?

    a. execute()

    b. enqueue()

    c. start()

    d. runBlocking {}

CHAPTER 12 WORKING WITH API AND NETWORKING

5. What is the primary advantage of Ktor over Retrofit?

    a. Ktor is synchronous by default.

    b. Ktor supports WebSocket communication.

    c. Ktor does not require coroutines.

    d. Retrofit is faster than Ktor.

6. Which Ktor module is used for JSON serialization?

    a. ktor-client-serialization

    b. ktor-client-gson

    c. ktor-client-json

    d. ktor-serialization-kotlinx-json

7. How do you define a GET request in Retrofit?

    a. @HttpGet("/posts")

    b. @Request(GET, "posts")

    c. @GET("posts")

    d. GET("posts")

8. What is the default HTTP engine used by Ktor Client?

    a. OkHttp

    b. CIO

    c. Apache

    d. None

9. Which function in Ktor makes a network call asynchronously?

    a. suspend fun

    b. runBlocking {}

    c. launch {}

    d. execute()

CHAPTER 12   WORKING WITH API AND NETWORKING

10. What is the main purpose of `ContentNegotiation` in Ktor?

    a. handling authentication

    b. enabling logging

    c. serializing and deserializing request/response bodies

    d. handling API errors

12.13 Answers

1. b
2. a
3. d
4. b
5. b
6. d
7. c
8. b
9. a
10. c

CHAPTER 13

Advanced Kotlin Programming

13.1 Introduction

The Alphabet, Inc. (then Google) declared Kotlin an official language for Android in 2017. In 2019, Google revised their former declaration about Kotlin and declared Kotlin the preferred language for Android app development. Intellij IDEA has two associations for Kotlin. The first association is .kt (DOT K-T) is used for Kotlin source code and treated as a Kotlin class. The second association is .kts (DOT K-T-S), which is used for Kotlin script or Gradle Kotlin DSL.

Kotlin enhances Android development by reducing boilerplate, improving safety, and simplifying asynchronous programming. Kotlin may call Java code and vice versa. This feature of Kotlin makes the migration of an existing Java project to Kotlin possible. Java allows null by default that leads to null pointer exceptions (NPEs). Kotlin has native null safety (? and !! operators) support to prevent NPEs and to reduce the possibility of runtime crashes [1]. Kotlin deals with the notorious null pointer exceptions in Java by focusing on null safety and integrating null safety operators in Kotlin [2]. In addition to null safety, this chapter also covers high order functions, lambdas, lazy initialization, and property delegation, as shown in Figure 13-1.

CHAPTER 13 ADVANCED KOTLIN PROGRAMMING

Figure 13-1. Advanced concepts in Kotlin

13.2 Null Safety

Kotlin offers several techniques to handle null values, including the non-null assertion (!!), safe call operator (?.), safe casts (as?), let scope function, and the Elvis operator (?:).

CHAPTER 13 ADVANCED KOTLIN PROGRAMMING

Safe Call Operator in Kotlin

The operator safe call (?.) in Kotlin allows accessing a property or calling a function only when the object is not null. Safe call is one of the three most used Kotlin features. The other two most used features in Kotlin are type inference and lambda [3].

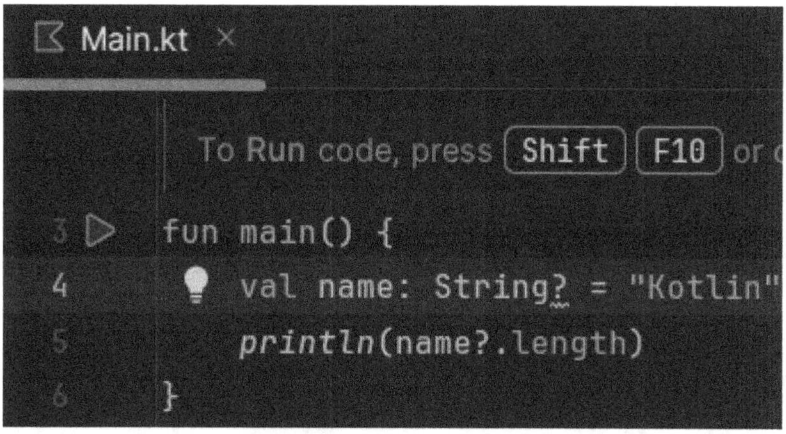

```
fun main() {
    val name: String? = "Kotlin"
    println(name?.length)
}
```

Figure 13-2. Safe call operator when value is not null

Output is 6 for the program shown in Figure 13-2. Here name is not null, which is why ?.length is executed.

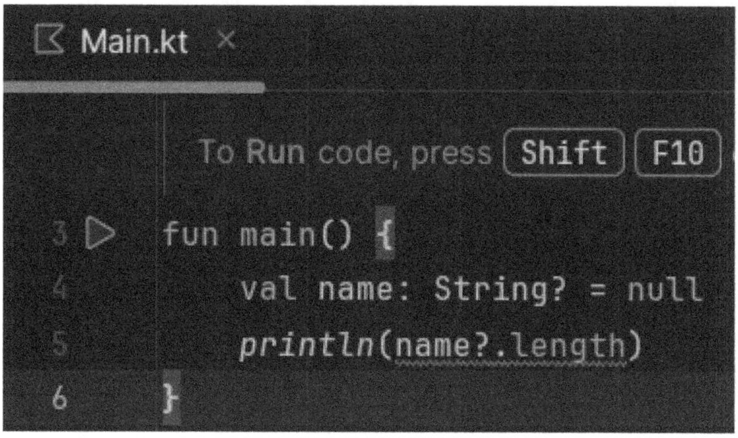

```
fun main() {
    val name: String? = null
    println(name?.length)
}
```

Figure 13-3. Safe call operator when value is null

We are getting null output after executing the program shown in Figure 13-3. Here name is null, and Kotlin returns null instead of throwing an error.

CHAPTER 13   ADVANCED KOTLIN PROGRAMMING

Elvis Operator in Kotlin

The Elvis operator (?:) provides a default value if the left-hand side of the Elvis operator is null [4]. The Elvis operator is developed in Kotlin to change the literal value associated with the Elvis operator in Kotlin code by changing the string literal to a constant string (shown in 13-5) as shown in Figure 13-4.

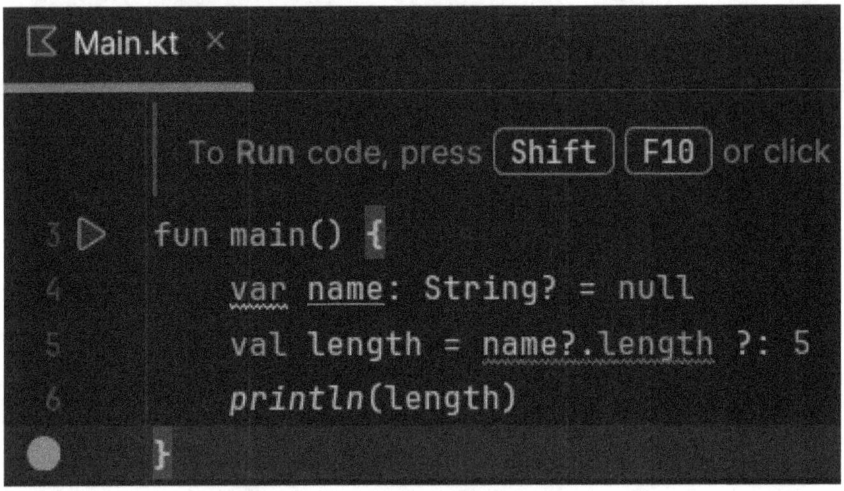

```kotlin
fun main() {
    var name: String? = null
    val length = name?.length ?: 5
    println(length)
}
```

Figure 13-4.   Elvis operator to assign some value when variable is null

Output is 5 for the Kotlin program shown in Figure 13-4, as the Elvis operator assigns a value of 5 to the `length` variable. The name "Elvis operator" refers to the fact that when its common notation, ?:, is not viewed with technical glass, it looks like the signature hairstyle of famous singer Elvis Presley, as shown in Figure 13-5 [5].

CHAPTER 13 ADVANCED KOTLIN PROGRAMMING

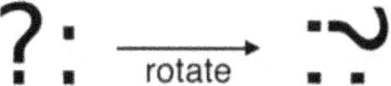

Elvis operator

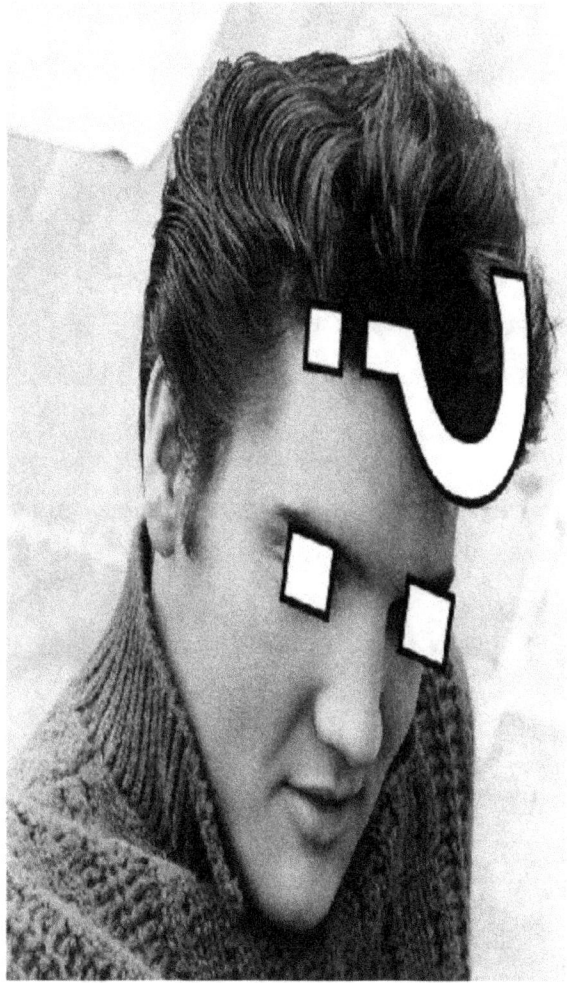

Figure 13-5. Elvis Presley signature hairstyle

CHAPTER 13 ADVANCED KOTLIN PROGRAMMING

Non-Null Assertion (!!) in Kotlin

The non-null assertion (!!) in Kotlin asserts that the variable is a non-null variable, throwing an NPE if it is actually null. Kotlin emphasizes type safety by introducing non-nullable types. This makes programs less prone to being null [2].

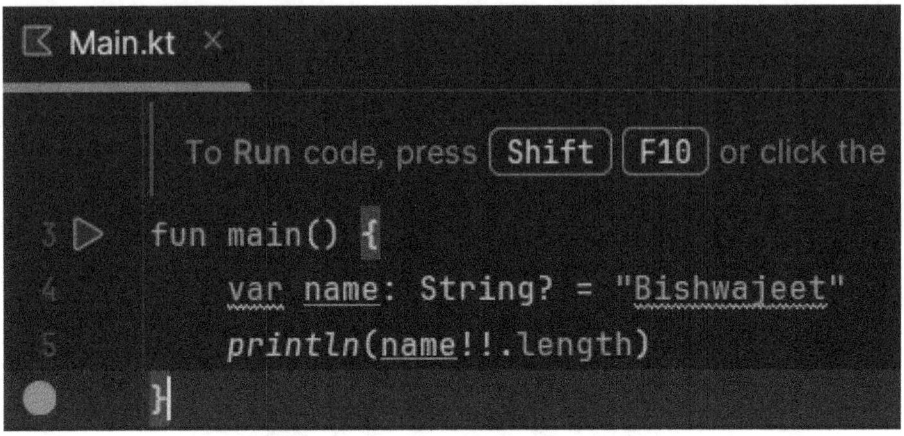

```
fun main() {
    var name: String? = "Bishwajeet"
    println(name!!.length)
}
```

Figure 13-6. Non-null assertion when variable is not null

Output is 10 when we execute the non-null assertion operator on a variable that is not null but has a length of 10 in Kotlin, as shown in Figure 13-6.

```
fun main() {
    var name: String? = null
    println(name!!.length)
}
```

Figure 13-7. Non-null assertion when variable is not null

CHAPTER 13 ADVANCED KOTLIN PROGRAMMING

In the Kotlin program shown in Figure 13-7, we unknowingly assert that name is not null but in reality it is null. Kotlin throws a null pointer exception as the String type variable name is null, as shown in Figure 13-8.

```
"C:\Program Files\Eclipse Adoptium\jdk-21.0.2.13-hotspot\bin\java.exe"
Exception in thread "main" java.lang.NullPointerException Create breakpoint
    at MainKt.main(Main.kt:5)
    at MainKt.main(Main.kt)

Process finished with exit code 1
```

Figure 13-8. *Kotlin program terminated with a NullPointerException at line 5 in Main.kt, indicating an attempt to access or operate on a null reference*

So, we conclude that we shall use a non-null assertion (!!) only when we are 100% sure that the variable is never null.

Safe Cast (as?)

The safe cast (as?) operator tries to cast an object but returns null if the cast fails, instead of throwing an exception. Kotlin's characteristic features are safety, compatibility with Java, and suitability for Android app development. These features have made Kotlin the second most preferred programming language for Android app development, following Java [6].

```
Main.kt
                    To Run code, press  Shift  F10  or click the
3   fun main() {
4       val obj: Any = "Bishwajeet"
5       val str: String? =obj as? String
6       println(str)
    }
```

Figure 13-9. *Kotlin program with safe cast*

CHAPTER 13 ADVANCED KOTLIN PROGRAMMING

Output is Bishwajeet when we execute the Kotlin program shown in Figure 13-9 because safe cast successfully type cast obj as String and store typecasted value on str.

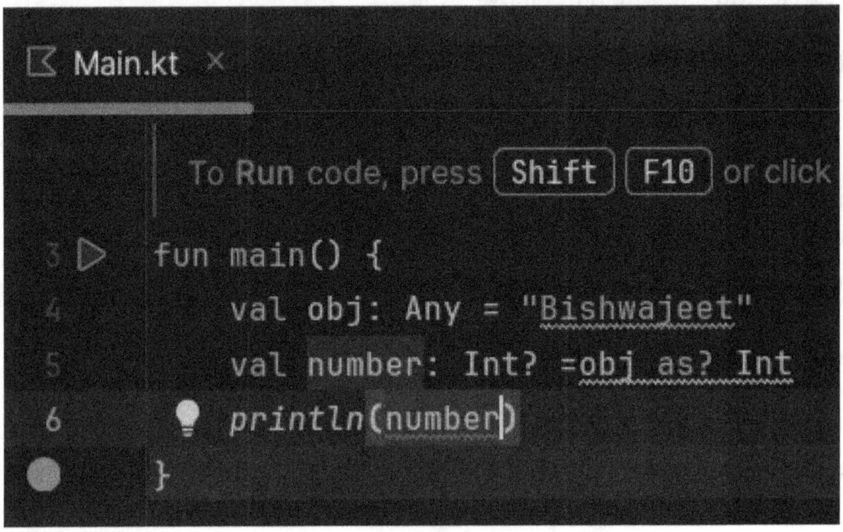

```
fun main() {
    val obj: Any = "Bishwajeet"
    val number: Int? =obj as? Int
    println(number)
}
```

Figure 13-10. Kotlin program with unsuccessful safe cast

Output is null as safe cast failed to type cast the obj as an integer based on the syntax of Kotlin program written in Figure 13-10.

let Scope Function

The let function executes code only if the variable is not null.

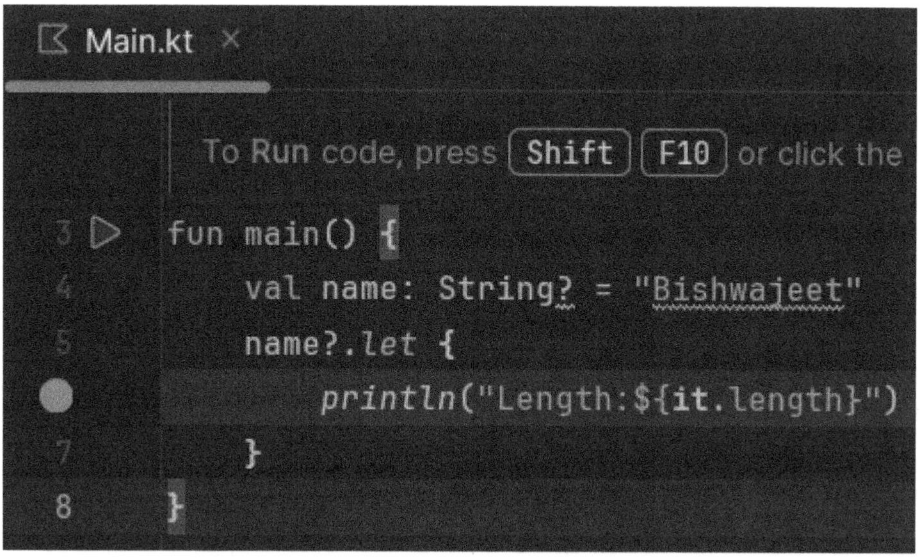
Main.kt
To Run code, press Shift F10 or click the
fun main() {
val name: String? = "Bishwajeet"
name?.let {
println("Length:${it.length}")
}
}

***Figure 13-11.** Kotlin program with let scope function*

Output is 10 when the Kotlin program using the `let` scope function is executed and when the variable has a value stored with a length of 10, as shown in Figure 13-11.

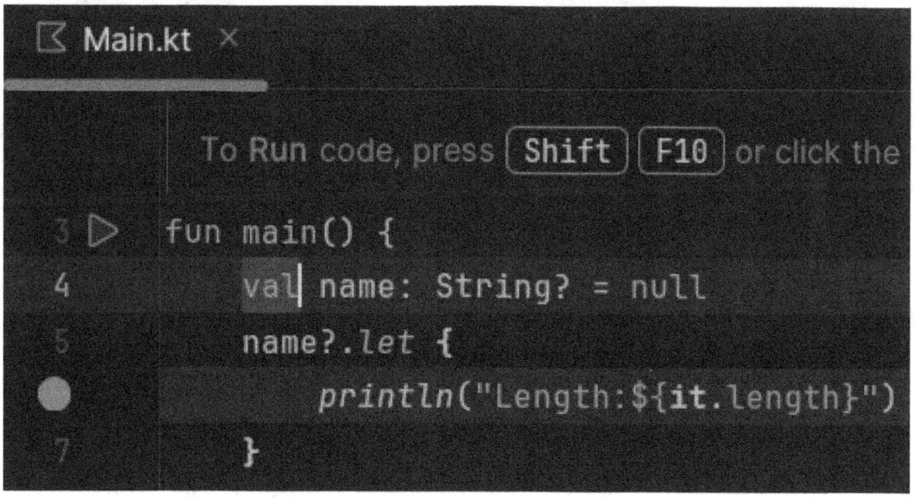
Main.kt
To Run code, press Shift F10 or click the
fun main() {
val name: String? = null
name?.let {
println("Length:${it.length}")
}

***Figure 13-12.** Kotlin program with let scope function*

There is no output as the `let` scope function did not allow it to execute because the variable is a null, as shown in the Kotlin program illustrated in Figure 13-12.

13.3 Higher-Order Functions and Lambdas

Java did not have functional features (e.g., streams, lambdas) till after Java 7. These functional features were first introduced in Java 8. Whereas, Kotlin has higher-order functions, such as lambda, that make functional programming easier as compared to traditional Java programming. A higher-order function is a special type of function that either takes another function as a parameter or returns a function. A lambda is an anonymous function that can be passed as an argument. Both Kotlin and Swift leverage higher-order functions extensively. Kotlin has rich support for higher-order functions that help developers in getting the benefits of encapsulation in mobile devices [7].

Higher-Order Function with Lambda

```kotlin
fun calculate (a:Int,b:Int, operation: (Int, Int)-> Int):Int{
    return operation(a, b) // Calls the Lambda Function
}

fun main() {
    //Passing Lambda Function
    val sum = calculate( a: 5, b: 3) {x,y -> x + y}
    val multiply = calculate ( a: 5, b: 3) {x,y -> x * y}
    println("Sum: $sum")
    println("Multiply: $multiply")
}
```

Figure 13-13. Kotlin program of higher-order functions with lambda

The Kotlin program shown in Figure 13-13 demonstrates the use of higher-order functions and lambda expressions and has the following explanation.

CHAPTER 13 ADVANCED KOTLIN PROGRAMMING

Explanation:

1. **Higher-Order Function (`calculate`):**

   a. It takes three parameters:

   a and b are two integers.

   An operation function that accepts a and b and returns an integer.

   b. Higher-order function calls the lambda function passed as operation on a and b.

2. **Main Function Execution:**

   a. Calls `calculate(5,3)`, passing a lambda function for addition (x, y -> x + y).

   b. Calls `calculate(5,3)`, passing a lambda function for multiplication (x, y -> x * y).

   c. Prints the results.

This showcases Kotlin's ability to use lambda functions to pass behavior as a parameter, making code more flexible and reusable.

```
"C:\Program Files\Eclipse Adoptium\jdk-21.0.2.13-hotspot\bin\java.exe"
Sum: 8
Multiply: 15
```

Figure 13-14. Output of Kotlin program of higher-order functions with lambda

The sum is 8 and result of multiplying is 15; these are the two outputs of the Kotlin program of higher-order function with lambda shown in Figure 13-14.

CHAPTER 13   ADVANCED KOTLIN PROGRAMMING

Higher-Order Function Returns a Function

```kotlin
fun operation(type: String): (Int, Int) -> Int {
    return when (type) {
        "add" -> { a, b -> a + b }
        "multiply" -> { a, b -> a * b }
        else -> { _, _ -> 0 } // Default case
    }
}

fun main() {
    val addFunction = operation(type = "add")           // Returns a function that adds two numbers
    val multiplyFunction = operation(type = "multiply") // Returns a function that multiplies two numbers

    println("Addition: ${addFunction(7, 2)}")           // Output: 8
    println("Multiplication: ${multiplyFunction(7, 2)}") // Output: 15
}
```

Figure 13-15. Returns a function from a higher-order function in Kotlin

In Kotlin, a higher-order function can return another function. Kotlin usually support higher-order functions that allow you to provide functions as parameters and return functions from other functions. Figure 13-15 is an example of a Kotlin program that demonstrates this concept, and has the following explanation:

1. `operation(type: String)` is a higher-order function in Kotlin returning a function of type `(Int, Int) -> Int`.

2. Based on the `type` parameter, it returns:

    a. a lambda for addition: `{ a, b -> a + b }`

    b. a lambda for multiplication: `{ a, b -> a * b }`

3. In `main()`, the returned functions are stored in `addFunction` and `multiplyFunction`, then executed with arguments; they give output shown in Figure 13-16.

CHAPTER 13 ADVANCED KOTLIN PROGRAMMING

```
"C:\Program Files\Eclipse Adoptium\jdk-21.0.2.13-hotspot\bin\java.exe"
Addition: 9
Multiplication: 14

Process finished with exit code 0
```

Figure 13-16. Output of Kotlin program returning a function from a higher-order function

Using Lambda with List Functions

Kotlin provides powerful **lambda expressions** that can be used with list functions like map, filter, forEach, reduce, any, all, count, and more. Figure 13-17 is an example demonstrating the use of lambda functions with a list.

```kotlin
fun main() {
    val numbers = listOf(1, 2, 3, 4, 5, 6, 7, 8, 9, 10)
    // Using filter: Get even numbers
    val evenNumbers = numbers.filter { it % 2 == 0 }
    println("Even Numbers: $evenNumbers")  // Output: [2, 4, 6, 8, 10]
    // Using map: Square each number
    val squaredNumbers = numbers.map { it * it }
    println("Squared Numbers: $squaredNumbers")  // Output: [1, 4, 9, 16, 25, 36, 49, 64, 81, 100]
    // Using forEach: Print each number
    numbers.forEach { println("Number: $it") }
    // Using reduce: Sum of all numbers
    val sum = numbers.reduce { acc, num -> acc + num }
    println("Sum of Numbers: $sum")  // Output: 55
    // Using any: Check if there's any number greater than 8
    val hasLargeNumber = numbers.any { it > 8 }
    println("Has number > 8: $hasLargeNumber")  // Output: true
    // Using all: Check if all numbers are positive
    val allPositive = numbers.all { it > 0 }
    println("All numbers are positive: $allPositive")  // Output: true
    // Using count: Count numbers greater than 5
    val countGreaterThan5 = numbers.count { it > 5 }
    println("Numbers greater than 5: $countGreaterThan5")  // Output: 5
}
```

Figure 13-17. Kotlin program of lambda expression with list function

CHAPTER 13 ADVANCED KOTLIN PROGRAMMING

The filter {it % 2 == 0} is used to filter even numbers. The map {it * it} is used to transform each element (squares it). The forEach {println(it) } is used to iterate and print each item. The reduce {acc, num -> acc + num} accumulates values (sum). The any {it > 8} returns true if **any** number is greater than 8. The all {it > 0} returns true if **all** numbers are positive. The count { it > 5 } counts elements greater than 5, as shown in Figure 13-18.

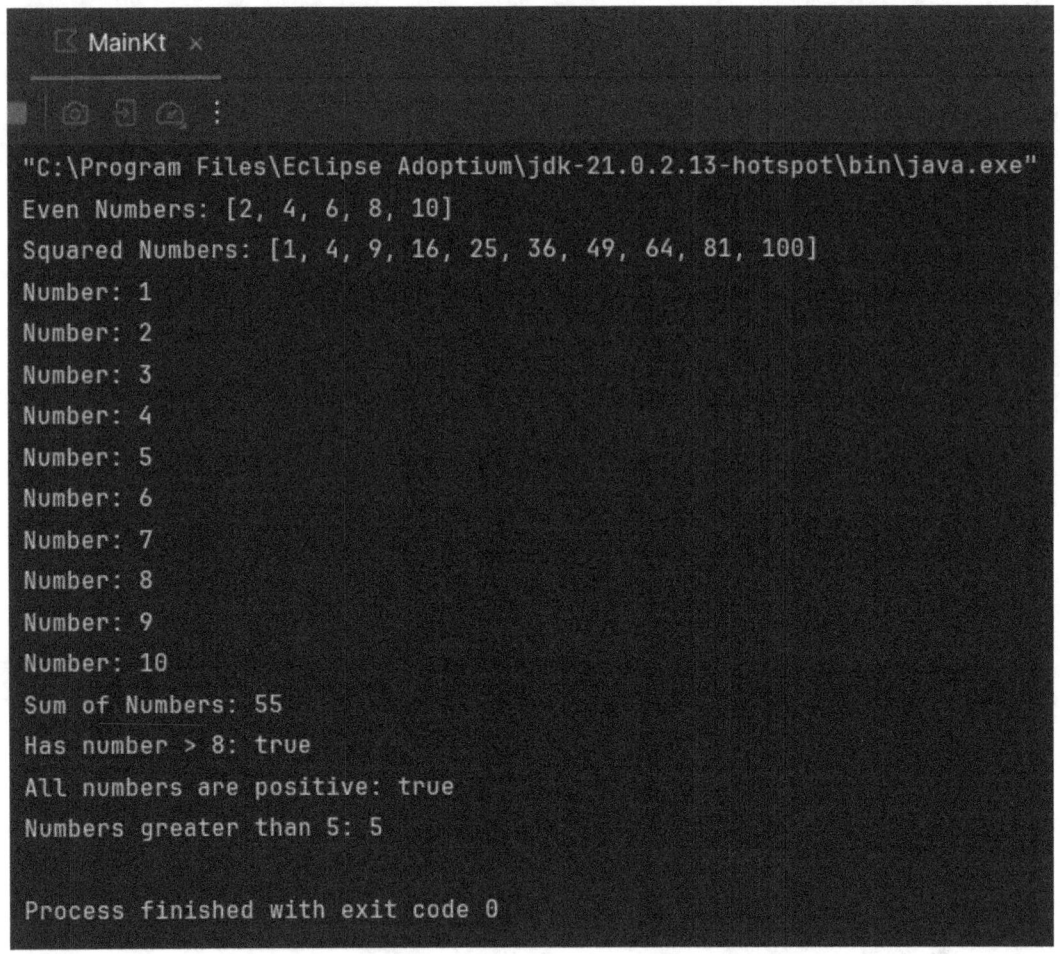

Figure 13-18. *Output of Kotlin lambda expression with list function*

13.4 Lazy Initialization

Lazy initialization in Kotlin is a mechanism where an object is initialized only when it is accessed for the first time rather than at the time of declaration. Lazy initialization improves performance and reduces unnecessary memory usage as it works on a principle called "If not needed then it never initializes." First access triggers initialization, and subsequent accesses return cached value, as shown in Figure 13-19.

```kotlin
class LazyExample {
    val lazyValue: String by lazy {
        println("Initializing lazyValue...")
        "Hello, Kotlin!"
    }
}

fun main() {
    val example = LazyExample()

    println("Before accessing lazyValue")
    println(example.lazyValue) // First access triggers initialization
    println(example.lazyValue) // Subsequent accesses return cached value
}
```

Figure 13-19. Kotlin program of lazy initialization

The code in Figure 13-19 has following explanation:

1. **lazyValue is initialized lazily using by lazy {}**

    a. The first time `lazyValue` is accessed, the block inside `lazy` executes.

    b. The result ("Hello, Kotlin!") is stored and reused for future accesses.

2. **In main():**

    a. `val example = LazyExample()` creates an object.

    b. "Before accessing lazyValue" is printed.

c. The first access (example.lazyValue) triggers **initialization**, prints "Initializing lazyValue...", and returns "Hello, Kotlin!" as shown in Figure 13-20.

d. The second access **returns the cached value** without re-initializing, as shown in Figure 13-20.

```
"C:\Program Files\Eclipse Adoptium\jdk-21.0.2.13-hotspot\bin\java.exe"
Before accessing lazyValue
Initializing lazyValue...
Hello, Kotlin!
Hello, Kotlin!

Process finished with exit code 0
```

Figure 13-20. *Output of Kotlin program with lazy initialization*

Lazy initialization (by lazy) delays object creation until it's needed. First access initializes the value, and subsequent accesses reuse it. This helps optimize memory and performance by preventing unnecessary computations. This technique is useful for initializing heavy resources, database connections, or API calls efficiently.

13.5 Property Delegation

A getter is a function that get the value of a property. A setter is a function that updates the value of a property. In Kotlin, we usually customize getter and setter for encapsulation, validation, transformation of data, and property delegation. Property delegation allows us to delegate the getter and setter logic of a property to another object instead of defining them manually.

CHAPTER 13 ADVANCED KOTLIN PROGRAMMING

```
import kotlin.properties.Delegates

class User {
    var name: String by Delegates.observable(initialValue = "Unknown") { _, old, new ->
        println("Name changed from $old to $new")
    }
}

fun main() {
    val user = User()

    user.name = "Alice"   // Triggers observer
    user.name = "Bob"     // Triggers observer
}
```

Figure 13-21. *Kotlin code of property delegation*

Kotlin provides built-in delegates like `Delegates.observable` to track property changes, as shown in the Kotlin program written in Figure 13-21. This code has the following explanation:

- `var name: String by Delegates.observable("Unknown")`
- Initializes `name` with `"Unknown."`
- Whenever `name` is changed, the **observer lambda function** is called.
- It prints the old and new values.
- **Setting** `user.name = "Alice"`
- The observer prints `"Name changed from Unknown to Alice"` as shown in Figure 13-22.
- **Setting** `user.name = "Bob"`
- The observer prints `"Name changed from Alice to Bob"` as shown in Figure 13-22.

301

```
MainKt

"C:\Program Files\Eclipse Adoptium\jdk-21.0.2.13-hotspot\bin\java.exe"
Name changed from Unknown to Alice
Name changed from Alice to Bob

Process finished with exit code 0
```

Figure 13-22. Output of Kotlin code of property delegation

13.6 Conclusion

In contrary to Java, which usually leads to null pointer exception, Kotlin offers several techniques to handle null values, including the non-null assertion (!!), safe call operator (?.), safe casts (as?), let scope function, and the Elvis operator. Kotlin provides powerful **lambda expressions** that can be used with list functions like map, filter, forEach, reduce, any, all, count, and more. Lazy initialization (by lazy) delays object creation until it's needed, which helps to improve perfromance and achieve memory optimization. Kotlin provides built-in delegates like Delegates.observable to track property changes.

13.7 Future Scope

In this era of ongoing evolution, every programming language is coming up with new versions with newer features; e.g., Python 1, 2,3 and Java 1,2,3,4,5,6,7,8,... and so on. Kotlin is also not a perfect language, and there is always scope for improvement. This book covers all available advanced concepts available at time of writing (null safety, property delegation, higher-order function, lambda, and so on), but when new features integrate in Kotlin, this advanced Kotlin programming chapter will need to be updated.

13.8 Real-Life Programming Practice

1. **Task Manager App:** This simple task manager app allows users to add tasks, check pending tasks, and mark tasks as completed.

   Concepts Covered:

   Null Safety: Safe call (?.), Elvis (?:), non-null assertion (!!)

   Higher-Order Functions & Lambdas: Functional programming for task filtering

   Lazy Initialization: Delaying the creation of a list until it's needed

   Property Delegation: Using `Delegates.observable` to track changes

   Code:

   ```
   import kotlin.properties.Delegates

   // Data Class for Task
   data class Task(val id: Int, var description: String, var isCompleted: Boolean = false)

   // Task Manager Class
   class TaskManager {
       // Lazy Initialization: Tasks list is created only when
           accessed
       private val tasks: MutableList<Task> by lazy { mutableListOf() }
       // Observable Property: Tracks changes in total tasks count
       var totalTasks: Int by Delegates.observable(0) { _, old, new ->
           println("Total tasks changed from $old to $new")
       }
   ```

```kotlin
        // Function to Add a Task (Using Safe Call Operator)
        fun addTask(description: String?) {
            val taskDescription = description?.trim() ?: "Untitled
            Task"   // Elvis Operator
            tasks.add(Task(tasks.size + 1, taskDescription))
            totalTasks = tasks.size   // Updates observable property
            println("Task Added: $taskDescription")
        }

        // Function to Display Pending Tasks (Using Higher-Order
           Function)
        fun showPendingTasks() {
            val pendingTasks = tasks.filter { !it.isCompleted }
            // Lambda
            if (pendingTasks.isEmpty()) {
                println("No pending tasks.")
            } else {
                println("Pending Tasks:")
                pendingTasks.forEach { println("- [ ] ${it.
                description}") }
            }
        }

        // Function to Mark a Task as Completed (Using Safe
           Call and !!)
        fun completeTask(taskId: Int) {
            val task = tasks.find { it.id == taskId }   // Finds
            task by ID
            task?.let {
                it.isCompleted = true
                println("Task Completed: ${it.description}")
            } ?: println("Task not found!") // Elvis Operator
        }
    }
```

CHAPTER 13 ADVANCED KOTLIN PROGRAMMING

```kotlin
// Main Function
fun main() {
    val taskManager = TaskManager()
    taskManager.addTask("Buy groceries")  // Adds task
    taskManager.addTask("Finish Kotlin project")
    taskManager.addTask(null)  // Handles null safely
    taskManager.showPendingTasks()  // Shows pending tasks

    taskManager.completeTask(1)  // Completes task 1
    taskManager.showPendingTasks()  // Shows pending tasks after completion
}
```

Output:

```
Total tasks changed from 0 to 1
Task Added: Buy groceries
Total tasks changed from 1 to 2
Task Added: Finish Kotlin project
Total tasks changed from 2 to 3
Task Added: Untitled Task
Pending Tasks:
- [ ] Buy groceries
- [ ] Finish Kotlin project
- [ ] Untitled Task
Task Completed: Buy groceries
Pending Tasks:
- [ ] Finish Kotlin project
- [ ] Untitled Task
```

13.9 Test Your Knowledge

1. What is a higher-order function in Kotlin?

   a. a function that takes another function as a a parameter or return a function

   b. a function with multiple parameters

   c. a function that can be overridden

   d. a function that has default arguments

2. What will be the output of the following code?

   ```
   fun calculate (a: Int, b : Int, operation: (Int, Int) -> Int): Int {
       return operation(a,b)
   }
   fun main() {
       Val result = calculate (4,2) {x,y -> x-y }
       println(result)
   }
   ```

   a. 6

   b. 2

   c. -2

   d. 4

3. What is lambda expression in Kotlin?

   a. a function without a return type

   b. an anonymous function that can be assigned to a variable or passed as an argument

   c. a function that must be declared inside a class

   d. a function that cannot take parameters

CHAPTER 13   ADVANCED KOTLIN PROGRAMMING

4. How do you write a lambda expression that multiplies two numbers in Kotlin?

   a. {a,b -> a * b}

   b. {a,b => a *b}

   c. fun (a,b) = a *b

   d. lambda (a,b) -> a * b

5. What does the ?. (safe call) operator do in Kotlin?

   a. forces a property to be non-null

   b. calls a method or property only if the object is not null

   c. converts a nullable type to a non-nullable

   d. throws a null pointer exception if the value is null

6. What is the output of the following code?

   ```
   Var name: String? =null
   Println(name?.length ?: "No Name")
   ```

   a. 0

   b. "No Name"

   c. Null

   d. Compilation Error

7. Which operator forces a nullable variable to be non-null, potentially throwing an exception?

   a. ?.

   b. ?:

   c. !!

   d. As?

8. Which built-in property delegate is used for lazy initialization in Kotlin?

    a. observable

    b. lazy

    c. vetoable

    d. delegate

9. What will happen if you access a lazy property before it is initialized?

    a. It will throw an error.

    b. It will return null.

    c. It will initialize the property on first access.

    d. The program will crash.

10. What will be the output of the following code?

    ```
    val numbers = listOf(1,2,3,4,5)
    val result = numbers.filter { it % 2 == 0 }
    println(result)
    ```

    a. [1,3,5]

    b. [2,4]

    c. [1,2,3,4,5]

    d. [2,4,6]

11. What is the purpose of the let function in Kotlin?

    a. executes a block of code only if the object is null

    b. executes a block of code only if the object is not null

    c. converts a nullable variable into a non-nullable one

    d. none of the above

12. What is the correct syntax to create a function that returns another function in Kotlin?

    a. fun getOperation(): (Int, Int) -> Int

    b. fun getOperation(): Int

    c. Fun getOperation() -> (Int, Int) -> Int

    d. Fun getOperation() : Function

13. In Android, which Kotlin feature is commonly used to avoid `NullPointerException` when accessing `SharedPreferences`?

    a. !! (Non Null Assertion)

    b. ?: (Elvis Operator)

    c. ?. (Safe Call)

    d. Observable

14. What does the following code do in Kotlin?

    `lateinit var text: String`

    a. initializes text with an empty string

    b. allows text to be assigned later before use

    c. makes text nullable

    d. prevents text from ever being null

13.10 Answers

1. a
2. b
3. b
4. a
5. b
6. b

CHAPTER 13   ADVANCED KOTLIN PROGRAMMING

7. c
8. b
9. c
10. b
11. b
12. a
13. c
14. b

CHAPTER 14

Data Analysis with Kotlin

14.1 Get Started with Kotlin Notebook

For data analysis, we use Kotlin Notebook, which is an interactive tool that lets you write clean code with visuals and analytics.

Following are the steps to install Kotlin Notebook.

> Step 1: Download and install the latest version of IntelliJ IDEA (Kotlin Notebook will require Ultimate Edition).
>
> Step 2: In IntelliJ IDEA, select IntelliJ IDEA ➤ Settings ➤ Plugins or File ➤ Settings ➤ Plugins.
>
> Step 3: In the Marketplace tab, browse to the Kotlin Notebook plugin and install it, as in Figure 14-1.

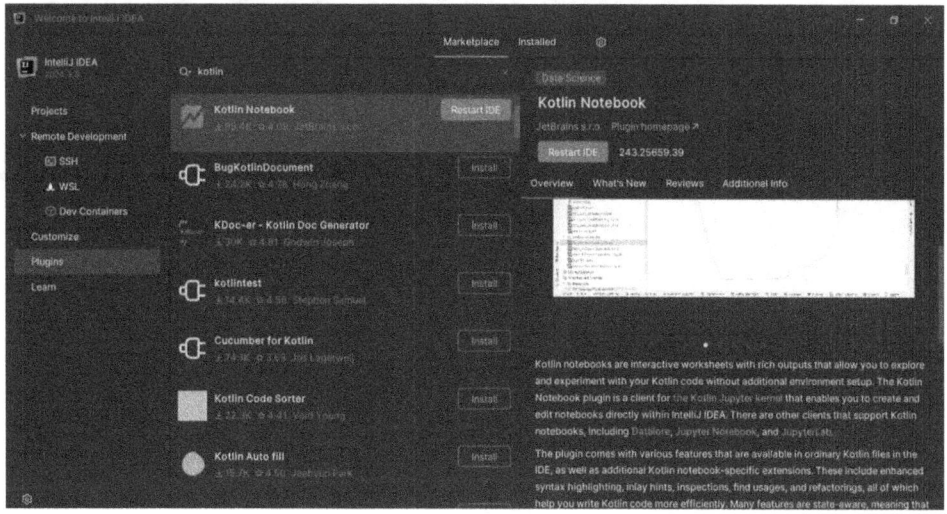

Figure 14-1. *Install Kotlin Notebook*

CHAPTER 14   DATA ANALYSIS WITH KOTLIN

Step 4: Click OK to apply changes and restart your IDE.

Next is to create a Kotlin notebook.

Step 1: Go to File ➤ New Project and give it an appropriate name, as in Figure 14-2.

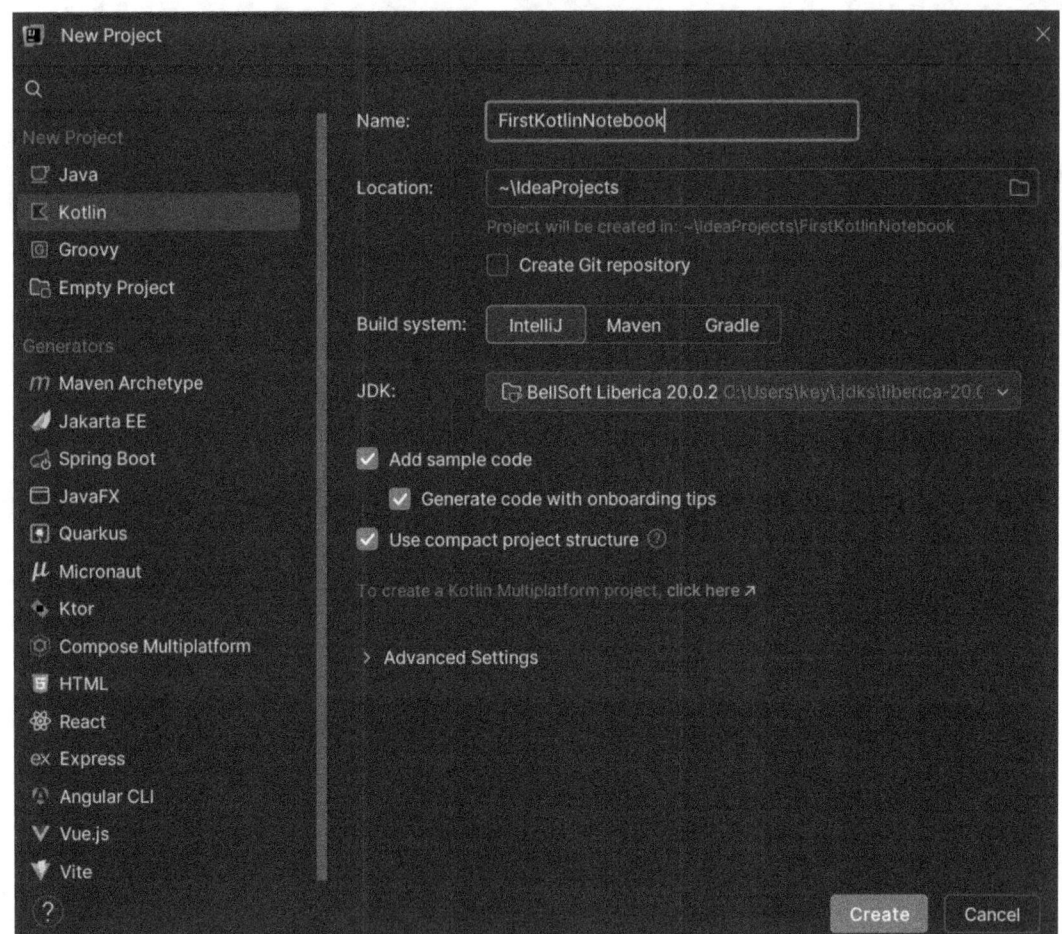

Figure 14-2. *Create a new project*

Step 2: After creating the project, select File ➤ New ➤ Kotlin Notebook and create one Kotlin notebook (Figure 14-3).

CHAPTER 14 DATA ANALYSIS WITH KOTLIN

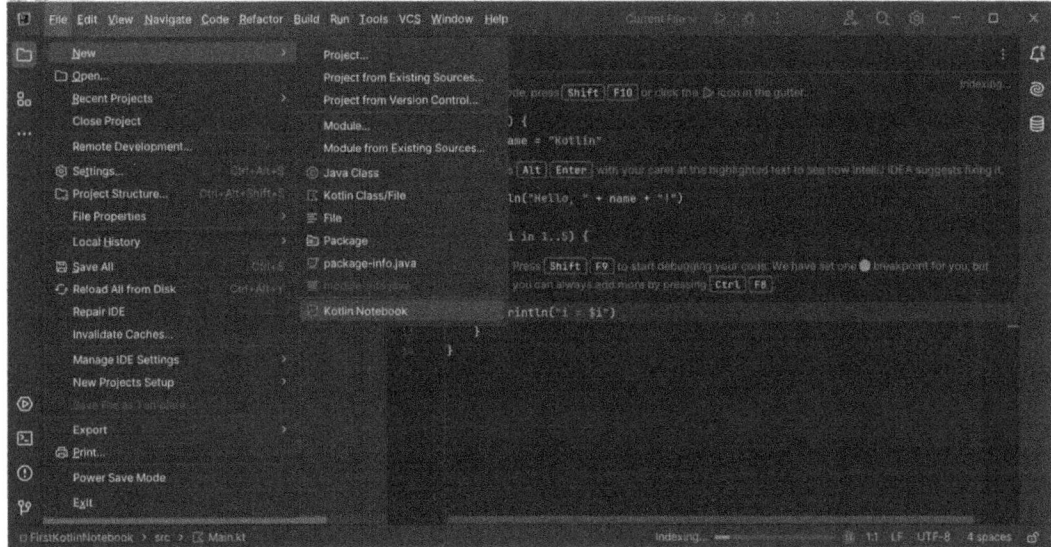

Figure 14-3. Create a notebook

Step 3: In an open tab, write the following code in the code cell:

println("This is my first kotlin notebook")

Step 4: To run the code cell, click the Play button or press Shift + Return (Figure 14-4).

```
▷ 1  println("Thin is my first notebook")
    ✓ [1] 559ms

        Thin is my first notebook
```

Figure 14-4. Run code

Step 5: Add a markdown cell by clicking the Add Markdown Cell button.

Step 6: Write any title, like New Operation, and run it like mentioned in Step 4.

313

Step 7: In a new cell, write 30+10 and run it (Figure 14-5).

Figure 14-5. *New Operations run*

Step 8: Add a new cell and declare one variable a = 10 and run it. After that, add a new cell and print a*a. See Figure 14-6.

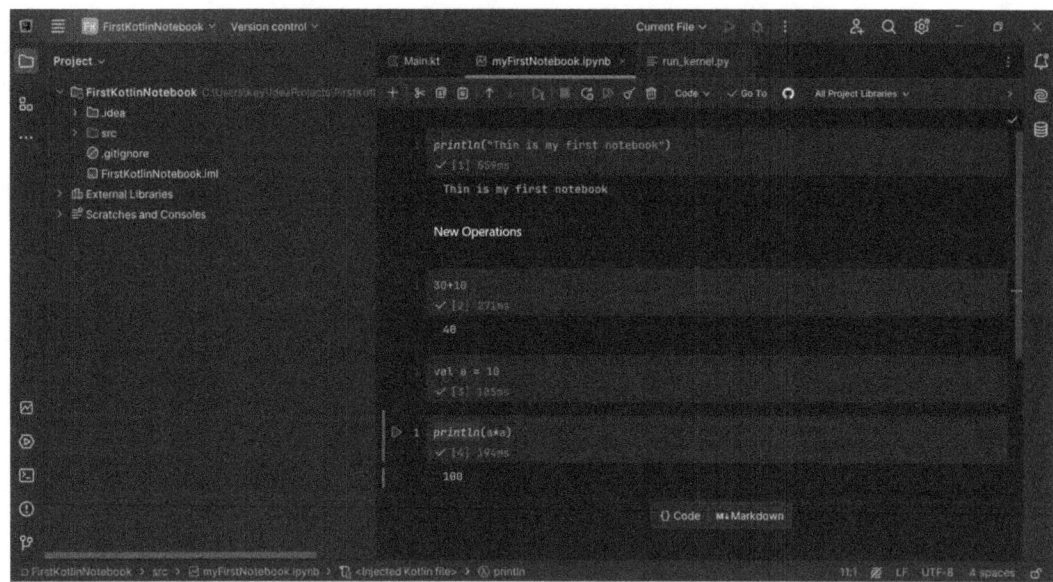

Figure 14-6. *Kotlin notebook with all operations*

Step 9: Run all code.

That's it. We have created out first Kotlin notebook successfully.

CHAPTER 14 DATA ANALYSIS WITH KOTLIN

14.2 Add Library to Kotlin Notebook

Let's add Kotlin library dependencies to the Kotlin library. We will add Kandy and Dataframe libraries, as follows.

Step 1: Create notebook and add code cell.

Step 2: Enter the code shown in Figure 14-7.

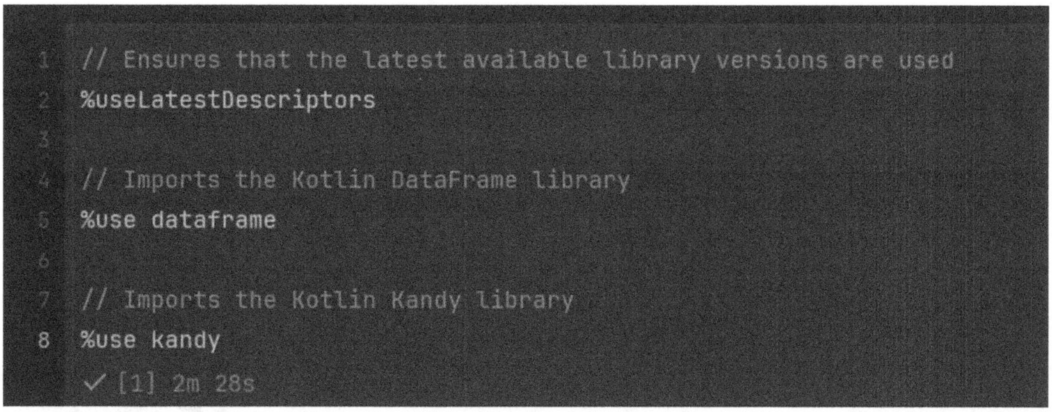

```
// Ensures that the latest available library versions are used
%useLatestDescriptors

// Imports the Kotlin DataFrame library
%use dataframe

// Imports the Kotlin Kandy library
%use kandy
```

Figure 14-7. Add libraries

Step 3: Run the cell. It will download all the required libraries, so it will take some time.

Step 4: To import a raw CSV file, write the code shown in Figure 14-8.

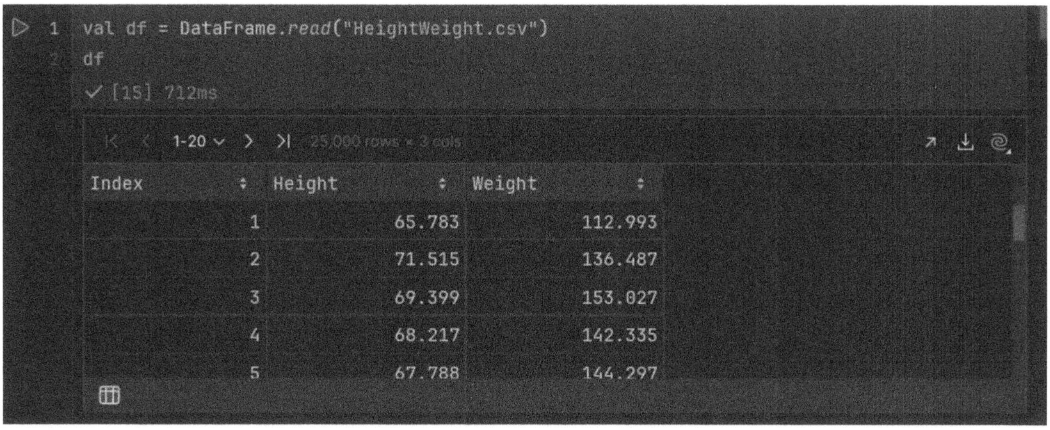

```
val df = DataFrame.read("HeightWeight.csv")
df
```

Index	Height	Weight
1	65.783	112.993
2	71.515	136.487
3	69.399	153.027
4	68.217	142.335
5	67.788	144.297

Figure 14-8. Read CSV file and print

315

CHAPTER 14   DATA ANALYSIS WITH KOTLIN

14.3 Working with Data Sources

We can read data from JSON files, and also we can update, add, filter, or remove data from such files. Following are the steps to follow.

>Step 1: Create a new project.

>Step 2: Create a new Kotlin notebook.

>Step 3: Add the `people.json` file (Figure 14-9).

Figure 14-9. The people.json file

>Step 4: In a new Kotlin notebook, add the required libraries, as shown in the previous section.

>Step 5: Read the JSON file. Figure 14-10 shows the code.

CHAPTER 14   DATA ANALYSIS WITH KOTLIN

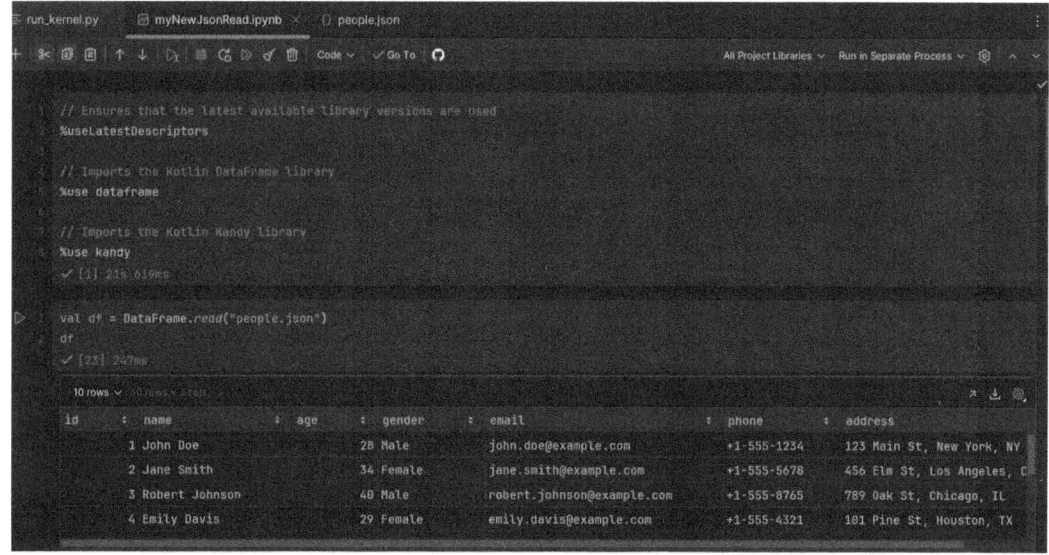

Figure 14-10. Read JSON file

Step 6: Let's check the type of each column in our dataset using the function schema(). Figure 14-11 shows that.

Figure 14-11. JSON file schema

Step 7: Let's use a filter function to filter a group of people having an age higher than 30. Figure 14-12 shows that.

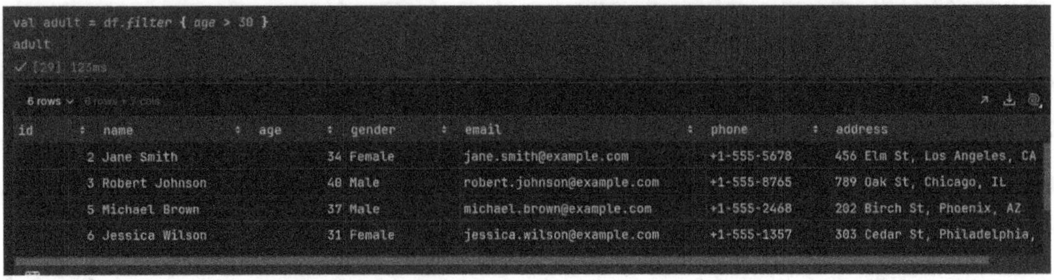

CHAPTER 14   DATA ANALYSIS WITH KOTLIN

Figure 14-12. The adult data filter

Step 8: Add a new schema named birthyear to the JSON file. Figure 14-13 shows that.

Figure 14-13. Add birthyear

Step 9: Remove the schema age. Figure 14-14 shows that.

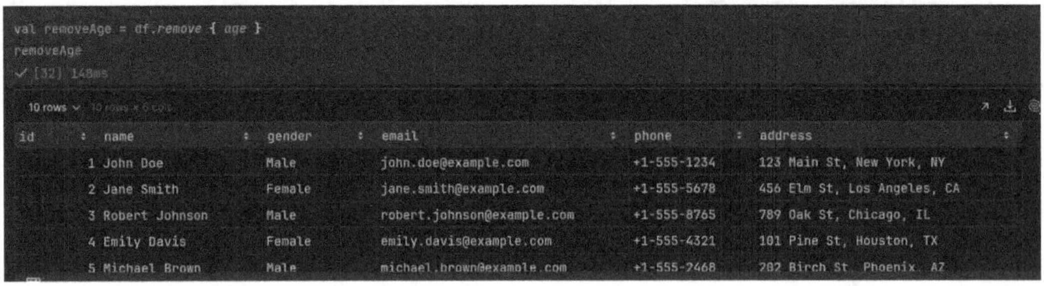

Figure 14-14. Remove age

Step 10: Save the removed age data to our people.json file using the writeJson() function. Figure 14-15 shows that.

CHAPTER 14 DATA ANALYSIS WITH KOTLIN

```
removeAge.writeJson("people.json")
✓ [46] 40ms
```

Figure 14-15. *Save JSON file*

Step 11: Convert this dataframe to an HTML table and open in a browser. Figure 14-16 shows how we can do so.

```
removeAge.toStandaloneHTML(DisplayConfiguration(rowsLimit = null)).openInBrowser()
✓ [48] 1s 86ms
```

Figure 14-16. *Convert dataframe to HTML table*

Step 12: Figure 14-17 shows the data converted from dataframe to HTML table.

id	name	gender	email	phone	address
1	John Doe	Male	john.doe@example.com	+1-555-1234	123 Main St, New York, NY
2	Jane Smith	Female	jane.smith@example.com	+1-555-5678	456 Elm St, Los Angeles, CA
3	Robert Johnson	Male	robert.johnson@example.com	+1-555-8765	789 Oak St, Chicago, IL
4	Emily Davis	Female	emily.davis@example.com	+1-555-4321	101 Pine St, Houston, TX
5	Michael Brown	Male	michael.brown@example.com	+1-555-2468	202 Birch St, Phoenix, AZ
6	Jessica Wilson	Female	jessica.wilson@example.com	+1-555-1357	303 Cedar St, Philadelphia, PA
7	David Martinez	Male	david.martinez@example.com	+1-555-9753	404 Maple St, San Antonio, TX
8	Sarah Taylor	Female	sarah.taylor@example.com	+1-555-7531	505 Walnut St, San Diego, CA
9	Daniel Anderson	Male	daniel.anderson@example.com	+1-555-8520	606 Spruce St, Dallas, TX
10	Olivia Hernandez	Female	olivia.hernandez@example.com	+1-555-3698	707 Aspen St, San Jose, CA

DataFrame [10 x 6]

Figure 14-17. *Converted HTML table data*

14.4 Data Visualization in Kotlin Notebook with Kandy

Kotlin offers powerful feature data visualization, using the Kandy library. We can access complex datasets and visualize data in the form of different techniques. Let's take one example of plotting different charts.

Create Line Chart

Step 1: Create New Project ➤ New Kotlin Notebook.

Step 2: Add required libraries Dataframe and Kandy using %use.

Step 3: Create a new dataframe that stores month, temperature, and city name. Figure 14-18 shows that.

```
val months = listOf(
    "January", "February",
    "March", "April", "May",
    "June", "July", "August",
    "September", "October", "November",
    "December"
)
// The tempBerlin, tempMadrid, and tempCaracas variables store a list with temperature values for each
  month
val tempCamden =
    listOf(5.2, 6.3, 8.3, 11.1, 14.3, 17.6, 19.5, 19.7, 16.1, 13.2, 9.1, 6.1)
val tempIndia =
    listOf(26.3, 27.9, 31.2, 39.9, 42.7, 34.1, 31.7, 29.2, 27.3, 26.4, 23.9, 21.6)
val tempFlorida =
    listOf(15.2, 16.4, 19.1, 22.6, 24.1, 27.3, 28.7, 28.4, 27.3, 24.2, 20.2, 17.1)

// The df variable stores a DataFrame of three columns, including records of months, temperature, and
  cities
val df = dataFrameOf(
    "Month" to months + months + months,
    "Temperature" to tempCamden + tempIndia + tempFlorida,
    "City" to List(12) { "Camden" } + List(12) { "India" } + List(12) { "Florida" }
)
```

Figure 14-18. New dataframe for storing temperature

CHAPTER 14 DATA ANALYSIS WITH KOTLIN

Step 4: You can see the structure of the data using the head method. Figure 14-19 shows that.

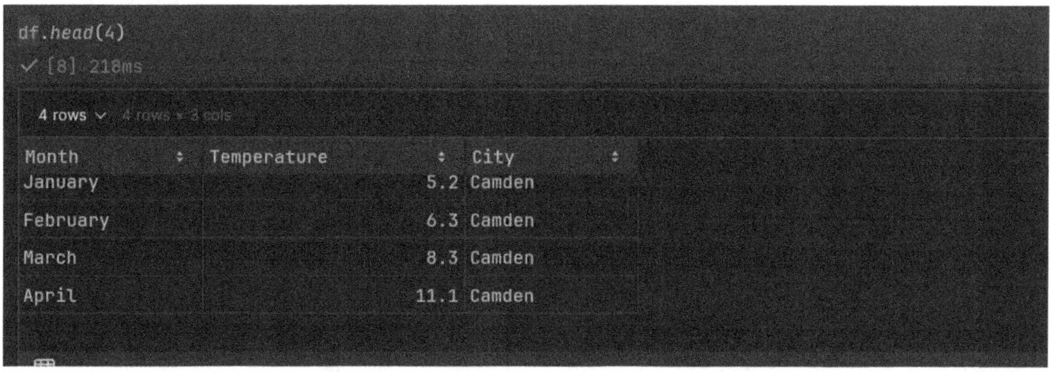

```
df.head(4)
✓ [8] 218ms

4 rows ✓   4 rows × 3 cols

Month      : Temperature  :  City      :
January                  5.2  Camden
February                 6.3  Camden
March                    8.3  Camden
April                   11.1  Camden
```

Figure 14-19. *Structure of data*

Step 5: Plot the graph using the following code. Figure 14-20 shows that, where line is the type of chart. The x and y show the axis of the chart and color shows the city-wise color differentiation.

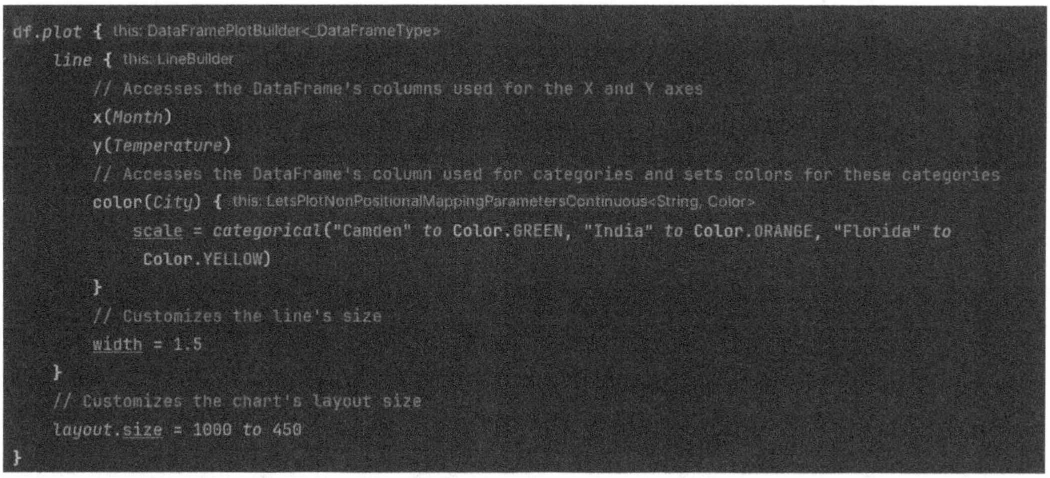

```
df.plot { this: DataFramePlotBuilder<_DataFrameType>
    line { this: LineBuilder
        // Accesses the DataFrame's columns used for the X and Y axes
        x(Month)
        y(Temperature)
        // Accesses the DataFrame's column used for categories and sets colors for these categories
        color(City) { this: LetsPlotNonPositionalMappingParametersContinuous<String, Color>
            scale = categorical("Camden" to Color.GREEN, "India" to Color.ORANGE, "Florida" to
                Color.YELLOW)
        }
        // Customizes the line's size
        width = 1.5
    }
    // Customizes the chart's layout size
    layout.size = 1000 to 450
}
```

Figure 14-20. *Code for plotting line chart*

CHAPTER 14 DATA ANALYSIS WITH KOTLIN

Step 6: Figure 14-21 shows the output of the line chart.

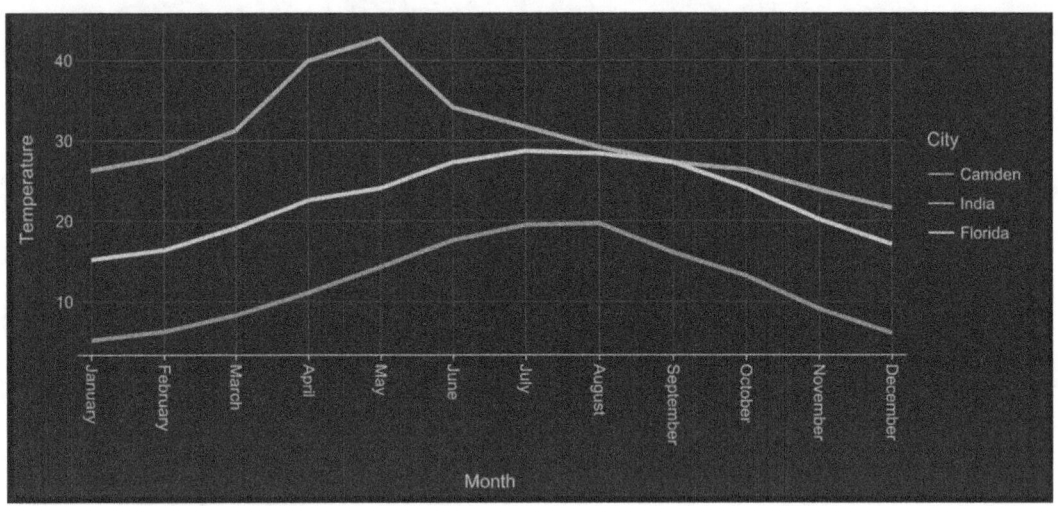

Figure 14-21. Line chart

Create Points Chart

Begin as in the preceding example, but you need to change in Step 5 (Figure 14-20), as shown in Figure 14-22.

```
df.plot { this: DataFramePlotBuilder<_DataFrameType>
    points { this: PointsBuilder
        // Accesses the DataFrame's columns used for the X and Y axes
        x(Month) { axis.name = "Month" }
        y(Temperature) { axis.name = "Temperature" }
        // Customizes the point's size
        size = 5.5
        // Accesses the DataFrame's column used for categories and sets colors for these categories
        color(City) { this: LetsPlotNonPositionalMappingParametersContinuous<String, Color>
            scale = categorical("Camden" to Color.LIGHT_GREEN, "India" to Color.ORANGE, "Florida" to
                Color.YELLOW)
        }
    }
    // Adds a chart heading
    layout.title = "Temperature per month"
}
```

Figure 14-22. Cde for points chart

Figure 14-23 shows the output of the points chart.

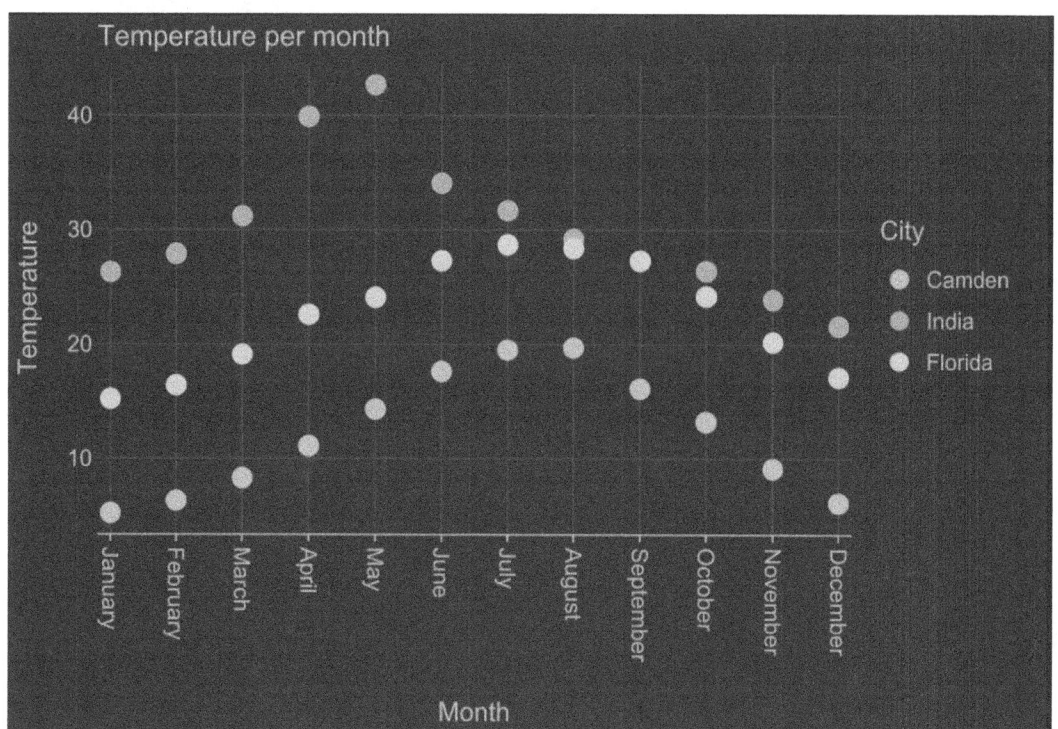

Figure 14-23. *Points chart*

Create Bar Chart

In this example you need to change in Step 5 (Figure 14-20), as shown in Figure 14-24.

```
// Groups by cities
df.groupBy { City }.plot {
    // Adds a chart heading
    layout.title = "Temperature per month"
    bars {
        // Accesses the DataFrame's columns used for the X and Y axes
        x(Month)
        y(Temperature)
        // Accesses the DataFrame's column used for categories and sets colors for these categories
        fillColor(City) {
            scale = categorical(
                "Camden" to Color.GREEN,
                "India" to Color.ORANGE,
                "Florida" to Color.YELLOW
            )
        }
    }
}
```

Figure 14-24. *Code for bar chart*

Figure 14-25 shows the output of the bar chart.

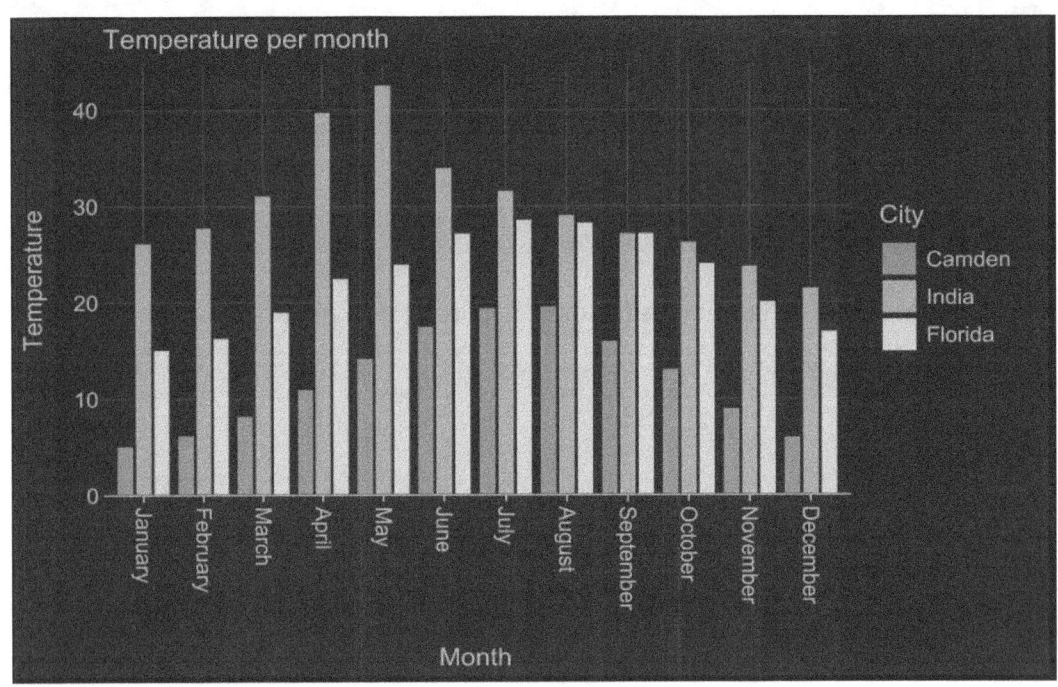

Figure 14-25. *A bar chart*

14.5 Libraries for Data Analysis in Kotlin

Kotlin provides multiple data analysis libraries for data collection, manipulation, and visualization. Table 14-1 shows the name of each library and its purpose.

Table 14-1. Data Analysis Libraries

Library Name	Purpose
Kotlin Dataframe	Data Collection, Data Cleaning, Data Processing
Kandy	Data Exploration, Data Visualization
KotlinDL	Model Building
Multik	Data Cleaning, Data Processing, Model Building
Kotlin for Apache Spark	Data Collection, Data Cleaning, Data Processing, Data Exploration, Data Visualization, Model Building
Lets-Plot	Data Exploration, Data Visualization
KMath	Data Cleaning, Data Processing, Data Exploration, Data Visualization, Model Building
Kravis	Data Exploration, Data Visualization

14.6 Real-Life Programming Practice

1. **Imagine you work for a retail company, and you need to analyze sales data from a CSV file. You will:**

    1. Load the CSV file into a Kotlin dataframe.

    2. Filter sales data for a specific product category.

    3. Summarize total revenue per category.

    4. Visualize the results using a bar chart.

CHAPTER 14 DATA ANALYSIS WITH KOTLIN

Code:

```kotlin
// Import necessary libraries
@file:DependsOn("org.jetbrains.kotlinx:dataframe")
@file:DependsOn("org.jetbrains.kotlinx:kandy")

import org.jetbrains.kotlinx.dataframe.api.*
import org.jetbrains.kotlinx.kandy.dsl.plot
import org.jetbrains.kotlinx.kandy.dsl.layers.bar
import org.jetbrains.kotlinx.kandy.lets.categories
import java.io.File

// Load sales data from a CSV file
val salesDF = DataFrame.readCSV("sales_data.csv")

// Display first few rows
salesDF.head(5).print()

// Filter sales for "Electronics" category
val electronicsSales = salesDF.filter { it["Category"] == "Electronics" }

// Summarize total revenue per category
val revenueByCategory = salesDF
    .groupBy("Category")
    .aggregate {
        sum("Revenue") into "Total Revenue"
    }

// Print summarized data
revenueByCategory.print()

// Visualize revenue per category using a bar chart
plot(revenueByCategory) {
    x(categories("Category"))
    y("Total Revenue")
    bar()
}
```

14.7 Summary

In this chapter, we have learned Kotlin data analysis, which is Kotlin with modern structure and syntax to process, manipulate, and visualize data. Kotlin is not a language like Python, but it provides data analysis through some libraries and functions.

14.8 Test Your Knowledge

1. **What is the primary purpose of Kotlin Notebooks?**

   a. writing and running Kotlin scripts interactively

   b. creating Android applications

   c. developing web applications

   d. managing databases

2. **How can you install Kotlin Notebooks in Jupyter?**

   a. by installing JupyterLab and adding the Kotlin kernel

   b. by using Android Studio

   c. by installing IntelliJ IDEA

   d. by using Kotlin Playground

3. **Which library is required to work with Kotlin dataframes in a Kotlin notebook?**

   a. kotlinx.serialization

   b. kotlin.reflect

   c. org.jetbrains.kotlinx.dataframe

   d. kotlinx.coroutines

4. **How can you add dependencies in a Kotlin notebook?**

   a. using `@file:DependsOn("<dependency>")`

   b. using `import dependency.kotlin`

CHAPTER 14   DATA ANALYSIS WITH KOTLIN

   c. using `dependency install <dependency>`

   d. using `@KotlinDependencies("<dependency>")`

5. **What is the default format for saving a dataframe using Kotlin?**

   a. JSON

   b. CSV

   c. Excel

   d. TXT

6. **Which of the following is NOT a supported data source for Kotlin dataframes?**

   a. CSV

   b. JSON

   c. XML

   d. Markdown

7. **Which Kotlin function is used to read a CSV file into a dataframe?**

   a. `DataFrame.loadCsv("file.csv")`

   b. `readCsv("file.csv")`

   c. `DataFrame.read("file.csv")`

   d. `DataFrame.fromCsv("file.csv")`

8. **What is the primary purpose of Kandy in Kotlin Notebooks?**

   a. data encryption

   b. visualizing data

   c. managing dependencies

   d. debugging Kotlin code

9. **How do you create a bar chart in Kotlin Notebooks using Kandy?**

   a. barChart(data)

   b. plotBar(data)

   c. plot(data).bar()

   d. dataFrame.barPlot()

10. **What is the recommended function to export a Kotlin dataframe as a CSV file?**

    a. df.writeCsv("output.csv")

    b. df.saveAsCsv("output.csv")

    c. df.write("output.csv")

    d. df.exportCsv("output.csv")

11. **What command is used to install a Kotlin dataframe and Kandy in Kotlin Notebook?**

    a. @file:DependsOn("org.jetbrains.kotlinx:dataframe")

    b. @file:Install("org.jetbrains.kotlinx:dataframe")

    c. import org.jetbrains.kotlinx.dataframe

    d. dependency install dataframe

12. **How do you filter rows in a Kotlin dataframe where a column named "Age" is greater than 25?**

    a. df.filter { it["Age"] > 25 }

    b. df.select { Age > 25 }

    c. df.filter { Age > 25 }

    d. df.where { it.Age > 25 }

13. **What is the function used to display the first few rows of a dataframe?**

    a. df.head(5)

    b. df.first(5)

    c. df.top(5)

    d. df.show(5)

14. **How do you add a new column to an existing Kotlin dataframe?**

    a. df.addColumn("NewColumn", value)

    b. df.insert("NewColumn", value)

    c. df.append("NewColumn", value)

    d. df.add("NewColumn") { value }

15. **Which format is commonly used for visualizing data using Kandy in Kotlin Notebook?**

    a. pie chart

    b. line chart

    c. heatmap

    d. radar chart

14.9 Answers

1. a
2. a
3. c
4. a
5. b
6. d
7. a

CHAPTER 14 DATA ANALYSIS WITH KOTLIN

8. b
9. c
10. a
11. a
12. a
13. a
14. d
15. b

CHAPTER 15

Kotlin Multiplatform

15.1 Introduction to Kotlin Multiplatform

Kotlin Multiplatform (KMP) is an innovative software development framework that allows the developers to create shared code that can be workable across numerous platforms, including iOS, Android, web, desktop, and embedded devices. It is a major component of the Kotlin system that aims to offer a balance between cross-platform code exchange and platform-specific customization. Unlike other cross-platform frameworks such as Flutter or React local, which generate user interfaces for several operating systems, KMP prioritizes the exchange of business logic, data models, and network logic, while ensuring that the user experience remains local to a given platform. It is developed and maintained by JetBrains, the same organization that created. The Kotlin KMP allows the development of common code in Kotlin while using platform-specific implementations as required. It has several advantages, such as better integration into existing projects and allowing the progressive adoption of the new standard without compromising the comprehensive rewrites of applications. An overview of KMP is shown in Figure 15-1.

CHAPTER 15   KOTLIN MULTIPLATFORM

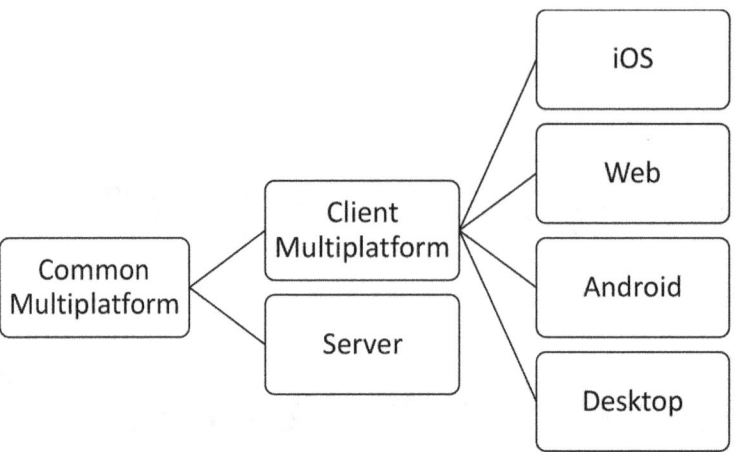

Figure 15-1. *Overview of KMP*

How It Works

KMP consists of multiple components, which allows the developers to share the code seamlessly over platform-specific customization. One of the generalized methods that is commonly used is shared module; i.e., Use Code Share Mechanism.

Sharing code among a certain group of like targets might occasionally be more advantageous. Kotlin Multiplatform offers a method to streamline the construction process with a preset hierarchy template. It comprises a predetermined list of intermediate source sets generated according to the goals specified in your project. To utilize platform-specific APIs from common code, one might employ another Kotlin feature: expected and actual declarations. This approach allows you to specify an expectation for a platform-specific API within shared code while offering distinct implementations for each target platform. This method may be utilized with several Kotlin concepts, including functions, classes, and interfaces. For instance, one can delineate a function in shared code while executing its implementation using a platform-specific library within the appropriate source set. KMP allows you to write the code for a specific environment, which is commonly known as platform-specific code; for example, Swift for iOS or Kotlin/Java for Android. Other supported platforms for KMP include the following:

- Native: For macOS, iOS, Windows, and Linux.
- WASM (Web Assembly): It allows you to write the code in a web browser.

- JavaScript: Used for web applications.
- Java Virtual Machine (JVM): For backend services.

Benefits of KMP

KMP allows developers to address the major challenges that arise in modern software development. The major benefits of KMP are the following:

- Native Platforms: Unlike most of the other cross-platform solutions that depend on interpretation layer or virtual machine, KMP allows you to compile the code as per the requirements. This guarantees enhanced performance and latency, making it suitable for responsive applications.
- Code Reusability: With the help of KMP, developers can use the code across multiple platforms and for multiple applications.
- Flexibility: KMP allows developers to incrementally present shared logic. They can begin with a limited area of the codebase, e.g., network operations or data storage, and then extend it to other regions.
- Interoperability: KMP allows developers to use Swift, Java, and JavaScript along with Kotlin, allowing steady adoption without the need for full-scale migration.

Use Cases

- Backend & Web Development: KMP shares logic, data validation, models, and APIs between backend services and web applications that are running on JavaScript.
- Mobile Development: It shares the logic between the mobile OSes, such as iOS and Android. Thus, the UI experience gets enhanced.

CHAPTER 15 KOTLIN MULTIPLATFORM

- Embedded and IoT: Native/Kotlin permits KMP to be used in Internet of Things (IoT) and embedded applications, allowing cross-platform firmware and software development.

- Desktop Applications: With the support for Native/Kotlin and JVM, KMP can be used to build cross-platform desktop applications for macOS, Windows, and Linux.

15.2 Setting Up a Multiplatform Project for iOS

While targeting a multiplatform project for iOS, a developer has to set up the integration of KMP with the iOS app using a shared module scheme. To do so, an iOS framework is generate, and then it is added with a local or remote dependency of the iOS project. Here there are two things a developer has to target: local integration and remote integration. The structure of a KMP integration is shown in Figure 15-2.

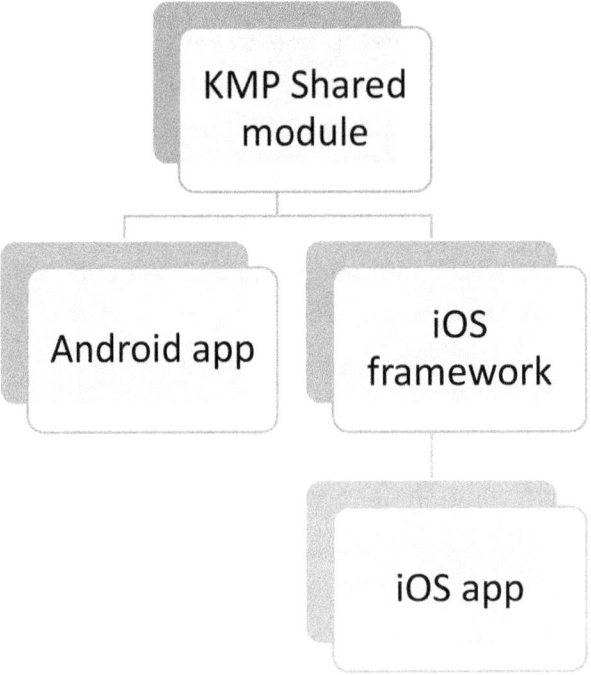

Figure 15-2. *KMP integration structure for project*

Local integration: In a local configuration, there exist two primary integration alternatives. Direct integration may be achieved using a specialized script, integrating the Kotlin build into the iOS build. Utilize the CocoaPods integration method if your Kotlin Multiplatform project includes Pod dependencies.

Direct integration: Integrate the iOS framework directly into the Kotlin Multiplatform project by incorporating a specific script into your Xcode project. The script is incorporated into the build process of your project's configuration settings. This integration approach is applicable if you do not use CocoaPods requirements in your Kotlin Multiplatform project. The KMP web wizard can be accessed at: https://kmp.jetbrains.com/?_gl=1*17n39m1*_gcl_au*NzM3Njc1MDAzLjE3NDAxMjcOMjA.*_ga*MTY4NDM2OTUwNC4xNzIONzY1MTEx*_ga_9J976DJZ68*MTcOMzEOMDk4OC44LjEuMTcOMzEOMTkzMi42MC4wLjA.

When creating a project in Android Studio, select the "Regular" framework option to enable automated setup generation. Utilizing the Kotlin Multiplatform web wizard results in direct integration's being implemented by default.

Integration of CocoaPods with a local podspec: The iOS framework from the Kotlin Multiplatform project may be integrated using CocoaPods, a widely used dependency management option for Swift and Objective-C applications.

This integration approach is applicable in the following cases:

- A mono repository configuration is established with an iOS project utilizing CocoaPods.

- You include CocoaPods dependencies in your Kotlin Multiplatform project.

To establish a workflow with a local CocoaPods dependency, you may either modify the scripts manually or utilize a wizard in Android Studio to construct the project.

Remote integration: Your project may utilize the Swift Package management (SPM) or the CocoaPods dependency management for remote integration to link the iOS framework from a Kotlin Multiplatform project.

Swift Package Manager using XCFrameworks: One may establish a Swift Package Manager (SPM) dependency utilizing XCFrameworks to integrate the iOS framework and the Kotlin Multiplatform project.

Integration of CocoaPods with XCFrameworks: The Kotlin CocoaPods Gradle plugin enables the creation of XCFrameworks, allowing for the independent distribution of common components from mobile applications via CocoaPods.

Set up compilations: Each target may possess numerous compilations for various objectives, often for production or testing, while also allowing for the definition of bespoke compilations.

Kotlin Multiplatform enables the configuration of all project compilations, the establishment of specialized compilations within a target, and the creation of distinct compilations. During compilation configuration, one can adjust compiler parameters, oversee dependencies, or establish compatibility with native languages.

Steps for Creating iOS Project

- Software required:
- macOS
- Xcode
- CocoaPods
- Android Studio or Intellij IDEA
- Latest Kotlin plugin
- JDK 11+ and Gradle7+

Creating Project using Android Studio or Intellij IDEA

To create a project, we have to follow a few steps, which are as follows:

    a. Open the Android Studio or Intellij IDEA.

    b. Go to New Project under File section.

    c. Select KMP of iOS or Android.

    d. Give a name to the project (e.g., ABC) and select the directory.

    e. Last is FINISH.

Defining Project Structure

The created project structure will appear as follows:

```
ABC
├── androidApp/        # Android-specific code
├── iosApp/            # iOS-specific code (Xcode project)
├── shared/            # Shared Kotlin code (business logic)
│   ├── src/
│   │   ├── commonMain/    # Shared business logic
│   │   ├── commonTest/    # Shared tests
│   │   ├── iosMain/       # iOS-specific implementations
│   │   ├── iosTest/       # iOS-specific tests
├── build.gradle.kts   # Root Gradle configuration
├── settings.gradle.kts
├── gradle.properties
```

Shared Module Configuration and Implementation

To configure the shared module, we have to open shared/build.gradle.kts and then add the KMP plugin, and then we have to target iOS. The code is given as follows:

```
plugins {
kotlin("multiplatform")
kotlin("native.cocoapods") // CocoaPods support for iOS
}

kotlin {
    iosX64() // For iOS Simulator
    iosArm64() // For physical iOS devices
    iosSimulatorArm64() // For Apple Silicon Macs

sourceSets {
valcommonMain by getting {
        dependencies {
            implementation(kotlin("stdlib"))
        }
    }
```

```
valiosMain by creating {
dependsOn(commonMain)
        }
    }
}
cocoapods {
    summary = "Shared Kotlin Code for iOS"
    homepage = "https://github.com/example/ABC"
ios.deploymentTarget = "14.0"
    framework {
baseName = "shared"
    }
}
```

This configuration is suitable for both iosArm 64 and iosX64, which support CocoaPods. To implement the shared code, we have to creagte a new file as Platform. kt: and to write the following code:

```
expect class Platform {
    fun getPlatformName(): String= "iOS"
}
```

It will permit the code to identify the platform and return "iOS" for Apple devices.

15.3 Multiplatform Libraries

Each software requires a collection of libraries to function well. A KMP project may rely on multiplatform libraries compatible with all target platforms, platform-specific libraries, and additional multiplatform projects. To incorporate a library dependency, modify your build.gradle(.kts) file located in the directory of your project that contains the shared code. Establish a dependent of the specified type (e.g., implementation) within the dependencies {} block, as follows:

```
kotlin {
sourceSets {
commonMain.dependencies {
```

340

```
            implementation("com.example:my-library:1.0") // library shared
            for all source sets
        }
    }
}
```

Dependency on a Kotlin Library

A dependency on a standard library (stdlib) in each source set is included automatically. The version of the standard library corresponds to the version of the KMP plugin. For platform-specific source sets, the relevant platform-specific variation of the library is utilized, while a common standard library is included for the remainder. The Kotlin Gradle plugin will choose the suitable JVM standard library based on the compiler options. jvmTarget compiler option in your Gradle build script.

- **Test libraries**

    For test purposes an API named Kotlin.test is available. While creating a KMP project we can add the test dependencies for each and every source set by using a common single dependency, such as commonTest:

    ```
    kotlin {
    sourceSets {
    commonTest.dependencies {
                implementation(kotlin("test")) // Brings all the
    platform dependencies automatically
            }
        }
    }
    ```

- **Kotlinx libraries**

    In case of shared code, the `kotlinx-coroutines-core:` library is used for the KMP project:

    ```
    kotlin {
    sourceSets {
    commonMain.dependencies {
    ```

```
                    implementation("org.jetbrains.kotlinx:kotlinx-
                        coroutines-core:1.10.1")
                }
            }
        }
```

Dependency on Another Multiplatform Project

One multiplatform project can be linked to another as a dependency. To do this, just incorporate a project dependency in the requisite source set. To utilize a reliance across all source sets, incorporate it into the common set. In this instance, alternative source sets will receive their versions automatically.

```
kotlin {
sourceSets {
commonMain {
            dependencies {
                implementation project(':some-other-multiplatform-module')
            }
        }
androidMain {
            dependencies {
                // platform part of :some-other-multiplatform-module will
                    be added automatically
            }
        }
    }
}
```

KMP is an important advancement in cross-platform programming, allowing the benefits of shared logic alongside a native experience. KMP provides a unified approach to writing stable and efficient code for mobile applications, web apps, and backend services.

15.4 Test Your Knowledge

1. **What is Kotlin Multiplatform primarily used for?**

    a. writing Android-only applications

    b. writing cross-platform applications with shared logic

    c. replacing Java in backend development

    d. creating UI frameworks for web development

2. **Which Gradle plugin is required for a Kotlin Multiplatform project?**

    a. kotlin-android

    b. kotlin-jvm

    c. kotlin-multiplatform

    d. kotlin-native

3. **How do you define a shared Kotlin function that requires platform-specific implementations?**

    a. using interface

    b. using sealed class

    c. using expect and actual keywords

    d. using abstract class

4. **Which tool is commonly used for dependency management in Kotlin Multiplatform projects?**

    a. CocoaPods

    b. Maven

    c. Gradle

    d. npm

CHAPTER 15   KOTLIN MULTIPLATFORM

5. **In a Kotlin Multiplatform project, which module contains the shared business logic?**

    a. androidApp/

    b. iosApp/

    c. shared/

    d. commonMain/

6. **Which Kotlin library is commonly used for networking in multiplatform projects?**

    a. Retrofit

    b. Ktor

    c. Volley

    d. OkHttp

7. **What is the purpose of the CocoaPods block in** `build.gradle.kts`**?**

    a. to enable iOS support in a Kotlin Multiplatform project

    b. to configure Android-specific dependencies

    c. to link external iOS libraries via CocoaPods

    d. both A and C

8. **Which Kotlin library is used for JSON serialization in Kotlin Multiplatform?**

    a. Gson

    b. Moshi

    c. kotlinx.serialization

    d. Jackson

9. **How do you run an iOS application in a Kotlin Multiplatform project?**

    a. using the Android Emulator

    b. running `./gradlewrunIos` in the terminal

c. opening the .xcworkspace file in Xcode and running the project

d. running flutter run

10. **Which statement is TRUE about Kotlin Multiplatform?**

   a. It forces developers to use a single UI framework for all platforms.

   b. It allows sharing business logic while keeping platform-specific UI.

   c. It does not support native iOS development.

   d. It requires writing duplicate code for each platform.

15.5 Answers

1. b
2. c
3. c
4. c
5. c
6. b
7. d
8. c
9. c
10. b

Index

A

Abstract class, 102
    multiple derived classes, 104
    override non-abstract method/
        property, 103
    syntax, 102
Address class, 196
Advanced Kotlin concepts, 286, 302
Android, 2
APIs, *see* Application programming
        interfaces (APIs)
Application programming interfaces
        (APIs), 281
    Android development, 270, 271
    categories, 269, 281
    cloud/backend, 275
    coroutines, 270
    database, 269
    database/storage, 272
    Google Maps, 270, 281
    graphical, 270
    IoT, 273, 274
    ML, 270, 273, 274
    MOTT, 270
    MQTT, 281
    multimedia, 274, 275
    networking, 269, 272
    UIs/graphics, 273
Apply function, 196
Arithmetic operators, 27, 28
ArrayIndexOutOfBound exception,
        134, 135

arrayOf() function, 34, 56
Arrays, 34
    arrayOf() function, 34
    element change, 35, 36
    length, 35
    loops, 36, 37
    in operator, 36
asReversed() function, 215
Assignment operators, 30, 31
average(), 156

B

BDD, *see* Behavior-driven
        development (BDD)
Behavior-driven development (BDD), 242
Blocking, 177, 188
Break statement, 43, 44
Build function, 197
build.gradle(.kts) file, 340

C

Calculator class, 236, 237
CD, *see* Continuous delivery (CD)
CI, *see* Continuous integration (CI)
Classes, 74
    abstract class (*see* Abstract class)
    class definition, 74
    constructors (*see* Constructors)
    data classes, 105–107
    enum, 108–110
    inner classes, 79, 80

INDEX

Classes (*cont.*)
   interfaces (*see* Interfaces)
   nested classes, 78
   property (*see* Property)
   sealed classes, 107
   syntax, class declaration, 74, 75
CocoaPods, 337
Collections, 147, 213
   arrays, 147
   filtering, 216–219
   immutable, 147
   lists, 147, 148 (*see also* Lists)
   maps, 147
   mutable, 148
   sets, 147
      advantages and disadvantages, 158
      basic functions, 156
      first and last elements, 155
      immutable set, 153
      indexing, 155
      mutable set, 154
   sorting, 213
      custom sorting, 214
      natural sorting, 214
      random sorting, 216
      reverse sorting, 215
   transforming, 219
   types, 147
Comments, 25
   multi-line comments, 25, 26
   single-line comments, 25
Comparison operators, 31
Constructors
   primary constructors, 81
      init blocks, 82, 83
      use default values, 83
   secondary constructors, 84

   call one constructor from another constructor, 85
   inside same class, 84
   types, 80
contains(), 156
containsAll(), 156
containsKey(), 162
containsValue(), 162
Continue statement, 44
Continuous delivery (CD), 240
Continuous integration (CI), 240
Contracovariance, 167, 168
Control flow
   else statement, 38
   else if statement, 39
   if statement, 37
   when statement, 40, 41
copy(), 107
Coroutines
   advantages, 177
   asynchronous tasks, 261
   cancellation, 184, 185
   CancellationException, 182, 183
   concurrency, 180
   CoroutineExceptionHandler, 183, 184
   create apps, 261
   creation, 178
   exception aggregation, 185, 186
   exceptions, 184, 185
   explicit job, 181
   extract function refactoring, 179
   food delivery application, 186, 187
   memory, 182
   scope builders, 179, 180
   structured concurrency, 178
   vs. threads, 182
   vs. traditional methods, 262

count(), 156
Covariance, 167
CSV file, 325
Custom exception, 137

D

Dagger Hilt, 270
Data analysis
    CSV file, 325
    libraries, 325
    use Kotlin Notebook (*see* Kotlin Notebook)
Data classes, 105
    copy(), 107
    equals(), 106
    hashCode(), 106
    Person(val name: String, val age: Int), 105
    toString(), 105
delete() function, 227
deleteRecursively() function, 227
Dependency injection (DI) frameworks, 270
Domain-specific language (DSL), 193
    Address class, 196
    advantages, 193
    apply function, 196
    builder pattern, 197, 198
    collections, 198–200
    creation, 194, 204–207
    @DslMarker annotation, 201, 202
    extension functions, 196
    external, 193
    HTML builder, 202, 203
    internal, 193
    lambda, 195
    Student class, 194, 196
    student function, 195
    uses, 208
do..while loop, 42
DSL, *see* Domain-specific language (DSL)
@DslMarker annotation, 201, 202

E

elementAt(), 155
else if statement, 39
else statement, 38
Elvis operator (?:), 288
Employee management system, 227–229
Enum class, 108, 109
    methods, 110
    properties, 109
equals(), 106
Exception handler, 183, 184
Exception handling, 127, 182, 183
    checked exception, 127
    database connection fails, 140
    finally block, 130, 131
    find square root of number, 141
    handle invalid user data, 139
    program for payment-processing system, 138
    request network connection, 141
    throw block, 132
    try-catch block, 128–130
    unchecked exception, 127
Extension functions, 196, 224

F

File handling, 226, 227
filter() function, 216
Filtering, 216–219

INDEX

filterIsInstance() function, 217
filterNot() function, 217
filterNotNull() function, 217
Finally block, 130, 131
Food delivery application, 186, 187
forEach {println(it) }, 298
for loop, 43
Function, 53
   advantages, 57
   body of function, 54
   and build real-life applications, 65
   built-in functions, 56
   call, 55
   with default arguments, 58–60
   disadvantages, 57
   with named arguments, 60–61
   parameters, 54
   recursive functions, 61
      normal function call, 61
      recursive function call, 63, 64
      tail recursive function, 64
   return value, 54
   standard library functions, 56
   user-defined function, 53
Functional programming, 2

G

Generics, 164
   contracovariance, 167, 168
   covariance, 167
   invariance, 165
   in Kotlin programs, 164
   online shopping platform, 170–172
   star(*) projection, 169
   syntax, 164
   type projections, 168

   variance, 165
      declaration-site, 165
      in keyword, 166, 167
      out keyword, 166
      use-site, 165
getOrDefault() function, 161
getValue() function, 161
Google Maps API
   add dependencies, 276
   API key to manifest, 276
   app run, 278
   enabling, 275
   features, 278
   load map, 277
   map fragment, 276

H

hashCode(), 106
Higher-order functions
   Kotlin program, 294
   lambda, 294, 295
   lambda expressions with list functions, 297, 298
   returns a function, 296, 297
HTML builder, 202, 203

I

IDEs, *see* Integrated development environments (IDEs)
if statement, 37
Immutable collections, 147
Immutable list, 148
Immutable map, 158
immutableNameList, 148
Immutable set, 153
indexOf() function, 155

INDEX

Inheritance, 86
    call secondary constructor from derived class secondary constructor, 90
    definition, 86
    in interfaces, 94
    Kotlin override property, 87
    multiple interface implementation, 95
    open keyword, 86
    parent class, 86
    with primary constructors, 88
    with secondary constructor, 89
    subclass, 86
Inner classes, 79, 80
Integrated development environments (IDEs), 13
Integration testing, 245
    in-memory databases/HTTP queries, 246, 247
    Ktor, 248, 250
    and unit tests, 249
IntelliJ IDEA, 13–15
Interfaces, 91
    calculator, 91
    default values and methods, 92
    properties, 93
    syntax, 91
Internal modifier, 97
Internet of Things (IoT), 270, 274
IoT, *see* Internet of Things (IoT)
isEmpty(), 156

J

Java, 1–4
Java virtual machine (JVM), 8, 335
Jump and return statements
    break statement, 43, 44
    continue statement, 44
    return statement, 45
JUnit, 241, 249
JVM, *see* Java virtual machine (JVM)

K

Kandy, 325
KMath, 325
KMP, *see* Kotlin multiplatform (KMP)
Koin, 270
Kotest, 241
Kotlin, 1
    Android, 264
    applications, 7
    benefits, 6
    companion objects, 5
    compilation time, 5
    concise, 4
    coroutines, 6
    data keyword, 2
    data classes, 4
    data stream, 258
    development environment
        command line, 8, 9
        create application, 15–18
        IntelliJ IDEA, 13–15
    drawbacks, 7
    DSL (*see* Domain-specific language (DSL))
    environment variable, 11
        advanced system settings, 10
        run files, 12, 13
        system variables, 12
        This PC option, 9, 10
    extension functions, 5
    features, 194, 250
    flows, 258

INDEX

Kotlin (*cont.*)
    higher order functions/lambdas, 5
    interoperability, 4
    KMP, 5
    lazy loading, 6
    null safety, 4
    output, 24
    patterns, 263
    products, cart, 49
    smart casts, 5
    structure, 23, 24
    student's eligibility, attendance, 48
    student's grade, percentage, 47, 48
    syntax, 23, 24
    syntax and capabilities, 249
    testing frameworks, 250
        JUnit, 241
        Kotest, 241, 242
        Spek, 242
    testing libraries, 249
    ticket price, amusement park, 46, 47
Kotlin Dataframe, 325
KotlinDL, 325
Kotlin for Apache Spark, 325
Kotlin function, *see* Function
Kotlin Gradle plugin, 341
Kotlin multiplatform (KMP), 5
    backend & web development, 335
    benefits, 335
    desktop applications, 336
    embedded and IoT, 336
    JavaScript, 335
    JVM, 335
    mobile development, 335
    multiplatform libraries, 340
        dependency on multiplatform project, 342
        dependency on standard library (stdlib), 341
        Kotlinx libraries, 341
        test libraries, 341
    multiplatform project for iOS
        CocoaPods integration, 337
        CocoaPods with XCFrameworks, 337
        create project using Android Studio/Intellij IDEA, 338
        define project structure, 338
        direct integration, 337
        KMP integration structure, 336
        local integration, 337
        remote integration, 337
        set up compilations, 338
        shared module configuration and implementation, 339, 340
        software, 338
        SPM dependency using XCFrameworks, 337
    native, 334
    overview, 333, 334
    platform-specific code, 334
    shared module, 334
    sharing code, 334
    WASM (Web Assembly), 334
Kotlin Notebook, 311
    add birthyear, 318
    add libraries, 315
    adult data filter, 318
    with all operations, 314
    converted HTML table data, 319
    create new project, 312
    create notebook, 312, 313
    data visualization, using Kandy library, 320
        create bar chart, 323, 324

INDEX

create line chart, 320–322
create points chart, 322, 323
function schema(), 317
to HTML table, 319
installation, steps, 311
JSON file schema, 317
new operations run, 314
people.json file, 316
read JSON file, 317
remove age, 318
run code, 313
save JSON file, 319
Kotlin system, 333
KotlinTest (Kotest), 241, 341
Kotlin *vs.* Java, 1, 3, 4
    Android, 2
    checked exception support, 2
    extension functions, 1
    languages, 2
    null value, 1
    smart cast feature, 2
    syntax, 1
    variables/fields, 2
    wildcards/ternary operators/and public fields, 2
Kotlinx libraries, 341
Kravis, 325
.kt (DOT K-T), 285
Ktor, 248, 250, 269, 272
.kts (DOT K-T-S), 285

L

Lambda expressions, 256, 294, 297, 298, 302
lastIndexOf() function, 155
Lazy initialization, 299, 300
lazyValue, 299

Let scope function, 292, 293
Lets-Plot, 325
Library classes, 225
listOf() function, 153
Lists
    access first and last elements, 150
    advantages and disadvantages, 153
    immutable list, 148
    mutable list, 149, 150
    sorting list, 152
    traversing methods, 150, 152
Live stock price updater, 264, 266
Logical operations, 29
Loops, 41
    do..while loop, 42
    for loop, 43
    while loop, 41, 42

M

Machine learning (ML), 270, 273, 274
main() function, 23, 55
main() method, 61, 296
map() function, 219
mapOf() function, 158, 161, 163
Maps, 158
    access values from multiple methods, 161
    advantages and disadvantages, 163
    empty, 161
    immutable map, 158
    keys, values and entries, 160
    key/value, 162
    mutable map, 159
    size, 160
    two different values to same key, 163
max(), 156

INDEX

Message Queuing Telemetry
    Transport (MOTT)
  add dependencies, 279
  app run, 281
  create project, 278
  explanation, 281
  features, 281
  implementation, 279, 280
Message Queuing Telemetry Transport
    (MQTT), 274
min(), 156
Mocking, 243, 249
MockK, 243, 249
  annotations, 243
    @Before, 245
    @MockK, 243
    @RelaxedMockK, 244
    @SpyK, 244
    @Test, 244
    @UnmockK, 244
  keywords and functions, 245
Multik, 325
Mutable collections, 148
Mutable list, 149, 150
Mutable map, 159
Mutable set, 154
mutableSetOf() function, 154

N

Nested classes, 78
Nested try block, 133
  multiple catch blocks, 134, 135
  catch blocks, 136–137
Null pointer exceptions (NPEs), 285, 290
Null safety, 285
  non-null assertion (!!), 290, 291
  safe cast (as?) operator, 291, 292
  Elvis operator (?:), 288
  let scope function, 292, 293
  null values, 286
  safe call operator (?.), 287
Null safety functions, 225
numArray, 134

O

Object-oriented programming
    (OOP), 1, 73
  abstraction, 74
  banking management system,
    111–118
  cinema ticket calculation
    system, 122–123
  classes and objects, 74
  encapsulation, 74
  geometric shape management
    system, 118–119
  inheritance, 74
  key concepts, 73 (*see also* OOP
    concepts)
  polymorphism, 74
  student management system,
    120–121
Objects, 75
  access member function of the
    class, 76
  attribute, 76
  behavior, 76
  create object, 76
  identity, 75
OkHttp, 269, 272
OOP concepts, 73, 74
  classes (*see* Classes)
  inheritance (*see* Inheritance)
  objects (*see* Objects)

Operators, 27
    arithmetic, 27, 28
    assignment, 30, 31
    comparison, 31, 32
    logical, 29
    vs. operands, 27
    types, 27

P, Q

partition() function, 218
print(), 56
println() function, 24, 56
Private modifier, 97
Property, 99
    access getter and setter, 101
    class properties, 99
    custom setter and getter, 101
    setters and getters, 100
    using val, 99
Property delegation, 300–302
Protected modifier, 98
Public modifier, 96

R

Reactive code, best practices, 263, 264
Reactive extension, 255
Reactive programming, 255–257, 264
Reactive programming patterns, 262
ReactiveX (Rx)
    cold/hot streams, 257, 258
    concepts, 256
    filter/distinct, 259
    Observable.interval(), 260, 261
    observables, 257
    RxKotlin, uses, 258
    streams, 257
    uses, 255
readText() function, 226
Recursive functions, 61
    normal function call, 61
    recursive function call, 63, 64
    tail function call, 64
rem(), 56
resolve() function, 226
Retrofit, 269, 272
Return statement, 45
reverseString function, 238
RxJava, 255, 256, 264
RxKotlin, 255
    API, 256
    features, 256
    uses, 258
    vs. RxJava, 255

S

Safe cast (as?) operator, 291, 292
Satatypes, 26
Sealed classes, 107
setOf() function, 155
Setter function, 198
Smart cast, 46
Software systems, 248
sorted(), 152
sortedDescending(), 152
Sorting, 213
    custom sorting, 214
    natural sorting, 214
    random sorting, 216
    reverse sorting, 215
Spek, 242
Standard library functions, 213, 229
star(*) projection, 169

INDEX

Streams, 257
String functions, 33, 34, 220–223
Strings, 32
    double quotes, 32
    functions, 33, 34
    length, 33
StringUtils class, 238
Student class, 194–196
sum(), 56, 156
Swift Package Manager (SPM), 337

T

Task Manager App, 303–305
Testing, 235, 250
    integration testing (*see* Integration testing)
    production-grade apps, 250
    unit testing (*see* Unit testing)
this() function, 85
throw block, 132
toInt(), 56
toLong(), 56
toLowerCase(), 56
toString(), 56, 105, 167
toUpperCase(), 56
Try-catch block, 128–130
Type checks, 45

U

UI, *see* User interface (UI)
Unit testing, 235
    advantages, 235
    discrete pieces, 235
    functionality-typically methods, 249
    identify defects, 249
    methodology, 249
    mocking, 243
    MockK, 243, 249
        annotations, 243, 244
        keywords and functions, 245
    strategies, 239, 240
    strings, different function, 236, 238, 239
    testing environment, 236
    two numbers, basic function, 236, 237
User-defined exception, 137
User-defined function, 53, 54
User experience (UX), 271
User interface (UI), 2
UX, *see* User experience (UX)

V

Variables, 26
Visibility modifiers, 96
    internal, 97
    private, 97
    protected, 98
    public, 96
Volley, 272

W

WebSockets, 269
when statement, 40, 41
while loop, 41, 42
writeText() function, 226

X, Y, Z

XCFrameworks, 337

GPSR Compliance

The European Union's (EU) General Product Safety Regulation (GPSR) is a set of rules that requires consumer products to be safe and our obligations to ensure this.

If you have any concerns about our products, you can contact us on

ProductSafety@springernature.com

In case Publisher is established outside the EU, the EU authorized representative is:

Springer Nature Customer Service Center GmbH
Europaplatz 3
69115 Heidelberg, Germany